Irish Paintings from the Collection of Brian P. Burns

Yale Center for British Art   September 25, 1997 – January 4, 1998

When the Brian P. Burns Collection was first shown at the McMullen Museum of Art at Boston College in early 1996, it came as a revelation to most American viewers. Here a lost dimension to modern Ireland was restored. The paintings added resonance to the familiar story of Irish history from the Great Famine to the struggles and troubles attending the creation of the Irish Free State. They invited comparison with Irish literature from the Celtic Twilight to the foundation of the Irish dramatic movement. The large group of works by Jack B. Yeats was a particular surprise and challenge. Unquestionably the finest and most important Irish painter to work in Ireland in the first half of the twentieth century, Yeats took his enigmatic imagery from Irish life, past and present, as did his brother the poet William Butler Yeats. What was the relationship between these two extraordinary brothers and what is the relationship between picture and poem?

There, on the mountain and the sky,
On all the tragic scene they stare.

The rich and remarkable story the collection unfolded made the prospect of an exhibition deeply attractive to the Yale Center for British Art. It would be the first time the Center had shown Irish painting. With enthusiasm, generosity, and grace, Brian Burns agreed to lend the collection for an extended period. After Boston, the collection was shown to great acclaim at the Hugh Lane Municipal Gallery of Modern Art in Dublin in the summer of 1996. Yale is the third venue, the first to present the collection in its greatly expanded form. About half again as many objects have been added to the collection by Mr. Burns, and the new acquisitions have sharpened the vision and deepened the revelation of modern Irish painting and its role in Irish history and culture. In turn, the Center has included a rich array of literary and historical manuscripts and books illustrative of key moments in Irish history and literature. These are drawn from the Beinecke Rare Book and Manuscript Library and Sterling Memorial Library at Yale, the John J. Burns Library at Boston College, the Woodruff Library at Emory University, and the Providence Public Library.

Every part of the collection has been strengthened: from the nineteenth-century landscapes and genre paintings to the work of Irish expatriate artists such as Roderic O'Conor, Sir John Lavery, Sir William Orpen, and William Leech. Most spectacularly, six new works by Jack B. Yeats have come into the collection since it was shown last year. Smaller versions of John Henry Foley's famous full-length bronzes of Oliver Goldsmith and Edmund Burke which stand in front of Trinity College and preside over College Green have also been added, as reminders of the Irish Enlightenment of the eighteenth century.

How have these additions sharpened the vision and deepened the revelation?

Firstly, they show how much the modern Irish artist embodies the complex fate of being Irish. The pattern of emigration, compelled or willing, runs through the ranks of modern Irish artists. None of the works by those expatriates mentioned above have Irish subjects, and that makes one dwell on the nature of national schools. Unconsciously, we think of the nativist strand as being the true and authentic voice of a national school. Paul Henry in Connemara or Séan Keating on Aran speak in an unmistakable Irish accent. Image and occasion reflect the Irish context and that alone. However enriching that context may be imaginatively, it could equally inhibit art and artist. To become a certain kind of artist and achieve a certain level of art, some Irish artists had to leave Ireland. Roderic O'Conor, whose reputation remains higher in continental Europe than elsewhere, is the classic example. His gifts were liberated through contact with Post-Impressionism and then, more remarkably, through Intimism to his brilliant flowering as a Fauvist. Although influenced by powerful figures around him, O'Conor is no mere follower in a fast-flowing stream but has a career unto himself. He never lived in Ireland after his early twenties; yet he remains indisputably an Irish painter oriented, tellingly, to Europe rather than Britain.

The second point follows quickly from the first: how different the story of modern Irish art is from modern British painting. Where eighteenth-century Irish art, architecture, and the decorative arts have been labeled "Irish Georgian," Irish painting of the late nineteenth and twentieth centuries cannot be so easily subsumed. The inclusion of additional paintings by Sir William Orpen and Sir Gerald Kelly—both Royal Academicians—reminds us how much Irish artists sought and found fame and success in London, yet how minimally the influence of British art flowed back across the Irish Sea. Even painters like William Leech, who spent most of his painting life in England after an extended period in France before World War I, shows scant influence of British art in a painting career of over fifty years.

Consistently Irish artists from the 1880s onwards looked to the Continent, to France and Belgium, for inspiration and guidance. The pattern of influence is so strong, running across different generations, that it suggests both the obvious—that Paris was more artistically interesting than London—and the political—that in matters of art the British could neither occupy nor dominate Irish artists. Irish art in its aptitude for European centers and models tacitly helped free Irish culture from a British straitjacket. It surely anticipates the Ireland of the present, viewing itself essentially as a part of modern Europe.

Thirdly, the addition of six works by Jack B. Yeats reminds us that such a thing as an Irish genius really does exist, that Ireland is not simply a cockpit of conflicting European and British influences and forces. Everything that Jack B. Yeats produced stems from the experience of Ireland; yet there is never a taint of the provincial or merely local. Those brilliant, puzzling presences in his paintings — a sea captain waiting by the misty shore for a boat to land, a blond head bending to a still rock pool—are born out of an inhabited landscape and an unforgotten history, a place where myth and reality collide.

Patrick McCaughey
Director

Henry Alken Jr. (1810–1894)
S. Spode Training Easter Bere, 1856
Oil on board
11 ¾ x 13 ½ in.

Anonymous, Irish
Lady Conyngham's Royal Pomeranian at Bifrons, Kent
Oil on canvas
19 ½ x 24 in.

James Brenan, RHA (1837–1907)
The Schoolroom (Empty Pockets), 1887
Oil on canvas
28 x 36 in.

James Brenan, RHA (1837–1907)
The Village Scribe (The Rent Collector), 1881
Oil on canvas
28 x 36 in.

Michael George Brennan (1839–1871)
The Acolyte
Oil on canvas
26 ¾ x 35 ¾ in.

George Campbell, RHA (1917–1979)
Jack B. Yeats, An Impression (Homage to Jack Yeats)
Oil on board
18 x 24 in.

Laurence Campbell, RHA (1911–1968)
Bust of Jack B. Yeats #9, 1944
Bronze
Height: 19 in.

Walter Chetwood-Aiken (1866–1899)
A Song to Spring, Ar Zon Amzer Nevez, 1897
Oil on canvas
27 ½ x 66 in.

J. A. Comyn
Fair Day in Connemara
Oil on canvas
17 ½ x 29 in.

Henry Robertson Craig, RHA, RUA (1916–1984)
A Dublin Drawing Room, c. 1958
Oil on canvas
20 ¾ x 25 ¼ in.

James Humbert Craig, RHA, RUA (1878–1944)
In County Mayo (Connemara Bog and Mountain Scene)
Oil on canvas
20 x 24 in.

Lilian Lucy Davidson, ARHA (1879–1954)
The Flax Pullers, exh. 1921
Oil on canvas
26 x 30 in.

F. J. Davis (active c. 1845)
The State Ballroom, St. Patrick's Hall, Dublin Castle, c. 1845
Oil on wood
37 ½ x 51 ½ in.

John Henry Foley, RA, RHA (1818–1874)
Edmund Burke
Bronze
Height: 38 in.

John Henry Foley, RA, RHA (1818–1874)
Oliver Goldsmith
Bronze
Height: 38 in.

Stanhope Alexander Forbes, RA (1857–1947)
The Forge
Oil on canvas
30 x 24 in.

Kathleen Fox (1880–1963)
Self-Portrait with Palette
Oil on canvas
24 x 20 in.

Letitia Marion Hamilton, RHA (1878–1964)
Fair Day at Castlepollard, Westmeath, c. 1948
Oil on canvas
25 ¼ x 36 in.

Paul Henry, RHA (1876–1958)
Spring in Connemara, c. 1930
Oil on canvas-board
24 x 28 in.

Nathaniel Hone, RHA (1831–1917)
Gathering Seaweed on the Strand, Malahide, c. 1890
Oil on canvas
25 x 36 in.

Nathaniel Hone, RHA (1831–1917)
St. George's Head, Kilkee, Co. Clare
Oil on canvas
24 ¼ x 39 ¾ in.

James Hore (active 1829–1837)
The Four Courts, Dublin, from the Quay
Oil on canvas
16 x 22 in.

John (Seán) Keating, PRHA (1889–1977)
An Aran Fisherman
Oil on canvas
33 ½ x 44 ¾ in.

John (Seán) Keating, PRHA (1889–1977)
King O'Toole, exh. 1933
Oil on canvas-board
26 x 30 in.

John (Seán) Keating, PRHA (1889–1977)
The Port Authority (Connemara Fisherman), c. 1940
Oil on canvas
30 ½ x 36 ½ in.

Sir Gerald Festus Kelly, RA, RHA (1879–1972)
Reclining Nude
Oil on canvas
22 ½ x 32 ¼ in.

Charles Vincent Lamb, RHA, RUA (1893–1964)
Flaherty's Pub
Oil on canvas
20 ½ x 24 ¼ in.

Sir John Lavery, RA, RHA, RSA (1856–1941)
The Drawing Room at Mount Stewart, c. 1925
Oil on panel
10 x 14 in.

Sir John Lavery, RA, RHA, RSA (1856–1941)
The Lakes of Killarney, 1913
Oil on canvas
25 x 30 in.

Sir John Lavery, RA, RHA, RSA (1856–1941)
Sunset – The Caravan
Oil on canvas
30 ¼ x 25 in.

William John Leech, RHA (1881–1968)
Morning Coffee and Biscuits
Oil on canvas
30 x 25 in.

William John Leech, RHA (1881–1968)
Statue of the Fragonard, Grasse
Oil on canvas
25 ½ x 32 in.

Patrick Leonard, ARHA (b. 1918)
After the Storm, The End of a Coaster
Oil on canvas
39 x 45 ½ in.

Theodor D. MacEgan ("The MacEgan") (1856–1939)
Interior National Gallery, Dublin, 1932
Oil on canvas
13 ¾ x 16 ½ in.

Maurice MacGonigal, PRHA (1900–1979)
Fishing Boats at Clogherhead (Harbour View), c. 1943
Oil on panel
12 x 16 in.

Maurice MacGonigal, PRHA (1900–1979)
Girl with Green Shawl (Cailin Og Iarthar), c. 1938
Oil on canvas
44 x 38 in.

William McEvoy (active 1858–1880)
Glengariffe from the Kenmare Road, Evening, 1862
Oil on canvas
28 x 52 in.

Frank McKelvey, RHA, RUA (1895–1974)
The Poultry Yard, 1923
Oil on canvas
17 x 22 ½ in.

Colin Middleton, RHA, RUA (1910–1983)
Cornfield, c. 1950
Oil on canvas
20 x 30 in.

R. A. Miley (active 1881–1888)
Down at the Start, c. 1880
Oil on canvas
17 ½ x 27 ½ in.

Richard Thomas Moynan, RHA (1856–1906)
Metropolitan School of Art, Dublin
Oil on canvas
30 x 24 in.

George Nairn, ARHA (1799–1850)
Knight of Tara, 1843
Oil on canvas
25 ½ x 35 in.

Erskine Nicol, ARA, RSA (1825–1904)
The Seanchai
Oil on canvas
18 ½ x 23 ½ in.

Erskine Nicol, ARA, RSA (1825–1904)
The Tenant, Castle Rackrent
Oil on canvas
20 ½ x 15 in.

Roderic O'Conor (1860–1940)
Geraniums
Oil on board
14 ¾ x 18 ⅛ in.

Roderic O'Conor (1860–1940)
Lovers in a Moonlit Garden ("Romeo and Juliet"), c. 1898–1900
Oil on canvas
25 ½ x 21 ¼ in.

Roderic O'Conor (1860–1940)
Reclining Nude
Oil on canvas
21 ¼ x 25 ¼ in.

Aloysius O'Kelly (1853–1935?)
Street Scene, Tangiers
Oil on canvas
13 ½ x 20 in.

Frank O'Meara (1853–1888)
Old Mill at Grez, c. 1878
Oil on canvas
18 x 22 in.

Sir William Orpen, RA, RHA (1878–1931)
Portrait of Miss Annie Harmsworth in an Interior
Oil on canvas
36 x 28 in.

Sir William Orpen, RA, RHA (1878–1931)
Portrait of Miss Annie Harmsworth in a Landscape, c. 1908
Oil on canvas
36 x 28 in.

Walter Frederick Osborne, RHA (1859–1903)
At the Breakfast Table, 1894
Oil on canvas
20 x 24 in.

Walter Frederick Osborne, RHA (1859–1903)
At the Racecourse
Watercolor
13 ½ x 20 ½ in.

Walter Frederick Osborne, RHA (1859–1903)
Seated Boy and Sea
Oil on board
5 ½ x 8 ¾ in.

Walter Frederick Osborne, RHA (1859–1903)
Study from Nature
Oil on panel
15 x 9 ¾ in.

William Osborne, RHA
A Moment of Liberty
Oil on canvas
14 ½ x 16 ½ in.

Albert Power, ARHA (1883–1945)
Head of William Butler Yeats, 1918
Bronze
Height: 17 ½ in.

George Russell (Æ) (1867–1935)
Celtic Twilight
Oil on canvas
24 x 30 in.

William C. Sadler II (c. 1782–1839)
Donnybrook Fair
Oil on panel
21 ¾ x 35 ¾ in.

Maria Spilsbury Taylor, RA (1777–c. 1823)
Henry Grattan, M. P. in a Library, c. 1815–20
Oil on canvas
37 ¾ x 31 ⅛ in.

Samuel Spode (active 1850)
Pembroke a Thoroughbred Horse
Oil on canvas
19 x 23 ½ in.

Bartholomew Colles Watkins, RHA (1833–1891)
Cloon Lake, Glencar, County Kerry
Oil on canvas
13 ½ x 20 in.

Bartholomew Colles Watkins, RHA (1833–1891)
Kylemore Lake, Connemara
Oil on canvas
13 ½ x 20 in.

Leo Whelan (1892–1956)
The Artist's Niece, Lena, Sewing, c. 1940
Oil on wood
12 x 10 ¼ in.

Jack Butler Yeats, RHA (1871–1957)
The Canal Water
Oil on board
9 x 14 in.

Jack Butler Yeats, RHA (1871–1957)
The Card Players
Watercolor
14 x 10 in.

Jack Butler Yeats, RHA (1871–1957)
The Derelict
Watercolor
14 x 10 in.

Jack Butler Yeats, RHA (1871–1957)
Duffy's Circus, c. late 1890s
Watercolor, pen and ink
5 ½ x 8 ¼ in.

Jack Butler Yeats, RHA (1871–1957)
The Embanked Road, c. 1945–46
Oil on panel
8 ½ x 14 in.

Jack Butler Yeats, RHA (1871–1957)
The Laugh
Oil on canvas
14 x 20 ½ in.

Jack Butler Yeats, RHA (1871–1957)
The Lonely Sea, c. 1940
Oil on canvas
14 x 21 in.

Jack Butler Yeats, RHA (1871–1957)
The Look Out (The Pilot House), c. 1911
Watercolor
9 ¾ x 13 ¼ in.

Jack Butler Yeats, RHA (1871–1957)
The Man Sure of His Welcome
Oil on panel
9 x 14 in.

Jack Butler Yeats, RHA (1871–1957)
A Misty Morning
Oil on panel
9 x 13 ¾ in.

Jack Butler Yeats, RHA (1871–1957)
On to Glory
Oil on canvas
18 x 24 in.

Jack Butler Yeats, RHA (1871–1957)
Patriotic Airs, c. 1923
Oil on canvas
14 x 18 in.

Jack Butler Yeats, RHA (1871–1957)
The Sea Captain (The Man off to Wexford)
Watercolor
4 x 7 ½ in.

Jack Butler Yeats, RHA (1871–1957)
A Silence
Oil on canvas
18 x 24 in.

ARA   Associate of the Royal Academy
ARHA   Associate of the Royal Hibernian Academy
PRHA   President of the Royal Hibernian Academy
RA   Royal Academician
RHA   Royal Hibernian Academician
RSA   Royal Scottish Academician
RUA   Royal Ulster Academician

America's Eye:
Irish Paintings from the Collection of Brian P. Burns

Edited by Adele M. Dalsimer and Vera Kreilkamp

BOSTON COLLEGE MUSEUM OF ART

Acknowledgements

First and foremost, we wish to thank Jennifer Grinnell, Coordinator of Exhibitions of the Boston College Museum of Art, for her unstinting commitment to the project. Without her talent, precision, and devotion, this exhibition and publication would not have been possible. Jennifer supervised the publication production from design to print, and consistently demonstrated her intelligence, thoroughness, and generosity.

Alston Conley, Museum Curator, designed the installation not only with an artist's awareness of the colors and forms of the works but also with a sensitive understanding of the social and historical concepts the editors sought to convey.

Kerry Leonard, undergraduate Research Fellow at the Boston College Museum of Art, meticulously kept track of the myriad details of the exhibition and catalogue. Kerry coordinated the photographs for the catalogue, and read, fact-checked and typeset the entries as they made their way between two continents. Her exceptional commitment was instrumental to the success of this project.

Honey Swartz, the Museum's Administrator, and Catherine McLoughlin, Administrative Assistant to the Irish Studies Program, nurtured and supported the project and us throughout.

By providing the editors and essayists with photographic reproductions of painting in the exhibition, Stephen Vedder of the Boston College Audio-Visual Department, made it possible for all of us to begin our work.

We are grateful for the fastidious and elegant copy-editing of Naomi Rosenberg.

We thank Anne Callahan of kor group who designed the catalogue, poster and invitation for the exhibition with an artist's eye.

Catherine Marshall, of the Irish Museum of Modern Art, Christina Kennedy and Daire O'Connell, of the Hugh Lane Municipal Gallery of Modern Art, provided us with informative catalogue copy.

The editors also wish to thank the eight essayists, who viewed the paintings from the prospective of their individual disciplinary backgrounds, but whose work collectively reveals the richness of Ireland's visual tradition as a scholarly resource.

Finally, we wish to thank Nancy Netzer, Director of the Boston College Museum of Art. Without her expertise and advise at every stage of this project, *America's Eye* would never have become a reality.

Table of Contents

Note to the Reader:

Numbered plates in this book
are works in the exhibition.
Additional plates are
designated as "figures."
References are listed in full at
the end of each essay.

Director's Preface

Serious collections of Irish art and antiquities are, in contrast with those of other societies, relatively recent phenomena. Although the Royal Irish Academy was founded in 1785 as a center for research on Irish civilization, George Petrie, the founder of scientific archaeology in Ireland, began to pull together all the native metalwork in its posession to form a National Museum of Antiquities only as recently as the middle of the last century. Indeed, the National Gallery of Ireland, the largest repository of Irish painting, was only founded after the Irish Industrial Exhibition in Dublin in 1853. Works that emerged from this post-Famine period provide a fitting starting point for, with a few notable exceptions, the collection of Brian P. Burns. Filled with works of art, Brian Burns's homes have become vessels of Irish civilization, so to speak. The Boston College Museum is pleased to have been able to select from them, probably the most extensive and important assemblages of Irish paintings in America, the works that comprise this exhibition. *America's Eye* celebrates more than a collector's legacy in the traditional sense: rather, more, it reflects a history of the developing attitudes and changing tastes that form part of the Irish-American experience in the second half of the twentieth century. The primary goal of the exhibition is to introduce an American audience to the riches of Irish painting, against an interdisciplinary backdrop.

In this regard, the Museum was fortunate to persuade two outstanding American scholars of Irish literature and culture, Professor Adele Dalsimer of Boston College and Professor Vera Kreilkamp of Pine Manor College, to serve as co-curators of the exhibition and co-editors of the catalogue. Their extraordinary knowledge of Ireland, their energy, and their literary gifts provided the mainspring of this undertaking. They worked tirelessly to select paintings that epitomize key elements of Irish culture and society between the mid-nineteenth and the mid-twentieth centuries and to gather together a group of renowned scholars from various disciplines to write essays that cast these works in a broad cultural context.

We also wish to express our thanks to Barbara Dawson, the director of the Hugh Lane Municipal Gallery of Modern Art in Dublin, for arranging for the exhibition to be shown there and for selecting three fine scholars, Christina Kennedy, Catherine Marshall, and Daire O'Connell, to write entries for this catalogue.

This, as all exhibitions, results from a complex collaboration. As always, logistics were efficiently handled by the Museum's administrator Helen Swartz. The Museum's coordinator of exhibitions, Jennifer Grinnell managed the production of the catalogue from beginning to end. Without Jennifer's passionate dedication to editing and layout, the undertaking would never have been completed. Naomi Rosenberg saw to copy editing of the catalogue; much additional help in entering corrections, organizing photographs and preparing information for bibliographies, provenance, and wall text came from the Museum's student research-assistant Kerry Leonard. Carolyn Kavanaugh edited the checklist of additional works in the Burns collection and helped with final proof-reading of the text. We also thank Anne Callahan for the handsome design of the catalogue.

Given the freedom that comes with movable walls our talented curator Alston Conley has designed rooms that correspond to and emphasize the larger themes of the exhibition. We are also grateful to the Museum's security staff, led by Alice Harkins, for its diligence and dedication.

From the outset Gregory Gromadzki, the conservator of the Burns collection, worked closely with the curators and Museum staff. He provided documentation on the collection and arranged for and supervised the photography, packing and transport of the works. His learned eye and skillful hand have ensured that the paintings are presented in a state as close to their original as possible. We also wish to make special mention of the valuable assistance Brian Burns received in the formation of his collection from his wife, Eileen, and several dealers, collectors and scholars in Ireland: Barbara Dawson, Helen Dillon, Val Dillon, the late Willie Dillon, the Honorable Desmond FitzGerald, Mr. and Mrs. James Gorry, Raymond Keaveney, Christina Kennedy, Muriel McCarthy, and Larry Powell. The organizers are particularly grateful to Eileen Burns for her support, enthusiasm, and keen eye for beauty in all aspects of this project.

As always, the avid support of the administration of Boston College, especially J. Donald Monan, S.J., Margaret Dwyer, Francis Campanella, William Neenan, S.J., Mary Lou DeLong, J. Robert Barth, S.J., Richard Spinello, Dennis Yesalonia, S.J., and Richard Landau, as well as that of the Friends of the Boston College Museum of Art, chaired by Nancy and John Joyce, was crucial to the success of this project.

Finally, we reserve our most profound gratitude for Brian Burns, whose foresight in assembling these visual records of Irish culture and whose generosity in lending them made this exhibition and scholarly endeavor possible. It is to him and to all that he has accomplished in collecting that this catalogue is dedicated.

Nancy Netzer, Director
Boston College Museum of Art

Foreword

The century of Irish art represented in *America's Eye: Irish Paintings from the Collection of Brian P. Burns* encompasses the stylistic diversity and range of subject matter that preoccupied Irish painters from the latter part of the Victorian period, through the evolution of modern Irish art in the first half of the twentieth century. The nineteenth century genre scenes included in this exhibition reveal the penchant of the age for stylized views of peasant life whilst the equestrian scenes attest to the enduring Irish passion for racing.

The revolutionary developments which occurred in art practice in the last decade of the nineteenth century in France and the resulting re-evaluation of critical criteria did not go unnoticed in Ireland. The appeal of the innovative teaching academies in Paris and the artists' colonies which proliferated in regions proved most attractive with Europeans, Scandinavians and Americans participating in Bohemian lifestyle. Brittany was a popular region for artists' colonies, the most famous being Pont-Aven. Artists were captivated by the traditional costume worn by the Bretons as is evident in Walter Chetwood-Aiken's splendid portrayal of a group of Breton women. With its unusual perspective, *A Song to Spring* has as its primary focus the distinctive Breton headdress for which the region was renowned. Sir John Lavery (nos. 4, 5), Walter Osborne (nos. 33-35), Roderic O'Conor (no. 38) and Frank O'Meara (no. 39) also worked in France evaluating and contributing to the ongoing artistic revolutionary processes; their approach to their art was highly individual, with the figure retaining an integral position, unlike the impressionists.

The spectacular scenery in the west of Ireland was the primary source of inspiration for artists such as Paul Henry (no. 7), Maurice MacGonigal (nos. 15, 16), and Jack B. Yeats (nos. 40-46). Yeats, perhaps our best known artist internationally, derived most of his subject matter from the way of life in County Sligo; the fairs, circuses — *Duffy's Circus* was the most famous Irish circus — horse races and fisherman are constant subjects in his work. Originally, a graphic designer, Yeats gradually used bolder and looser brushwork. His later, more abstract work was likened to that of his friend, the Austrian artist Oscar Kokoschka. Like Yeats, Maurice MacGonigal drew on the west of Ireland for his subject matter. He and Séan Keating used themes from the west to express their nationalism, treating their subjects as icons of pure Irish culture.

This exhibition *America's Eye* provides audiences at the Boston College Museum of Art with an excellent opportunity to assess the evolution of Irish art from the mid-nineteenth century to the 1950s. We are delighted to be associated with this exhibition, as it has particular relevance for us at the Hugh Lane Municipal Gallery of Modern Art in Dublin. At the beginning of this century, in 1904, Hugh Lane organized what was to be the first public exhibition of Irish art at the Guildhall in London. It was an outstanding success and provided him with support to establish a collection of Modern Art in Dublin. Just as this exhibition attempts to bring together the most significant Irish artists of the period, Hugh Lane assembled the best collection of modern Irish of the time, together with significant examples of modern European painting. Our congratulations to Brian Burns for making his collection available to American and Irish audiences; to Boston College for initiating the exhibition, in particular Professor Nancy Netzer, Director of the Museum of Art, Professor Adele Dalsimer, Co-Director of the Irish Studies Program, and Professor Vera Kreilkamp, of the English Program at Pine Manor College. This catalogue of paintings and the collection of essays place Irish art in an interdisciplinary context. I also wish to congratulate Christina Kennedy, Catherine Marshall and Daire O'Connell who wrote the catalogue entries, and Jennifer Grinnell, Kerry Leonard and Stoney Conley of the Boston College Museum of Art.

While Irish literary prowess is widely acknowledged, our visual tradition, with the exception of contemporary practice, remains relatively unknown. This imbalance can only be addressed by focused international exposure. The collection of Brian Burns on exhibit at the Boston College Museum of Art provides one such showcase for Irish art.

Barbara Dawson, Director
Hugh Lane Municipal Gallery of Modern Art

Introduction

America's Eye:
The Irish Art of Brian P. Burns

Adele M. Dalsimer and
Vera Kreilkamp

*" ... Ireland not as she is displayed in guide book or history, but Ireland seen
because of the magnificent vitality of her painters, in the glory of her passions."*

— William Butler Yeats, speech at the Banquet of the Irish Academy of Letters,
    17 August 1937

In 1992, when the exhibition *Master European Paintings from the National Gallery
of Ireland* brought the work of Claude, Gainsborough, and Chardin from Dublin to
Boston's Museum of Fine Arts, many puzzled viewers asked where the Irish artists were.
Even to the casual museum-goer, the answer seemed painfully evident. With the exception
of Jack Yeats, known to Americans as much for his illustrious brother as for his own
work, Ireland had produced no eminent artists since anonymous monks created the *Book
of Kells*. Although rich in literary and musical traditions, Ireland appeared to Americans as
a nation without a visual imagination. With *America's Eye: Irish Paintings From the
Collection of Brian P. Burns*, Boston College corrects this misreading by presenting Ireland
as William Butler Yeats would, in all the "magnificent vitality of her painters."

But what is Irish art? Rather than enter into the current debate that locates the source of
the nation's post-Famine visual art either in nationalism[1] or in international Modernism,[2]
the curators of this exhibition propose a less politicized definition. The works in this
collection, produced in the nineteenth and the first half of the twentieth centuries, have
been designated Irish for a variety of reasons. Most frequently their creators were Irish-
born, but some, Erskine Nicol or H. Robertson Craig, for example, were foreign-born
painters who produced considerable work in Ireland. The paintings generally depict Irish
subjects — landscapes, individual or group portraits, interiors, genre scenes, still lifes —
but several Irish artists like Frank O'Meara, Roderic O'Conor, and John Lavery, chose
settings in Paris, Brittany, Antwerp, or even Tangiers. The Irish art in *America's Eye*, then,
is a loosely defined entity created by men and women who were either born in or produced a significant body of work in Ireland.[3]

Such an inclusive definition of the national art suggests that, like serious professional
artists elsewhere, most Irish painters were not provincial in their approach to their craft.
In fact, in *Irish Art and Modernism*, S. B. Kennedy argues that unlike the writers of
the Literary Revival, whose poetry and prose were "closely associated with the separatist
revolutionary politics of the time," contemporary Irish artists "forged a broader and
less isolationist philosophy" (1). Thus, *America's Eye* presents works influenced

---

[1] In short, the rise of Irish painting, like the rise of Irish literature, is linked inseparably with Ireland's belated progress toward political
independence" (Fallon 15).

[2] "The overall thrust in the visual arts, unlike the literary arts, was ... inspired by the international Modern Movement" (S.B. Kennedy 2).

    [3] In *Irish Painting*, Brian Kennedy offers a similarly inclusive definition (7).

by European artistic movements of the last two centuries. In the mid-nineteenth century, Irish peasant life inspired anecdotal Victorian genre paintings, themselves influenced by an earlier Dutch tradition. From 1850 on, Irish artists traveled abroad and were influenced by the naturalistic landscapes of the Barbizon school and particularly by such figures as Corot and Millet. After the turn of the century, when Hugh Lane introduced the nation to modern French art, Irish painters could view European masterpieces in Dublin's Municipal Gallery.[4] As a result of their exposure to impressionism and post-impressionism, landscape painters absorbed continental influences, even as they continued to depict the scenery of the west of Ireland so central to the ideology of cultural nationalism. Walter Osborne's late works in this exhibition, for example, exhibit quintissential impressionistic techniques, while paintings by Roderic O'Conor and Colin Middleton evidence post-impressionist influence.

Other groups of paintings suggest further relationships between Ireland and Europe. Representations of painters in their studios, palettes in hands, by Kathleen Fox and Richard Thomas Moynan allude to a self-conscious trope that dates from the seventeenth century. Working in a similarly self-referential genre, William MacEgan and Robinson Craig create a visual narrative of their professions in paintings indebted to the *Kunstkammer* (painting gallery) tradition, which emerged in seventeenth-century Antwerp. This exhibition also contains unabashedly heroic portrayals of rural men and women by Seán Keating and Maurice MacGonigal; their propagandistic canvases on behalf of Irish nationalism are the most explicitly political works in the collection. But even Keating, regarded by patriotic admirers as the "Green Hope of national painting" (Fallon 167), can be viewed in the wider context of early twentieth-century socialist realism. Thus, collectively, these works demonstrate not that Irish art, even in its most nationalistic manifestations, exists in isolation from a larger world, but rather that it absorbs from and participates in the development of European painting.

But *America's Eye: Irish Paintings from the Collection of Brian P. Burns* does more than bring important but unfamiliar paintings to the United States; it also demonstrates the powerful and evolving role of the diaspora in Ireland and America. Brian Burns's leadership role in collecting and preserving Ireland's cultural heritage reverses the older patterns of discrimination that denied his nineteenth-century ancestors the opportunities of his generation. The trajectory of emigrants, who initially moved from impoverished lives in their homeland to economic and social marginalization in their adopted nation, culminates in Mr. Burn's success in America and his expression of social and cultural responsibility toward Ireland. *America's Eye*, and the publication of a catalog and collection of interdisciplinary essays in the field of Irish Studies attest, moreover, to the way in which the visual arts, too often viewed as irrelevant to the lives of ordinary Irish men and women, have helped to shape Irish history and identity.

An Irish-American Collector

In his dual nationalities, Brian Burns is a citizen of state newly reimagined by Irish President Mary Robinson to include both the homeland and the diaspora. Her non-territorial definition of Irishness encompasses not only the five million men and women who inhabit the island, both north and south, but also those seventy million people worldwide who claim Irish descent and who define themselves by their identity with Ireland: "men and women whose pride and affection for Ireland [had] neither deserted them nor deterred them from dedicating their loyalty and energies to other countries and cultures." As philanthropist, art collector, economic adviser,[5] and entrepreneur in Ireland and America, Brian Burns's life exemplifies the dual loyalties and energies President Robinson celebrates.

But growing into maturity in the 1950s and 1960s, Mr. Burns lived among Irish-Americans eager to assimilate, to shed an earlier collective guilt and sadness about leaving the homeland — and thus among many who would reject their earlier historical identities as products of a tragic emigration saga. In *Emigrants and Exiles*, Kerby Miller describes the nineteenth and

---

[4] Known today as the Hugh Lane Municipal Gallery of Modern Art.

[5] Mr. Burns is a member of the Ireland-America Economic Advisory Board to the Prime Minister, 1995-1998.

early twentieth-century Irish-American experience as imbued with a sense of loss, victimization, and forced exile. Although the United States was the land of opportunity and promise for most emigrants, for the new Irish-American it was a refuge from a wrenching expulsion, from a separation so final that those departing were often mourned in an "American wake." [6] Indeed, Mr. Burns speaks of his grandfather's unwillingness to encourage his American-born son to visit Sneem, County Kerry, the village from which the elder Burns emigrated 1892. Thus Burns's father, although an advocate of Irish-American affairs, never returned to the family home: "There was too much sadness" (Interview).[7]

Such an identification of the past with loss and exile shaped the creation of an Irish-American self-image. In 1972, as other groups were beginning to explore the sources of their cultural identities, Andrew Greeley criticized the failure of Irish-Americans to legitimize their heritage. He observed that the Irish had failed to make themselves "count" when the Office of Education in Washington was offering support to programs in Mexican, Scandinavian, Jewish and Black Studies (3). Writing four years later, with an even darker assessment of Irish-American cultural aspirations, Lawrence McCaffrey condemned the movement from urban ghetto to suburb as a "journey from someplace to no place" (176). McCaffrey interpreted the assimilation of the Irish-American as social impoverishment: becoming successful Americans, Irish immigrants and their descendants abandoned most reminders of the historical and cultural forces that had shaped them.

Brian Burns's career exists in striking contrast to Greeley's and McCaffrey's gloomy scenarios. Rather than shedding his ethnic history or embracing a sentimentalized vision of it, Mr. Burns has made the preservation of Ireland's cultural heritage a central preoccupation of his life. In the very decade that Greeley and McCaffrey were issuing their jeremiads, he purchased his first works of Irish art and assumed a leadership role in Irish-American philanthropy.[8] As he was cited as among the nation's most prominent Irish-American business leaders,[9] Brian Burns was creating a major collection of nineteenth and early twentieth-century Irish paintings.

Like another Irish-American, John Quinn, the celebrated turn-of-the-century lawyer, philanthropist, and patron, Brian Burns finds the expression of his personal and ethnic history in Irish arts and letters. Quinn recognized, nurtured, and collected the work of writers and painters of early twentieth-century Ireland. Tellingly, Nathaniel Hone's *Gathering Seaweed on the Strand, Mahahide*, in the current exhibition, was part of his original collection (no. 1). Indeed, in discussing Quinn's pivotal role in American art history, the critic Aline Saarinen could be describing Burns: "Law was his livelihood, but in his Irishness [he] first found his identity, and Ireland was his path to splendor" (211).

Brian Burns's recent philanthropy proclaims a similar commitment to Irish art and literature. The stereotypical icons of Irishness in America — shamrocks and leprechauns, wolfhounds and harps — have little to do with the cultural enterprises that he has supported. While continuing to acquire works of visual art, Mr. Burns has become increasingly active as a patron of literary and historical scholarship in Ireland, England, and America.[10] In light of this continuing commitment to the nation's culture, he remains aware of the ethical dilemma raised by a collection of Irish paintings in the United States: should all Irish works of art

---

[6] The Irish language offers no equivilent word for the English "emigration." The Irish use the word *deoraíócht* or "exile" to describe that experience.

[7] In 1987, Mr. Burns established a handicraft center in Sneem to provide local employment.

[8] In 1978, Mr. Burns became the youngest director of the American Irish Foundation, an organization established by John F. Kennedy and President Eamon de Valera to encourage American charity for Ireland. As director, in 1987 Burns accomplished the successful merger of that foundation with the Ireland Fund, thereby creating the American Ireland Fund, the largest and most effective Irish charitable organization in the United States.

[9] *Irish America* Oct. 1991: 6.

[10] In Dublin, he organized a fund to restore and support Marsh's Library, and in Cork he established the American Law Library. At Cambridge University, he helped found the Charles Stuart Parnell Chair at Magdalen College. In honor of his late father, Mr. Burns founded the John J. Burns Library of Rare Books and Special Collections at Boston College and endowed the University's Irish Collection, the largest archive of its kind in America. Acknowledging the importance of scholarly dialogue between Ireland and America, he created the Burns Visiting Scholar, a chair in Irish Studies at Boston College for Irish academic, cultural, and political leaders. In 1993, Mr. Burns enabled the library to acquire the most comprehensive group of W. B. Yeats manuscripts outside Ireland.

remain on the island, available primarily to its five million citizens? He has asked whether removing art treasures from Ireland diminishes rather than preserves the national heritage. The most persuasive argument for an American collection of Irish art lies in President Robinson's new, broader definition of her nation.[11] If Boston, New York, Chicago, and San Francisco are truly Ireland's next parishes, then Irish-American leaders must make the national heritage accessible to a diaspora too long unaware of its cultural legacy.

Irish Studies and the Visual Arts

Brian Burns's growing support of arts and letters emerged just as American academics were responding to the failure of the universities to acknowledge a distinct Irish social experience. Before the 1970s, most college courses studying Great Britain either ignored or co-opted Irish events and achievements. They typically treated the Great Famine, the watershed of nineteenth-century Ireland, as a regional footnote to British history. W. B. Yeats was taught as the "last romantic" of an English tradition; James Joyce, the product of a Catholic nationalist Dublin family, was presented almost exclusively in relation to international literary modernism. In the visual arts, the achievements of Early Christian Ireland were assimilated into the study of European medievalism.

Irish Studies courses began to proliferate on American campuses in response to such appropriations;[12] and with these additions to the curriculum came the centrality of a national, rather than imperial, narrative in literary and historical scholarship. By stressing the particularities of the Irish experience, academics recontextualized, reinterpreted, and thus reclaimed not only Joyce and Yeats, but also Jonathan Swift, George Bernard Shaw, Oscar Wilde, and Samuel Beckett from British literature. Similarly, the evolving merger of Irish and post-colonial studies focused historical research on the experience of the colonized rather than the imperial nation. Today, in contrast to the academic shortcomings Greeley decried in the 1970s, at least ten percent of American post-secondary institutions offer courses in Irish Studies.

But because most of these new, often interdisciplinary courses sought to explore the nationalist perspective, modern Irish visual art had little place in the curriculum — even though images can be as effective as documents in revealing the past.[13] Preoccupied with reconstructing the world of the colonized, the Irish Studies classroom generally ignored eighteenth- and nineteenth-century paintings produced by upper- and middle-class men and women, usually members of the Anglo-Irish colonial establishment. Such classrooms turned with increasing interest to rural archeology, Irish language and literature, and indigenous art forms to image a nation previously neglected by American scholars. Nevertheless, the artifacts produced for the dominant class can provide indirect access to the experiences of the whole nation. In elite art, the voices of the colonized are sometimes most audible in their silences, most visible in their absences. In *The State Ballroom in St. Patrick's Hall, Dublin Castle*, for example, F. J. Davis depicts a festive ritual of the Ascendancy during the years of the Great Famine (no. 24). Elegantly uniformed and fashionably dressed members of the imperial establishment dance, mindless of the million country people — invisible and mute in the painting — who are dying of starvation and disease. Only the viewer who insists on remembering what Davis omits, the viewer who can register absences as well as presences, will comprehend the implications of the painting. During a year of devastating national trauma, a celebratory social life proceeds in the opulent seat of imperial power.

Such a contextualizing of a painting in history retrieves social commentary in other works as well. James Brenan's *The Schoolroom* (no. 14) depicts handsome, ruddy-cheeked children, whose charms survive their rags, bare feet and disorder. The young boys are indifferent to the proper business of the schoolroom — two argue about possessions, others chat or play —

---

[11] Forty-four million Americans identify themselves as Irish-American.

[12] The growth to 1600 current members (1994) of the American Conference of Irish Studies, the professional organization guiding and supporting scholars, mirrors the development of the field.

[13] Two recent interdisciplinary works have begun to examine Irish art from such a historical perspective: *Visualizing Ireland: National Identity and the Pictorial Tradition*. Ed. Adele Dalsimer. London: Faber and Faber, 1993; *Ireland: Art into History*. Ed. Brian Kennedy and Raymond Gillespie. Dublin: Town House, 1994.

and the work alludes to popular motifs in Victorian genre paintings. But knowing that by 1887, when he painted *The Schoolroom*, Brenan was a leader in the field of art education and headmaster of the Cork School of Art, we can move beyond formalist criticism. We can read the work not only as an example of a popular Victorian form, but also as a subtle indictment of the national school system. By the late-nineteenth century, a colonial state bureacracy had displaced the native Irish hedge school — an indigenous response to the suppression of eduction for rural Catholics. Ironic pictorial details suggesting Brenan's criticism of the state education — books with broken spines and missing pages, the floor strewn with papers, the vague outline in the picture on the wall of a figure wielding a club over a small child — reveal much about the effects of a proliferating imperial bureaucracy on the native population. Reading *The Schoolroom* in the context of social history suggests how visual art, like literature, decodes the human meaning of political systems. Just as Brian Friel's play *Translations* illustrates the trauma that the decline of the hedge schools inflicted on a traditional culture, Brenan's painting calls into the question the progressive values of an imperially mandated national school system.

While this exhibition argues that the visual arts provide powerful resources for the study of Irish political, social, and economic history, it also contributes to the growing reputation of artists whose works were themselves victims of that history. After independence, the new nation's rejection of the emblems of a colonial past — of which the neglect of Anglo-Irish architecture is the most striking manifestation — accompanied a general isolation and provincialism. And without sufficiently influential champions, nineteenth- and early twentieth-century painters failed to enter the account book, as it were, of a world aesthetic. The very success of Irish literature in the cultural marketplace fostered the lingering misperception of Ireland as a country without a tradition of visual art — or more pointedly, as a nation without a visual imagination. For an international public preoccupied with the nation's literary achievements, Irish art was "something which never happened, a historico-cultural non-event" (Fallon 11). Only in recent years, with increasing museum and gallery space, growing sales, traveling exhibitions, and a proliferating bibliography, have Irish paintings become valued commodities on the world market.

Comprehensive private collections like Mr. Burns's raise awareness about cultural artifacts; through their acquisitions collectors declare their aesthetic convictions and shape the taste that governs the marketplace. Auctions and gallery sales bring paintings formerly confined to private domestic spaces to the public, to scholars and connoisseurs, as well as to potential purchasers. But most important is the effect of exhibiting such a collection in a museum setting and thus making Irish painting available to the university community and the general public. Since relatively few United States museums have mounted shows of Irish art, Americans have had little opportunity to view the work of Irish artists in their national context. Thus, with an educator's zeal, Boston College presents *America's Eye: Irish Painting from the Collection of Brian P. Burns* to the public.

Reading the Paintings

Inviting eight scholars — literary and cultural critics, economic and feminist historians, a celtic linguist, a museum curator, and a calligrapher/paleographer — to respond to objects in the Burns collection, the editors of this volume seek to demonstrate how the language and methodology of various academic disciplines can illuminate Irish paintings, cultural expressions too often neglected in the Irish Studies classroom. The essays implicitly assert that visual materials are essential resources for the study of Irish civilization. Kevin Whelan, for example, arguing that historians must look beyond traditional archival resources to amplify voices silenced by traditional methodologies, turns to a painting by a Scots-born artist to retrieve the buried experience of Irish Famine victims.

We share Whelan's belief that scholars must become receptive to new forms of evidence and hope that this exhibition and publication, underwritten by a university with a thriving Irish Studies curriculum, will foster the interdisplinary examination of the Irish visual tradition. Faculty and students will view and discuss the paintings in *America's Eye* not only as aesthetic objects, but also as heuristic resources. Just as the University's research collections of Irish print materials have served Boston College well, this enterprise demonstrates the educational value of a comparable resource in its museum.

In *Visualizing Ireland*, historian Kevin O'Neill notes how formalist criticism has obscured the ideological role of Irish art and neglected popular visual representations that properly belong to the nation's aesthetic heritage (58). As if in answer to O'Neill's concerns, several essayists in this volume offer alternative readings of this heritage, readings that broaden the definition of the art object. For example, Angela Bourke demonstrates how an Ulster Protestant painter acknowledged an indigenous artistic production in the most "Catholic and western" of Irish counties. Bourke sees the turf stacks in J. H. Craig's unpeopled landscape *In County Mayo* (no. 6) as carefully aligned and symmetrical works of art: each a "temporary installation" in the countryside. Interpreting the iconography of an elite painting, she draws upon her familiarity with rural customs and history and expands the definition of Ireland's visual tradition to include the objects that country people produced in the course of their daily lives.

Bourke's interest in indigenous visual representation — and in undermining the traditional hierarchical distinction between elite and popular art— is shared by Peter Murray, who writes on painter James Brenan's second career as art educator. Murray celebrates the artist/ administrator's introduction of classes in lacemaking and embroidery into the curricula of the nation's art schools. Margaret MacCurtain's essay on Walter Osborne's *A Study From Nature* (no. 35) turns to yet another non-traditional artistic genre produced by women, the Irish domestic garden. Such landscapes reflect not the formal ideal of the the grand Anglo-Irish demesne, but a middle-class, suburban version of rurality. Even when overshadowed by the formal plantings of the eighteenth-century Big House, these gardens survived as intimate elements in the nation's landscape. In her reading of Osborne's painting, Mac-Curtain emphasizes the enduring role of Irish women in creating and maintaining this popular domestic art form.

Viewing a controversial nineteenth-century artist from different disciplinary perspectives, two essayists arrive at divergent assessments of his work. Although praised for his technical mastery as a genre painter, Erskine Nicol stirs uneasy responses among his critics (Brian Kennedy 20). John Koch notes that Nicol's "Paddy" series of paintings, depicting boorish Irish rustics, reflects Victorian racist attitudes disseminated, for example, by *Punch* magazine in simian-featured caricatures. Calling upon his training in celtic linguistics, Koch argues that the protagonist of Nicol's *The Seannachie* (no. 10) is not the revered story-teller of an indigenous Gaelic tradition, but rather an outsider's hostile interpretation of that popular figure. By pursuing latent stereotypes in Nicol's work, Koch emphasizes the artist's failure to transcend the political attitudes of his British market.

Economic historian Kevin Whelan, on the other hand, finds more to praise in Nicol's depiction of mid nineteenth-century Ireland. Whelan first contextualizes *The Tenant, Castle Rackrent* (no. 11) by offering exhaustive documentation of British hostility toward its famine-racked colony; he then reads the painting as the artist's layered response to the injustices of a colonial land tenure system. Unlike Koch, this critic argues that Nicol recognizes — albeit with ambivalence— the claims to the land of the indigenous Irish. According to Whelan, Nicol's "flesh-and-blood" tenant embodies a moral and historical relationship between the land and people. He asserts a claim based on family, community and memory, while his landlord's tenure rests on the abstract legalities of property, power, and money.

Several essayists address twentieth-century works by artists actively committed to political independence. By 1922, the tenant in Nicol's nineteenth-century painting possessed the land legally as well as morally. However, the actualities of statehood disappointed some Irish artists and intellectuals — even those who had enthusiatically supported independence. Jack Yeats expresses his hostility in *Patriotic Airs* (no. 42), a painting haunted by ironic absences, which, according to Philip O'Leary, expose discrepencies between the dream of a free Gaelic nation and the "gentrified brand of bourgeois patriotism" of post-treaty Ireland (50). Set in 1923, a year of increasing urban poverty and political violence, the painting depicts a prosperous audience listening to patriotic music in the Gaiety Theater. The complacency of the Dublin burghers belies the national trauma that accompanied the end of Ireland's Civil War. O'Leary's description of Yeats as an active and long-standing participant in the Irish language movement accounts for much of the painting's irony: a bored English-speaking audience betrays the ideals of linguistic cultural nationalism in the very theater that offered the first Irish language play to Dubliners only two decades before.

Although O'Leary reads *Patriotic Airs* as Yeats's satire of a post-independence "packaged … culture," Tim O'Neill's essay reveals Seán Keating's far less hostile response to the new nation. In the years before and after independence, Keating called for an explicitly ideological iconography. His *Men of the West* and *Men of the South*, and his later allegoric series for the Shannon Hydro-electric Scheme, formulated triumphantly nationalistic visual symbols. But in 1933, when he paints *King O'Toole* (no. 19) as the last descendant of an ancient Gaelic family, Keating reflects the inward-looking ideals of Eamon de Valera's conservative nation. Although he embraces and builds on the patriotic romanticism of nineteenth- and early twentieth-century cultural revivalism, Keating offers a visual trope for the new nation's Gaelic heritage with some ambivalence. O'Neill's essay underscores how far the ancient Gaelic familes had fallen in modern Ireland. With neither an economic nor social role, deserted by continuing emigration from the countryside, Keating's old, shabby *King O'Toole* is as much victim as ideal. The essay's description of O'Toole as "proud and sadly defiant" (53) captures Keating's ambiguous iconography.

In the final essay, Kristin Morrison turns to a seemingly apolitical genre of nautical canvases painted in the 1940s by Maurice MacGonigal and Seán Keating, and contextualizes them in Irish literature. She questions why — unlike novelists, playwrights, and poets — visual artists with avowed Republican sympathies, and working within memory of civil upheaval, should insistently depict tranquil ocean settings of moored boats and peaceful harbors. Morrison relates such timid iconographic choices to the needs of the isolationist state of the 1940s: "To have secured one's boat, to be safely home, may indeed have been comforting, and such imagery may have been intended to consolidate a sense of national identity, but is not such an identity inward-looking and provincial" (37)? Of all the nautical scenes in the Burns collection, only Jack Yeats's suggestively titled *The Lookout* (no. 41), painted in 1911 before the armed hostilities of the twenties, the economic trauma of the 1930s, and the isolation of state neutrality during World War II, is willing to face the turbulence of an unknown future.

Collecting History

The evolution of this collection from the early 1970s to 1996 mirrors an important shift in Ireland's cultural self definition: from an inward-looking post-colonial country preoccupied with issues of nationalism to a particpant in the international community. The early acquisitions commemorate a lost rural world shadowed by the memory of the Famine and its aftermath. The anonymous *Lest We Forget* (fig. 1), James Brenan's *The Village Scribe* and *The Schoolroom* (nos. 13, 14), Maurice MacGonigal's *Cailin Og Iarthar* (or *Girl in Green Shawl*) (no. 16), and Seán Keating's *King O'Toole* are examples. Thus the early history of the collection reflects one side of a schism that divided those who looked inward and saw "the key to future … within the island," from those who looked outward and saw that Ireland would thrive only with the infusion of "new influences … from the wider European community" (Murray 9).

The inward looking aspect of these early acquisitions reflects two related impulses: the efforts of generations of cultural nationalists to reconstruct the debased image of a colonized country, and the Irish-American collector's parallel desire to turn a deracinated ethnic group's sense of loss into gain.[14] Like the Literary Revivalists, some nineteenth- and early twentieth-century painters conceived of the western landscape and rural people as the sources of a national identity, and thus attempted to memorialize a disappearing world by making it the

---

[14] "The Irish American knows very little of himself. Too often he remembers only the emigration experience and fails to take pride in the life his grandparents' led" (Interview).

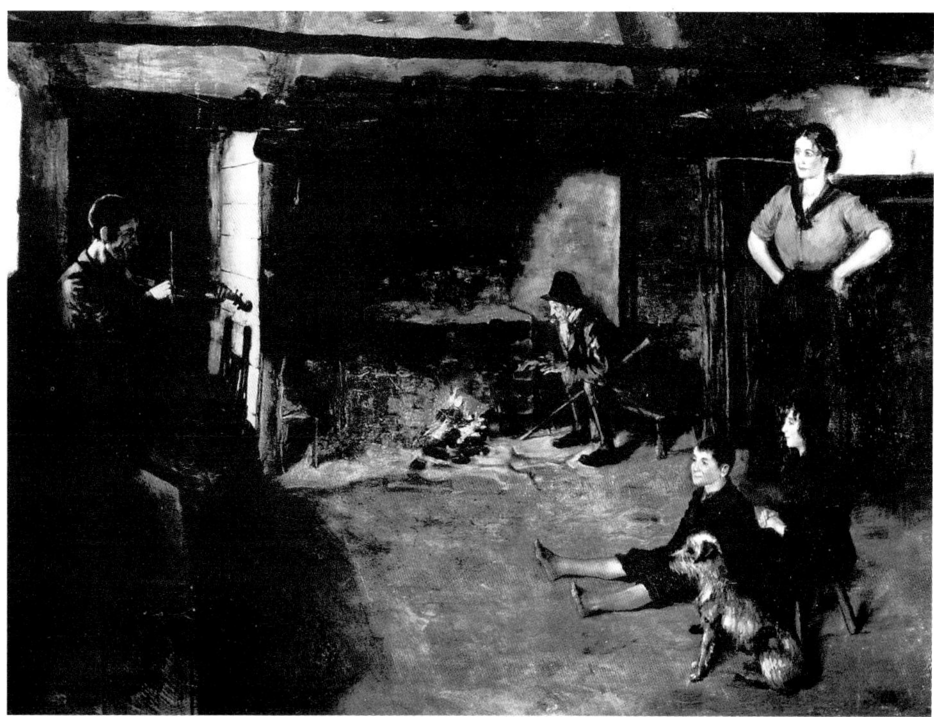

subject of art for elite audiences. In Brenan's nineteenth-century works, for example, peasant society is the "real" Ireland, even when painted by an urban, middle-class artist. MacGonigal's and Keating's more recent heroic portraits similarly celebrate a rural nation rooted in a celtic people, but in their case, by artists who held strong political ties to the twentieth-century Republican movement. These early aquisitions emphasize Mr. Burns's initial desire to reframe his grandfather's memories of exile into the shapes and patterns of a vital people and landscape — and thus to reconfigure the trauma of post-Famine emigration.

Although, from its inception, this collection has included works by women as well as men, by artists from the north as well as the south, Mr. Burns has recently expanded his notion of subjects appropriate for Irish paintings. He continues to acquire works sympathetic to issues of national identity, as, for example the recently purchased *The Artist's Niece Lena, Sewing*, by Leo Whelan (no. 12), in which a Dublin kitchen scene becomes a staged depiction of a traditional west-of-Ireland rural cottage. But the collection now also includes several works depicting a broader range of social classes: professional artists and patrons, sometimes in urban settings, as well as scenes of middle-class and gentry Protestant life.[15] Although several artists represented here — Nathaniel Hone, John Lavery, and Frank O'Meara, for example — executed *plein air* paintings in France and Belgium, only recently in 1990 did Mr. Burns acquire Walter Chetwood-Aiken's *Ar Zon Amzer Nevez* (*A Song to Spring*) (no. 36), and introduce non-Irish settings into his collection. This visually splendid canvas suggests the collector's expanding perspective; in acquiring *Ar Zon Amzer Nevez*, Brian Burns has moved from an exclusively nationalist or "inward looking" side of the social division described by Peter Murray, to the perspective of "those who [are] outward looking." Acquiring the work of a hitherto unknown Irish artist working in France and painting Breton women in a spring orchard, Mr. Burns embarked on a new direction in collecting, a direction that mirrors Ireland's contemporary role in a larger European community.

---

[15] Despite Mr. Burns's stated preference for paintings of rural life produced between 1850 and 1950, one of the early purchases for the collection, *Portrait of Henry Grattan*, by Maria Spillbury-Taylor (1777-1823), was motivated by his sense of a professional kinship with a famous eighteenth-century Irish lawyer/statesman. That Henry Grattan belonged to the Protestant Ascendancy, and that the setting of the painting, a lawyer's library, has nothing to do with rural landscape or the Catholic country people of Mr. Burns' own ethnic roots, suggests, in even the earliest acquistions, this lawyer-collector's openness to a "catholic" vision of Irishness.

The arrangement of the works in this exhibition and catalogue thus illustrates dual pressures on Irish painters. Unlike French or English painters, who felt far less obliged to articulate a national identity, Irish artists turned insistently to the western landscape and rural genre scenes — or alternatively to the Ascendancy world of the Big House and Dublin Castle — to define the special characteristics of the colony or nation. On the other hand, paintings of middle-class life, of the art world, as well as those with European settings, suggest less localized preoccupations. A separate grouping in the exhibition offers works by Jack Yeats, Ireland's most celebrated twentieth-century artist. Paradoxically regarded as the nation's "European genius," Yeats refused to ally himself with any international aesthetic (Pyle 95), and turned repeatedly to settings in the west of Ireland.

Viewers will see Yeats's individualistic relationship to a narrative subject matter, national politics, and avant garde techniques. His earliest work on display here, the watercolor *Duffy's Circus* (no. 40), reveals how the matter of the rural west of Ireland attracted the young painter. But another watercolor, *The Lookout*, moves beyond the merely local and resonates with a heroic mythologizing of the western countryman. In the 1923 oil, *Patriotic Airs*, however, Yeats's response to Irish politics following the War of Independence, the Civil War, and the formation of the Free State becomes explicitly topical and ironic. The late oils of the 1940s, *On to Glory* (no. 43), *The Lonely Sea* (no. 44), *Misty Morning* (no. 45), and *The Embanked Road* (no. 46), express even more vividly the complexity of Yeat's mature work. While employing traditional Irish motifs exploited by cultural nationalists like J. M. Synge or W. B. Yeats — the rose, the sea, the horse, the road — these expressionist works create personal allegories of beauty, freedom, and escape in the isolated Irish nation of mid-twentieth century.

Refusing to espouse the artistic dogmas of either Keating's or MacGonigal's didactic nationalism, or of a European-centered post-impressionism, Yeats is at once the most eccentric and representative of Irish artists. The seven paintings in this exhibition, but a small portion of his oeuvre, support the judgment that even in his striking originality, Yeats embodies and synthesizes both the "inward looking" and "outward looking" directions of Irish art that *America's Eye* presents.

Works Cited

Brian Burns. Interview, April 27, 1995.

Dalsimer, Adele. Ed. *Visualizing Ireland National Identity and the Pictorial Tradition*. Winchester, MA: Faber and Faber, 1993.

Fallon, Brian. *Irish Art 1830-1990*. Belfast: Appletree Press, 1994.

Greeley, Andrew M. *That Most Distressful Nation: The Taming of the American Irish*. Chicago: Quadrangle Books, 1972.

Kennedy, Brian. *Irish Painting*. Dublin: Town House, 1993.

Kennedy, Brian and Raymond Gillespie. Eds. *Ireland: Art into History*. Dublin: Town House, 1994.

Kennedy, S. B. *Irish Art and Modernism*. Dublin: Hugh Land Municipal Gallery of Modern Art, 1991.

Miller, Kerby. *Emigrants and Exiles: Ireland and the Irish Exodus to North America*. New York: Oxford, 1985.

McCaffrey, Lawrence J. *The Irish Diaspora in America*.Washington, D.C.: Catholic University Press, 1976/1984.

McConkey, Kenneth. *A Free Spirit: Irish Art 1860-1960*. London: Antique Collectors' Club, 1990.

Murray, Peter. *Irish Art 1770-1995: History and Society*. Cork: Crawford Municipal Gallery, 1995.

O'Neill, Kevin. "Looking at the Pictures: Art and Artfulness in Colonial Ireland." *Visualizing Ireland*. Dalsimer 55-70.

Pyle, Hilary. "Jack B Yeats — 'A Complete Individualist.'" *Irish Arts Review Yearbook 1993*. V.9: 86-101.

Robinson, Mary. *Address by Mary Robinson On the Occasion of Her Inauguration as President of Ireland*. 3 December, 1990.

—— 'Cherishing the Irish Diaspora.' *Address to the Houses of the Oireachtas by President Mary Robinson On a Matter of Public Importance*. 2 February 1995.

Saarinen, Aline, *The Proud Possessors*. New York: Random House, 1958.

Zilczer, Judith. *"Noble Buyer:" John Quinn, Patron of the Avant-Garde*. Washington, D.C.: Smithsonian Institute Press, 1978.

Essays

In County Mayo J. H. Craig:
The Loneliness of the Long-Distance Landscape

Angela Bourke

The blues, greens, and peaty browns of J. H. Craig's *In County Mayo* (no. 6) suggest the freedom of an empty landscape. A northern Ireland bourgeois Protestant's view of that most Catholic and peasant western county, Craig's painting includes no figures of the people who live there. Even so, this airy outdoors manages to evoke the domestic: the coziness of houses and the work of human hands. Courteously, even shyly, it contemplates the life being lived and its sculptural expression. The Irish Catholic tradition is famous for talk, writing and music, but is credited with little visual art. Yet Craig's landscape is ordered around the forms of turf stacks, which, like the dry stone walls and the elegantly parallel cultivation ridges or "lazy-beds" of the west of Ireland, are as aesthetic as they are practical reponses to the challenges that environment presents and the materials it provides.

Here, sedges and feathery white bog-cotton blow in the clean wind; spongy ground with rocks breaking its surface stretches away toward a small lake and the mountains beyond. The intense blue of the lake, a long horizontal streak flowing into the right frame just below the picture's mid-point, and the piling forms of cumulus clouds mean that the day is fine, most probably a summer afternoon. There is no paved road; no house or other building; there are no fences. This is a turf bog, the "Bogland" of Seamus Heaney's poem.

In American English "turf" may mean territory. In Britain it suggests horseracing or green lawns. In Ireland its primary meaning is peat cut for fuel. In the left of the painting a meandering line of light suggests a bog road, one of the narrow, white, dry ways along which turf for heating and cooking is drawn off the bog, sometimes by car and trailer, sometimes, when the surface is too soft, by a donkey slung with panniers of woven willow, as would have been the custom in Craig's time.

There are machines now which extract turf from the bog, but turf-cutting by hand is still an important part of the summer's work in parts of rural Ireland. Day after day, starting usually in April, the driest month, teams of men methodically cut into what Heaney has called the "kind, black butter" of the bog (85-86), using the narrow, straight-shafted turf spade, called a "slane" (Irish *sleán*). The steel blade of the slane has a wing at right angles to its surface, allowing a good cutter to extract the sod intact with one cut, and he works with such rhythm and efficiency that all emerge the same size and shape and there is no waste. The waterlogged, heavy sods, each larger than a shoebox, are spread on the ground in rows to dry. When they have dried enough to stand on end, they are propped against each other in little wigwam shapes, to let the wind reach as many of their surfaces as possible. This step is called "footing," and is often done by women and children. Like a home-baked loaf, a hand-cut turf-sod carries the signature of the man who cut it. Months later, a woman cooking with turf on her open fire or range can tell the difference between her husband's and her son's cutting.

Burning turf gives off an unmistakable fragrance that incomparably evokes the domestic life of rural Ireland. The turf bog, too, even when empty of human figures, may recall the satisfaction of work and relaxation shared. By its nature it lies at some distance from houses and from cultivated land, so before they had cars, cutters walked or cycled to the bog, and stayed for hours on end. They became ravenously hungry as they worked, and their families carried great quantities of picnic food to them, which men, women and children ate together, sitting on the heather, drinking from bottles of cold milky tea, or boiling up a kettle on a campfire.

As summer wears on, turf cutters assemble the footed sods into larger and larger heaps, and finally, before carrying them home, build them into a stack which can be nine feet high. These are the stacks, or ricks, that Craig shows us. The dried sods of turf, light and narrow enough now to lift easily in one hand, have been laid in careful courses, plaited almost, with short sides facing out and down, to build a shape that hunkers against the wind and throws off rain (only dry turf will burn hot enough to bake bread or heat a house). Later these stacks will be dismantled and carried off the bog in cartloads to be piled in sheds or rebuilt, close to houses, as lean-tos against gables or as free-standing replicas of themselves. Each one represents a year's fuel for a household.

In the painting, a straight-sided watery channel in the bog's surface leads the eye diagonally from the lower left-hand corner into the center. This long rectangle marks where the turf has been extracted, where water has seeped in and reflects the sky; the vertical cut-marks of the slane are still visible along its walls. Dominating the right half of the painting, at the end of the channel, is stack of turf seen head on. The uninitiated eye could see it as simply round: a humpy cone with its tip missing, and indeed some small turf stacks are built this way, but to the left and behind are two further stacks, showing their gabled shape and sloping sides.

The gabled or hipped oblong repeats the shape of the low thatched houses of Irish vernacular building, and of potato clamps, where the tubers are covered with earth for storage. Estyn Evans's *Irish Folk Ways* shows sheaves or "beets" of flax built into the same shape for outdoor storage. The symmetry and alignment of the turf stack is a source of pride to its builder. It is a deliberate, temporary installation in the landscape, and although its construction is dictated by practical

tradition, its detail expresses something of his personality.

Craig, like most of the painters in this exhibition, came from a Protestant background, but his vision of unpopulated bogland is not that of the Anglo-Irish gentry, who built their Big Houses to look out upon landscapes cleared of peasants and their distressing poverty. Such was the eighteenth-century Ascendancy's desire for privacy and a utopia within the walls of its demesnes that many landlords evicted the indigenous people who spoiled their views. Craig contemplates a landscape that is quite without walls, yet bears clear signs of human working. Still, his turning his back on the paved road and on towns and villages is significant.

There is, and was, much more *In County Mayo* than rolling bogland. In August 1879, the year after Craig's birth, fourteen people in the tiny village of Knock reportedly saw an apparition of the Virgin Mary accompanied by St. Joseph and St. John the Evangelist. This apparition led to Knock's becoming a center of Catholic pilgrimage, and, in recent years, acquiring its own airport. Several commentators have linked it with a crisis in agricultural production and land tenure in the years up to 1879. Following a series of disastrous harvests, over 1,000 families were evicted in Ireland that year, large numbers of them in County Mayo. Protest meeetings were held in Knock and elsewhere, and that same autumn the Land League, later led by Charles Stewart Parnell, was founded in nearby Irishtown. Squalid poverty, violent agrarian disputes, and intense Marian devotion, all inevitably fields of disquiet and incomprehension for a prosperous Protestant visitor from County Down, lie just outside the frame of this painting.

Dermot Healy's recent novel, *A Goat's Song*, introduces another northern Protestant into Mayo. This visitor is not a painter, but an officer of the Royal Ulster Constabulary, at the height of the "troubles" in Northern Ireland. For the fictional Jonathan Adams, as perhaps for James Humbert Craig, the turf stack with its sculptural order is a mediator between two cultures.

When Jonathan Adams and his family entered the town of Belmullet, Co. Mayo, "[d]ogs fought. Goats butted the sideboards of carts. Men sat on steps eating sandwiches. Cows shat on pavements. Men sat on tractors eating ice-cream cones. It was like watching some medieval pageant" (118-19). Like a Breughel painting, the human environment described here exhibits all the rackety, rabelaisian disorder conventionally ascribed in Unionist

discourse to Catholics and Irish-speakers, and
Adams is at once alienated and fascinated.
Later, reading about the apparition at Knock,
he realizes:

> He had entered Mayo—a county of graven
> images; pilgrimages with bagpipes; fiddles
> and whiskey; apparitions. The wanton songs
> of men and women. Images that should
> nowise be worshipped. There shall be
> no making of images, nor bowing down to
> them, nor to idolaters, Augustine cried.
> (138)

Gratefully, he turns his eyes instead to the
majestic emptiness of landscape, but, eventually,
turf comes to symbolize his acceptance of and
by Mayo:

> He watched the lines of tractors bearing turf
> home, and bought a trailer load. The farmer
> heeled it up against the side of the house
> and the family in the evenings tried building
> the sods into pyramid-shaped stacks like
> those of their neighbours.
>
> Attacked by midges, they persevered
> haphazardly throughout the weekend, but
> only succeeded in leaving behind them a
> crumbling, half-finished stack of sods, all
> awry and proud and shapeless, when they left
> for home. Three weeks later they returned
> to find that some nameless neighbour had
> finished it in their absence. It stood beside
> the gable wall, tidy and perfect as a hermit's
> beehive hut. This was a miracle in Jonathan
> Adams' [sic] eyes. He tried to imagine from
> the look in the eye of neighbours passing
> who it was who had built his *turf house* for
> him, but no one owned up. (146)

These Ulster Presbyterians, whose whole
measure of pride is in their order, method,
and thrift, must concede that in building a turf
stack the people of Mayo, for all their appari-
tions and whiskey-drinking, are capable
of a tidiness and a perfection which they cannot
achieve. The reference to "a hermit's beehive
hut" is the novelist's wink at his reader, for
beehive huts — the tiny, round, corbelled stone
buildings of early Christian times, found chiefly
in the Dingle peninsula of west Kerry would
surely be outside the mental world of Jonathan
Adams and his family, for whom all such icons of
Irish cultural nationalism are quite exotic. But
this comparison and the reference to the stack as
a turf house confirm its kinship to building and
shelter. Stacked and ready, the turf that heats the
house and scents the air around it is, itself,
house-like.

Seamus Heaney has written of the tiny, perfect
Gallarus Oratory in County Kerry, cousin to
those beehive huts, that entering its stone space
is "like going into a turf-stack"(52). Other
commentators have compared its oblong shape
to an upturned boat. Built at least 800 years
ago, and probably much earlier, as a place
of prayer, it has the same form, the same water-
shedding sturdiness, as Craig's turf stacks.

The turf stacks in this painting quote the shape
of the mountain on the left behind them, and
we are free to read them as part of an uninhab-
ited landscape. But in their environment of time
as well as space, they are known for the recent
work of nearby human hands. Like Gallarus,
these stacks could probably endure for hundreds
of years, but they will be dismantled soon. Their
references are not bare, lonely mountainsides,
but houses, places built and lived in; safe against
the wind and rain, dry inside.

Works Cited

Carroll, Michael P. *The Cult of the
Virgin Mary: Psychological Origins.*
Princeton, N.J.: Princeton University
Press, 1986.

Evans, E. Estyn. *Irish Folk Ways.*
London: Routledge and Kegan Paul,
1957.

Healy, Dermot. *A Goat's Song.*
London: Harvill. 1994.

Heaney, Seamus. *Poems 1965-1975.*
New York: Farrar Strauss Giroux,
1980.

Somerville-Large, Peter. *The Irish
Country House: A Social History.*
London: Sinclair-Stevenson, 1995.

When a Seanchaidhe is not a Seanchaidhe and a Paddy is not a Paddy

John T. Koch

The Seannachie, painted by the Scottish genre artist Erskinee Nicol (1825-1904), reveals an outsider's view of native Irish society. The painting's central figure (the dark ragged man, seated and gesturing at the center) is not a *seannachie* from the traditional Gaelic perspective, a great and real authority and pillar of the social order. Nicol's figure reflects, rather, a long-standing Anglo-Irish interpretation of that Gaelic-speaking story monger. He is an itinerant who seeks illegitimate material entitlements from Anglicized families of modest substance. Moreover, the iconography of the painting derives from neither native Irish nor Scottish representation of the *seannachie,* but from the figure of a sinister tall-hatted huckster invented by the prolific Dutch genre painter Jan Steen (1626-1679). That villain's many incarnations include quack doctors, false clerics, popular entertainers, and an alchemist. Cultivating a typical satirical Victorian view of Ireland, Nicol adapts this traditional Dutch genre figures to his Irish themes.

The seventeenth-century Dutch artist's avaricious purveyor of bogus learning perfectly conveys Nicol's interpretation of the Gaelic *seannachie.* To the colonizers, the charismatic learned man belongs to the alien and inferior culture of the colonized; he is a witch-doctor attempting to enthrall ordinary folk with dark superstition and incomprehensible mumbo jumbo. In the painting, his intended prey are the young and innocent mother and child who stand before their cottage. This humble but virtuous little household — inhabited by the neatly dressed woman and toddler— alludes to British Protestant morality rather than Catholic Irish squalor. Although presumably located in Ireland, the home Nicol's *seannachie* visits could be, just as well, a Scottish or English cottage.

To unpack the resonances of Nicol's painting, we must begin with the word *seannachie* itself, in the native language and culture. It signifies, very broadly, a custodian of traditional history. Within pre-modern Irish society, *seanchaidhthe* formed one of many orders of learned professionals, organized into what we might loosely term 'guilds,' who jealously maintained entitlements from which they derived their livelihoods. Well over a thousand years old, the term and institution are attested as *senchaid* in Old Irish texts (Vendryes S-83-4). The related word for the oral repertory of the *seanchaidhe* is *seanchas,* usually inadequately translated 'tradition.' This word also goes back to the first bloom of vernacular literature in early Christian times, where it refers to a wide range of old stories, historical material, genealogy, and legend. The scope and prestige of *seanchas* can be illustrated by the title of the largest collection of early Irish law codes, which carried the personal authorization of St. Patrick and was termed *Senchus Már 'The Great Seanchas'* (Kelly 242-46). The *seanchaidhe* as custodian of *seanchas* becomes fully meaningful only when we see *seanchas* as uniquely Gaelic in its extent, prestige, and centrality to the culture. *Seanchas* itself is transparently derived from the more basic word *sean* "old," which carries a more positive range of meanings than the English synonym.

For example, *seanmháthair* and *seanathair* are 'grandmother' and 'grandfather;' traditional *sean-nós* singing is singing in the 'old manner;' a *seanfhocal*, literally 'old-utterance,' is a proverb.

What a *seanchaidhe* was (and to some extent, at least, still is) in Irish-speaking society tells us little about Nicol's painting. Neither a member of that society nor sympathetic toward it, Erskinee Nicol was hardly inclined to give us an accurate ethnographic presentation of an Irish *seanchaidhe*. Whether portrayed as quaintly appealing as in *The Tenant* or more often satirically as in his "Paddy" series, Nicol's rustic Irish — in costume, custom, beliefs, and genetic type — appear as distinct from and inferior to the social class of the artist and his English patrons. We have abundant graphic evidence of his negative attitude towards Irish-speaking society, and his short humorous book, *Jim Blake's Tour from Clonave to London* (1867) is a first-person, non-stop spoof of a good-hearted, but abjectly ignorant, Hibernian buffoon. Furthermore, his art is rooted in the tradition of his native pre-Victorian Lowland Scotland, and thus to a style heavily indebted to the Dutch masters. Consequently, Nicol's learned stock of genre types could not have included any uniquely Gaelic cultural figure.

Nicol was raised in greater Edinburgh, and none of the biographical evidence suggests his knowledge of the Irish language, spoken or written. But he need not have known any Irish to have painted a *seanchaidhe*, for the word and concept had long since passed into English. The borrowing of a word from one language to another, as English has borrowed *seannachie* from Gaelic, means either or both of two possibilities: (1) that the two languages are in close and intimate contact with a sizable number of bilinguals in common, (2) that the borrowing language has no precisely suitable word because it has no precisely corresponding cultural institution.

English has no word to cover even approximately the range of meanings of *seanchaidhe*. "Storyteller" lacks the strong sense of authority within the community and the strong sense of professional calling, and a "storyteller" does not necessarily possess a vast repertory founded on ancient tradition, as does the Gaelic *seanchaidhe*. A mere teller of tales or accounts is an Irish *scéalaí*, whose stock and trade, *scéalta*, need not bear the magisterial authority of *seanchas*. English "historian" will not do either; for its connotation is a scholar expert in book learning, as opposed to the primarily oral material of the *seanchaidhe*. There is no native Anglo-Saxonism or Romance borrowing to convey the notion of an individual in more-or-less full command of a vast inventory of otherwise inaccessible oral cultural information.

In passing between societies as different and unequal as those of the colonized native Irish and colonial English, a loan-word may retain its original referent, but shift sharply in its moral valence. And it is just so in the first English occurrence, dating to 1534 and belonging to the state papers of Henry VIII:[1] "That no Yryshe mynstrels, rymours, shannaghes, ne bardes, unchaghes,[2] nor messengers, come to desire any goodes of any man dwelling within the Inglyshrie." This sixteenth-century reference is illuminating in showing the *shannaghe* to be but one specialization among an array of master performers in native learned traditions. Of the six classes of oral performers, three are sufficiently exotic to require words of Gaelic origin. The key legal point is that these professionals had recognized economic claims upon landed native Irish, but emphatically not upon Anglo-Irish, patrons. This *shannaghe* belongs to the "other" Irish society, non-English-speaking and non-Anglicized. He is an implicit threat, subversive to the Tudor regime, a potential corrupting influence, actively seeking to insinuate Gaelic values (in the most literal, socio-economic sense of the word) into Anglo-Irish society.

This early Anglo-Irish view of the *shannaghe* fits Nicol's painting better than does the nativitist notion of the esteemed storyteller of pre-colonial rural Ireland. Like the *Inglyshrie* of the sixteenth-century statute, Nicol's mother and child have an established dwelling and goods. With the *mynstrels, rymours, shannaghes, bardes*, we are not so far from the social rôle of Jan Steen's tall-hatted comic villains — the quack doctors, alchemist, false clerics. Nicol's seated male figure likewise has no fixed abode and offers some sort of animated oral performance, perhaps in exchange for hospitality, a share of the frugal comfort and security of the cottage household.

---

[1] The following passage is taken from the OED, sn. *sennachie*.

[2] *Unchaghe* looks like another loan from Irish and/or Scottish Gaelic. The OED, citing only this example, glosses the word 'a foolish or wanton woman' with a derivation from 'Ir. *óinseach*'. Phonetically, this etymology is workable, but the word had a wider range of meanings in the late Middle Ages, including 'strolling *jongleurs*, clowns' (*Dictionary of the Irish Language*, s.n. *óinseach*), which would be more appropriate in this context.

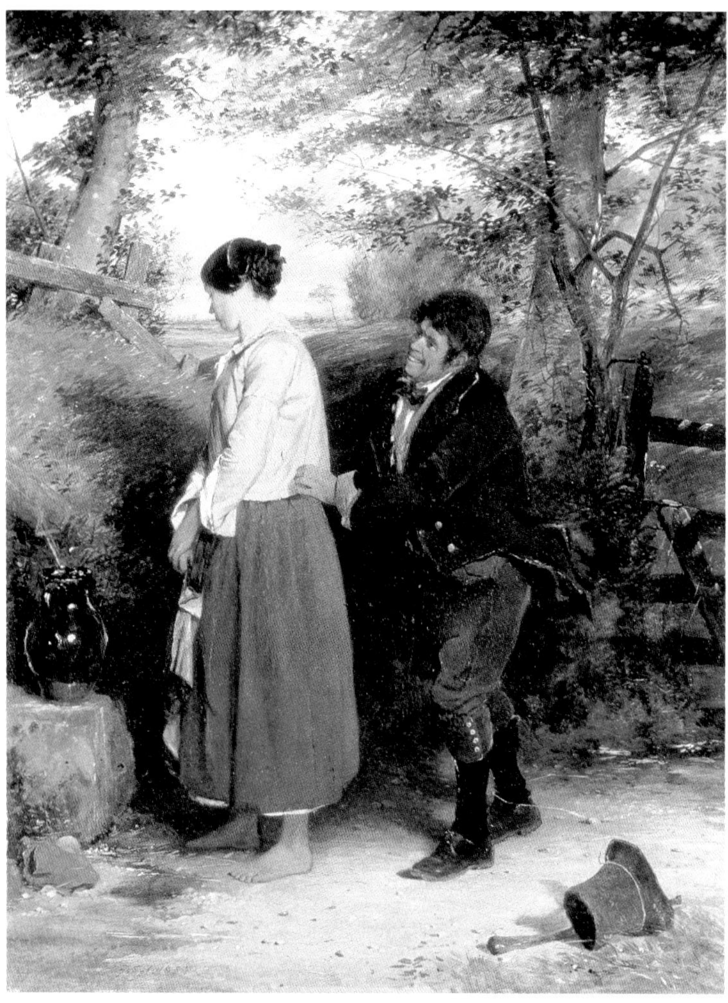

But the young mother sweeping out clumps of dust with her broom blocks the threshold.

Nicol's identity as a Scottish, rather than an English, painter is a crucial link in understanding the moral and ethnic spin he gives to the figure of the *seannachi*. The terms *Gael* and *Gaelic* have long referred — and still do — both to the population, culture, and language of the native Irish and to their closely related counterparts in the Scottish Highlands and Western Isles.[3] Rather less well known, the term *Irish* and its byform *Erse* also formerly referred indifferently to both Irish and Scottish Gaels — and among the older generation in Lowland Scotland, this usage is still not uncommon. By Nicol's young adulthood, the long-standing cultural friction between Lowlander and Gael had been rearticulated within the prevailing pseudo-scientific doctrine of Anglo-Saxon racial superiority, as in the following extract from *The Fifeshire Journal* of 11 September 1851.

> Ethnologically the Celtic race is an inferior one, and attempt to disguise it as we may, there is naturally and rationally no getting rid of the great comical fact that it is destined to give way — slowly and painfully it may be, but still most certainly — before the higher capabilities of the Anglo-Saxon.
>
> In the meantime, a part of the natural law which had already pushed the Celt from continental Europe westward, emigration to America is the only available remedy for the miseries of the race, whether squatting listlessly in filth and rags in Ireland, or dreaming in idleness and poverty in the Highlands and Islands of Scotland. (qtd. in Fenyo)

In this racial formulation, the Irish and Scottish Gaels are one in their abysmal Celtic status and inevitable American exile, though the stereotypical imagery differs somewhat. And for Nicol, issues of Irishness and Celticity would have hit close to home. As a Scot, his identification with the dominant Anglo-Saxons could not be taken for granted, and thus had to be demonstrated unambiguously to his English patrons. Before he arrived in Ireland in 1845/6, Nicole was no doubt already thoroughly familiar with the Gaelic word and institution of the *seannachie*, as borrowed from Scottish Gaelic *seanachaidh*. Among the books that

---

[3] Historical linguistics can explain why modern Scotland and Ireland possess so closely related Celtic languages that they are virtually local dialects of a single language. In the earlier Middle Ages, only one as yet dialectically undifferentiated language was common to Ireland and Northwest Scotland. This language's name for itself was *Goidelg*, i.e. Gaelic. Its modern Irish and Scottish descendants call themselves *Gaeilge* and *Gàidhlig*, respectively. Today, when speaking of the period about AD 600-900, the common mother language is usually called 'Old Irish'. Understandably, a few Scottish scholars prefer 'Old Gaelic'.

were popular during his Edinburgh youth, the introduction to Sir Walter Scott's *Chronicles of the Canongate* and the first novel in that group, *The Highland Widow* (both 1827), have a developed Highland setting. They use and explain, always correctly, a number of Scottish Gaelic names and terms. In the former, we find the following exchange.

> ". . . all I know about the Gael is but of little consequence—Indeed, I gathered it chiefly from Donald MacLeish."
>
> "And who might Donald MacLeish be?"
>
> "Neither bard nor sennachie [sic.], I assure you, nor monk nor hermit, the approved authorities for old traditions. . ." (97)

The second source contains this revealing passage:

> Her memory carried her far back into former days, and her stores of legendary history, which furnish at all times the principal amusement of the Highlander in his moments of repose, were augmented by an unusual acquaintance with the songs of the ancient bards, and the traditions of the most approved seannachies and tellers of tales. (145)

In both passages, Scott presents a culture that differs in language and religion from that of his English and Lowland Scots readership. And the revered authorities of that alien culture hold social positions that do not exist in the English- and Scots-speaking world. The centrality of oral tradition in Gaelic life has, in fact, no analog in the social structure known to Scott's readers. In this sense, Scott's seannachie, with his store "of legendary history," forms an important element in the literary construct of the alien Gael. Accordingly, Scott is as ambivalent to the seannachies as he is to the Highlanders in general. Though semi-romanticized, Scott's Highland Gaelic culture is clearly primitive, less civilized, prone to chaos and inevitable tragedy, generally inferior to that of his audience. To my knowledge, at least to 1900, the English usage of "seannachie" (&c.) never refers to storytellers of the Scots-speaking (i.e. Scottish English-speaking) Lowlands nor to English-speaking Irish, but rather only to the more remote Gaeldom of the Highlands and Western Isles and the Irish *Gaeltacht.*

As a Lowland Scot transforming himself into a Victorian "Briton" in Ireland, Nicol's attitude to the *seanchaidhe* and his Gaelic world was a complex blend of deep familiarity and hostile alienation. Remarkably, Nicol spent the years 1846-1850 in Ireland[4] — the entire duration of the Famine — and yet that national trauma seldom registers in his numerous representations of the Irish poor.[5] It is hard to imagine that Nicol, an accomplished draftsman with an eye for naturalistic detail, could have been so insulated from the disturbing images of the famine years (cf. McConkey 19). Surely this gap must be understood as intentional and meaning-ful, rather than merely anomalous. The greater the suffering of the Irish, the more vociferously English Victorians reinforced the notion of Celtic inferiority as the only possible exculpation of a imperial world order in which one million died of starvation in a nearby colony.

Contemporary cultural critics, particularly those in the fields of Irish or Post-Colonial Studies, will find much to dislike in Nicol's *corpus.* His "Paddies" have the disturbing quality of an ethnic joke whose only point is to reinforce a damaging stereotype. The archetypal Irish rustic is often cast as a crude fool with the familiar apish features of Victorian political cartoons (cf. Crookshank and Knight of Glin 1994, 178). Nicol's series shows Paddy implicitly illiterate, hankering for home-brewed liquor, and sporting the sly but foolish grin of a masher. Ugly, dark-skinned, and ill-kempt, Nicol's Paddy reflects an ideology of racial types akin to the Darwinian "Index of Nigrescence" of Dr. John Beddoe (1826-1911; see Curtis 19-20). In *Don't Say Nay* (fig. 2), a swarthy, simian-featured, and semi-erect Paddy steals up behind a barefoot countrywoman as she collects water from a spring in a glazed black jug. Standing upright, she is taller than he, neat and fair-skinned.[6] Although she appears only in one-quarter view, her features appear to be delicate and refined.

---

[4] He held a teaching appointment with Department of Art and Science in Dublin from 1846-50 (Kennedy 20; Crookshank and Knight of Glin 1994, 178).

[5] *An Ejected Family* (painted in Edinburgh in 1853) may be the closest Nicol came to reflecting the social conditions of the famine that he had witnessed a few years before. It shows the exterior of a thatched cottage and the pitiful evicted family young man, wife, infant, two older children, and an old man (Kennedy 20).

[6] One can only wonder if it was this series that first drew Nicol's famous granddaughter, anthropologist Mary Leakey, to the subject of primate evolution.

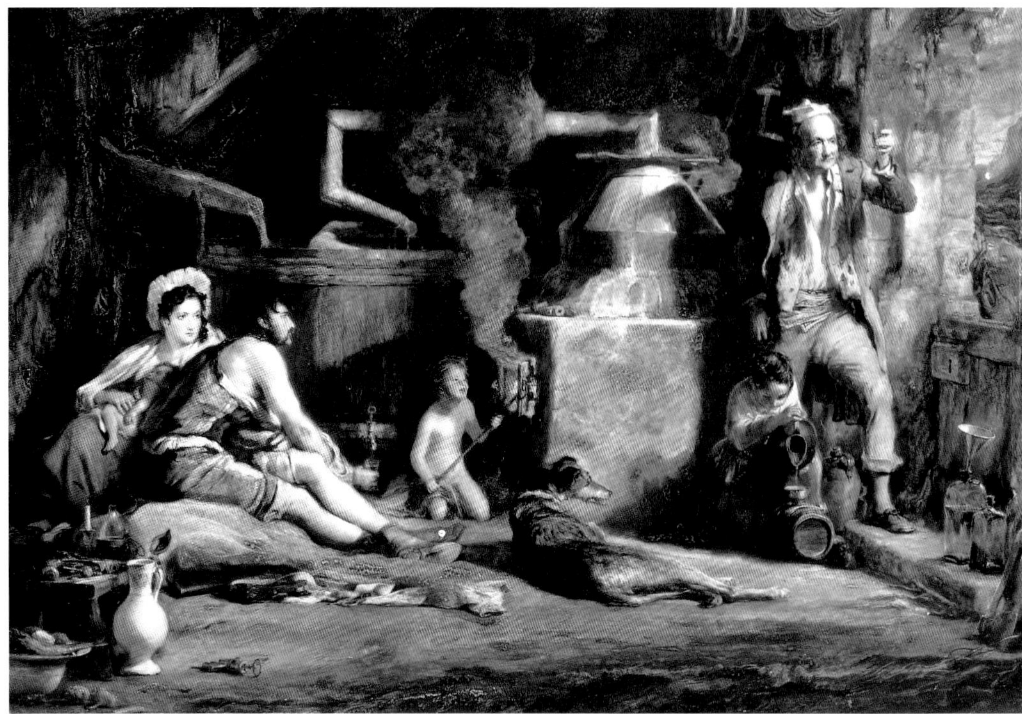

Though Nicol's taste may raise hackles, he usually shows condescension rather than hostility toward his Irish subjects. He is clearly fond of his Hibernian literary persona Jim Blake, a fast friend devoted to his Irish family and native bog. Likewise, his Paddy figure can appear as a central *paterfamilias* in a charming cottage interior. *The Tenant* is typically Irish in his rustic costume and walking stick, but his handsome ruddy features and sad intelligent expression are not Paddy's. The map of "Castle Rackrent" (with its two prominent "bogs") behind him, an allusion to Maria Edgeworth's first novella, will set straight any viewer who has failed to register the other ethnic clues.[7] But Nicols leaves no doubt, even in his most affectionate depictions of the native Irish, that these degraded and demeaned colonial subjects are far inferior to the Victorian middle class for whom he paints.

Although *The Seanchaidhe* lacks the broad ethnic caricature of many of Nicol's other paintings, clues that the central figure is Irish are nonethe-

less present.[8] His facial features are not simian, he lacks the usual green coat, and he is older than any of the artist's images of Paddy. But the *seanchaidhe's* hat is of the same type as has fallen off Paddy's head in *Don't Say Nay* and as the inverted hat of *The Tenant* (no. 11). (Jim Blake has the same sort in some of the book illustrations.) The *Seanchaidh's* short face and pointy chin, implying his toothlessness, and his ragged clothes help mark him as a rural Irishman. The woman and her hair style are similar to those in *Don't Say Nay*, as is her black glazed jug and even its position.

If the old man in this painting is indeed a Nicol Irishman, why is he a different sort of Nicol Irishman? Like the Paddy of *Don't Say Nay*, *The Seanchaidhe* may be read as an idle would-be seducer, seeking the attentions of an industrious housewife. But Paddy, guileless, sneaks up oafishly from behind, while *The Seanchaidhe* is neither an oaf, nor a forgivable simple soul. Because he has more craft and charm, he is more

---

[7] On this painting, see further Whelan's essay in this volume.

[8] Assuming that *The Seanchaidhe* is the intended title, it is clear enough that the man cannot be a Scottish *seanachaidh*, or any sort of Highland Gael. Nicol would give any Highlander his tam, tartan, and other telltales. The lack of overt poverty and general tidiness of the cottage in *The Seanchaidhe* does not constitute any kind of an argument for a Highland Scottish, as opposed to Irish, setting. Neither the reality nor the reputation of the Highlander was notably better than that of the Irish in the mid nineteenth century. Gaelic Scotland was not exempt from the potato famine, and the infamous compulsory eviction and emigration, the so-called 'Highland clearances,' continued to this period.

dangerous. Casting his spell in plain view, his motive must be something more subtle than straightforward lust. The painting suggests, moreover, elements of moral allegory: the more virtuous figures, younger and better dressed, are bathed in light, while the old rascal moves in dark shadow. He beckons from the west, as the wholesome young household in the east hesitates. The mother sweeps the gray dirt from her house out to the stranger's dark exterior ground.

Nicol's artistic vices are principally the cliched prejudices of England in the Victorian Age. However, his enduring virtues — composition, naturalistic detail, and occasional social empathy (albeit condescending) — can all be traced back to his pre-Victorian predecessor Sir David Wilkie (1785-1841) and especially to Wilkie's earlier and more popular 'Dutch' style of 1804-1825.[9] A minister's son from Fife, Wilkie (like Nicol) was a Lowland Anglophone Protestant, and like Nicol, he was educated in Edinburgh (MacMillan 165-78; Errington). Probably Nicol's repeated journeys to Ireland were inspired in part by Wilkie's tour of Dublin and the west in 1835 — as well as his friendship with Maria Edgeworth. Wilkie's one Irish painting *The Irish Whiskey Still* (1840) (fig.4) may, in its subject, have contributed to some of Nicol's "Paddy" paintings, but the elder artist's still-keeping family, though ragged, are physically idealized, reminiscent of Ossianic heroes, and oddly, the illicit nature of their activity escapes any moralistic disapproval (Errington 15-17).

Wilkie chose to paint mostly Lowland Scottish themes that sometimes looked back a generation or more from the painter's time. But more important was his attitude towards his subject. He never set himself above, or apart from the humble and disadvantaged characters in his scenes to side with his wealthy English patrons. The shy children who attend transfixed Wilkie's *Blind Fiddler* (1806) seem possible prototypes for the shy toddler of Nicol's *Seanchaidhe*. The ragged but dignified fiddler differs from Nicol's *Seanchaidhe*, showing Wilkie's respect for traditional folk art, in recognizing this itinerant as a humble heir to Homer and the romanticized Gaelic bard Ossian (MacMillan 171).

The best spirit of the Scottish reformers is alive in Wilkie's paintings and remains accessible and admirable today.[10] As well as Maria Edgeworth's *Castle Rackrent*, Wilkie's 'rent paintings' (which became popular subjects of *tableaux vivantes*) are necessary background to Nicol's *Tenant* and *Ejected Family*. But for Wilkie and Edgeworth, the plight of the tenantry was a leading social issue. In Nicol's paintings, these themes may be construed as nostalgic, rather than groundbreaking, lying within an accepted canon of imperial subject matter. His Irish paintings only serve to emphasize his relative lack of involvement with the starker humanitarian disaster he had lived through.

In Nicol's favor, we see that his sense of humor was far richer than Wilkie's; he seldom took his subject or himself altogether seriously. If we wonder how Nicol could bear to give so much time and painstaking workmanship to subjects for which he plainly had no respect (such as Paddy, Jim Blake, or *The Seanchaidhe*), the spiritual kinship of the clown artist for his clown creations may be our answer. Wilkie and Nicol were alike enough in their cultural background, genre tradition, and technical ability. The disparity that separates the major painter from the minor lies surely in the differences in social conscience and empathy.

---

[9] As opposed to the 'Spanish' style of his later career, which shows influence from El Greco and Velázquez.

[10] Though he was appointed Painter to the King in 1830, at one time Wilkie's social conscience jeopardized his patronage. The moving *Distraining the Rent* (1815) was coolly received. Wilkie's friend Haydon wrote of the episode: 'The aristocracy evidently thought it an attack on their rights. Sir George [Beaumont] was very sore on the private day, and said Wilkie should have shown why the landlord had distrained; he might have been a dissipated tennant' (MacMillan 174).

Works Cited

Crookshank, Anne, and the Knight of Glin. *The Watercolours of Ireland: Works on Paper in Pencil, Pastel and Paint*, c. *1600-1914*. London: Barrie & Jenkins, 1994.

Curtis, L. Perry, Jr. *Apes and Angels: The Irishman in Victorian Caricature*. Washington, DC: Smithsonian Institution Press, 1971.

Dictionary of the Irish Language, Based Mainly on Old and Middle Irish Materials (Compact Edition). Dublin: Royal Irish Academy, 1983.

Errington, Lindsay. *David Wilkie 1785-1841* (Scottish Masters 10). Edinburgh: National Galleries of Scotland, 1988.

Fenyo, K. 'Highland Clearances: A Form of Ethnic Cleansing,' *West Highland Free Press*, 3 July 1995.

Kelly, F. *A Guide to Early Irish Law.* Dublin: Institute for Advanced Studies, 1988.

Kennedy, S. B. *Irish Art and Modernism, 1880-1950*. Belfast: Queen's University Press, 1991.

McConkey, Kenneth. *A Free Spirit: Irish Art, 1860-1960*. London: Antique Collectors' Club in association with Pyms Gallery, 1990.

MacMillan, D. *Scottish Art, 1460-1990*. Edinburgh: Mainstream Publishing, 1990.

N[icol], E[rskine]. *Jim Blake's Tour from Clonave to London*. Dublin: M. H. Gill, 1867.

OED = *Oxford English Dictionary*. 2nd ed. Oxford: Oxford University Press, 1989.

O'Leary, Philip. *The Prose Literature of the Gaelic Revival, 1881-1921: Ideology and Innovation*. University Park: Pennsylvania State University Press, 1994.

Scott, Walter. *Chronicles of the Canongate*. 1827. Boston: Estes and Lauriat, 1894.

Vendryes, J. *Lexique étymologique de l'Irlandais ancien*. Dublin and Paris: 1959.

Reflections on Walter Osborne's
Study from Nature

Margaret MacCurtain

The repose of Walter Osborne's *Study from Nature* (no. 35) draws the beholder into the picture to observe a seated woman in a wide-brimmed straw hat, comfortable apron and dark skirt — the garb of the woman gardener of the last hundred years. She sits on the ground gazing at her harvest of freshly-dug potatoes, having plunged the trines of her pitchfork into the trench. Nothing in the stillness of the central figure suggests pressure.

In the right-hand corner, shafts of light and shade play over a bluish-green cabbage. Behind the foreground of what appears to be the corner of a vegetable plot, a wood-rail fence holds back from the potato patch an exuberance of natural vegetation, a branchy fruit bearing tree, and the abundance of tall wildflowers at its base. Still further behind, a larger fence separates the scene from the more distant background. Having given his painting so general a title, Osborne invites the beholder, as well as the central figure, into a reverie withdrawn from outside distraction. Some viewers may see in the delicate range of blues and greys the dawn of an autumn day. The muted greens and whites, the shading of the dug clay, the counterpoint of amethyst shades in the woolen blouse, and the warm russet tones of the potatoes demonstrate the artist's understanding of composition. The longer the eye observes the subtle shading, the more secrets it will reveal. Is that a ladder mingling with the lower branches of the fruit-tree? How the spread branches relieve any monotony of sky the milky dawn light casts! Is that tall spire, behind the pitch-fork, an onion

flower, *Allium cepa Proliferum*? Notice the tones of the wicker basket and how the light plays on the hand of the woman holding the twig.

Walter Osborne's popularity has grown steadily. A wider public came to honor his paintings during and since the exhibitions of his work at the National Gallery of Ireland and the Ulster Museum in 1983. His *Apple Gathering, Quimperlé* (1883), which hangs in the National Gallery of Ireland, shows two small country girls collecting fruit. Like *Study From Nature*, it evokes the pleasures of an unsophisticated seasonal farm ritual. As a landscape artist, Osborne preferred to paint the light and shadow of farmland, with fields, hedges and trees, and rural-looking buildings, rather than dramatic scenery (Sheehy 27). He often peopled his landscapes with a lone figure, as in *Seated Boy* and *Study from Nature*. If he chose to establish an evocative autumnal mood, for example, he drew his subject-matter from life, and painted out-of-doors to capture its particular light.

Osborne belonged to the generation of Irish painters who acquainted their viewers with what was then a relatively new phenomenon in late nineteenth-century Dublin: the suburban, middle class garden. The son of an artist, Osborne grew up in Rathmines, just outside Dublin City on Castlewood Avenue, and he finished his life in the same house. Before the turn of the century, today's suburban Rathmines was partly in the countryside, and Castlewood

Avenue houses possessed back gardens with trees, flower beds and vegetable plots. Quietly but insistently Osborne's paintings of suburban and rural life projected the aspirations of the *plein-air* circle of artists to which he belonged. This group invariably worked out-of-doors, endeavoring to infuse their subjects with the sensibility of nature as they saw it at that moment.

In *Study from Nature,* Osborne depicts a domestic landscape evoking a suburban version of rurality that accompanied major changes in economic and social life after the mid-nineteenth century. Although the painting was created in the French countryside, in the canvas Osborne celebrates the intimate garden landscape of Ireland as well as the continent. In choosing such informal scenes as subject matter, Osborne broke from the earlier convention of painting the vast geometric landscape gardens of aristocratic patrons. Placing a woman at the center of his canvas, moreover, suggests the role Irish women have played in creating and maintaining domestic gardens throughout the centuries.

Prior to the Great Famine of the 1840s, gardens were the prerogative of the aristocracy, the ostentatious extension of the castles and great houses of Ascendancy Ireland. Ornamental shrubbery and park lands set off the houses of the nobility; herbal and flower gardens were cultivated by lesser mortals, such as Mrs. Delany, in the rectory garden at Delville[1], and by Maria Edgeworth, the novelist, for pedagogical instruction of her father's numerous children at Edgeworthstown. But the Irish laboring classes could ill-afford the space even for a cottage garden, as the demand for potato cultivation invaded every available foot around their hovels.

Pre-Famine Ireland was a map of tessellated landscaped demesnes with forbidding boundary walls protecting their inmates from wild countryside, and wilder inhabitants who roamed it. Unless they were estate villages, towns had little aesthetic consciousness about parks or landscaping. Absorbed in surviving the tides of poverty-stricken families that fled the countryside in the decades of rising population before the 1840s, Irish towns were bleak, inhospitable refuges for the poverty stricken.[2] The appearance of urban back-gardens in post-Famine towns and cities signified a return to normality. These new garden forms represented a defensive response to the ravages of the Great Famine, and a withdrawal into an aestheticized domesticity by an expanding Victorian bourgeoisie.

In Osborne's generation, middle-class women themselves tended their flowers and vegetables, distant in both time and mentality from the elegant eighteenth-century ladies, who paced the avenues of their estates, excluded by the laws of propriety from "working" in the gardens of their demesnes. Osborne's woman gardener is closer in spirit to a seventeenth-century settler's wife who tended the small house garden adjacent to Tully Castle in County Fermanagh. Built as a fortified tower-house in 1618 (in reality a planter's castle), its ruins today overlook the Erne river (Waterman 123-26). The castle was destroyed after a massacre, witnessed by the woman of the house, in the fateful 1641 Ulster Rising. Its garden, which she cultivated, was situated in the bawn, or open space, in front of the castle.[3] This Scottish planter's wife grew the flowers and herbs she loved: heartsease, love-in-a-mist, marigold, larkspur, pink campion, cornflower, and the herbs lemonbalm, marjoram, bergamo, rosemary, sweet cecily, lovage, Welsh poppy, chives, fennel and tansey. Loyal to the Scottish King James I, she planted Scottish Rose, Rose of York and Lancaster, and Jacobite Rose with older strains like the Rosa Mundi, much favored by medieval herbalists, and Maiden's Blush.[4]

Máire Rua O'Brien's seventeenth-century is less gloomy. She re-designed the fortified house at Leamaneh in County Clare after her marriage to Conor O'Brien, adding a courtyard and an adjoining pleasure garden. In his 1900 ground plan of Leamaneh, T. J. Westropp, the antiquarian scholar, shows an ornamental walk, a summer house and a fishpond. Close by, a small ruined turret, called to this day "Máire Rua's seat," overlooks the Burren countryside where alpine and arctic plants grow amid Mediterranean species. Leamaneh, with its four stories and bartizan in its southwest wall (Westropp 403-

---

[1] Against the wishes of her aristocratic family, Mary Granville married Dr. Patrick Delany, an Irish clergyman of humble origin and modest means. Her letters and diaries, her flowered collages, and her witty personality establish her as one of the most remarkable observers of eighteenth-century Irish life. Her gardens at Delville, her painting, shell work, and needle work were, in different ways, a celebration of the flower.

[2] See *Irish Country Towns,* and *More Irish Country Towns,* Ed. Anngret Simms and J.H. Andrews, Cork: Mercier Press, 1994, 1995.

[3] This garden has been recently reconstructed and put in the care of the Department of the Environment for Northern Ireland.

[4] The history of Tully Castle and its flowers is available from the Historic Monuments and Buildings Branch, Department of the Environment for Northern Ireland.

07), stood sturdily on a Gaelic frontier, yet even today visitors standing in the shadow of this fortress ruin can trace the walls of a deer park, a reminder of Máire Rua's dramatic renovations to her home on the eve of the Cromwellian conquest.

With the final subduing of the rebellious Irish at the end of the seventeenth century, the victors, loyal supporters of their monarchs William and Mary, settled down to enjoy the land that was their reward. A period of ninety years ensued, uninterrupted by rebellion or invasion. The most spectacular feature of this age of property was the building boom of the new landed gentry. All over Ireland, landowners built themselves imposing residences—Palladian, Gothic-revivalist and neo-classical in style. On these spectacularly landscaped demesnes, women's personal gardening space disappeared, as professionally designed and maintained gardens took over. Care of the estate, including the demesne, was perceived to be men's work.

Like those houses of an earlier period, the classical eighteenth-century great house was designed for defense. Heavy locks, chains, and a deep moat or ditch protected entries and ground windows from unlawful entry. Beyond the trenches stretched lawns, bounded by low ditches or sunken fences, that dropped to the parks dotted with trees. Then, in a long curve as far as the eye could see, the demesne kept people out as much as they restrained animals from wandering. In her memoir of her family seat, *Bowen's Court,* Elizabeth Bowen exposes the vulnerability of the Big House and its demesne: "the isolation is innate; it is an affair of origin" (248).

On these isolated demesnes, in the pre-Famine years of dense population and cheap labor, scores of gardeners tended the Big House grounds. By then, the enclosed and locked "walled garden" had become a feature of the Big House landscape. Placed close to a side-door of the mansion, such gardens permitted family and friends to enjoy the herbaceous borders, the yew and oak walks, the rock gardens and water gardens, yet remain discreetly out of sight. If space permitted, the kitchen garden, originally located some distance from the house, was incorporated within the walled garden; clipped beech hedges outlined the four quadrants of its French *potager-jardin* layout. The kitchen garden's popularity continues, and recently, Lanning Roper, the designer of Glenveagh Castle Gardens in County Donegal, has recreated its early nineteenth-century beauty in a splendid mixture of flower, fruit and vegetable.

Were it not for the testimony of an upper-middle-class clergyman's wife in her letters and diaries, and in the artistic precision of her flower collages, women as gardeners would have been overlooked in the construction of the great demesne landscapes of those centuries. Mrs. Delany's delight in her Delville garden in Glasnevin, and in the countryside around the deanery in Downpatrick, County Down, is reflected in a March 1746 letter to her sister: "I have been planting sweets in my 'Pearly Bower' — honeysuckles, sweet briar, roses and jessamine to climb up the trees that compose it, and for the carpets, violets, primroses and cowslips" (qtd. in Hayden 64)! For Mrs. Delany, the ability to recognize the ability a well planned garden became a touchstone of good taste. Commenting on a friend's lack of appreciation, she wrote "no eyes nor under-standing to see that it was not a common vulgar garden." Returning from her rambles with "handfuls of wild plants," she would, "search for their names and virtues in Hill — but he is not half so intelligible as old Gerard," (qtd. in Hayden 68) referring to her ever-present botany books. An early botanist, she identified rare specimens and classified them scientifically. Popularizing wild flowers, she rebelled against the absurdities perpetrated in the interests of formality: "Today," she writes in her diary,

> we dine at Lord Chief Justice Singleton's at Drumcondra. He has given Mr. Bristowe full dominion over house and gardens, and like a conceited connoisseur, he is doing *strange things* building an absurd room, turning fine wild evergreens out of the garden, *cutting down,* full-grown elms and planting twigs! (qtd. in. Hayden 79)

Mary Delany's gardening letters return us to the world of Walter Osborne's *Study from Nature.* He too, was a naturalist, and for years he worked in the open air, lodging in cottages and in small country inns, until winter arrived. But in the hundred years since Osborne painted *Study from Nature,* a transformation in the Irish landscape has occurred. Gone is the formally landscaped demesne of the Big House, isolated from and at odds with the world outside its walls. While its hold on the literary imagination remains hypnotic, in popular perception the Big House has been stripped of its aloofness. It has become a place to visit and to reclaim as a national heritage, an accomplishment linked to the transformation of the nation. At weekends,

Irish families explore house and gardens, a testimony to the new leisure interest in gardening that has seized that very section of society for which Elizabeth Bowen expressed her class repugnance. "The democratic smell of the Dublin bus" (*Irish Stories,* 10) that Bowen abhorred now mingles with the scent of old roses and lavender; the gate of the walled garden swings open to admit visitors once deemed intruders.

The suburban flower garden flourishes, its pleasures replenished from the retail garden centers that have sprung up throughout the country. The "Tidy Towns" competition has brought trees and plants to the bare streets of Irish municipalities, and has restored elegance to neglected stone work. In their acclaimed compilation, *In an Irish Garden* Sybil Connolly and Helen Dillon describe the gardens of "castles, Georgian mansions, small country houses, vicarages, town houses, modern bungalows and cottages in the four corners of Ireland"(8). The past, educating the present, has given us back the Irish garden that Osborne painted.

Works Cited

Bowen, Elizabeth. *Bowen's Court.* London: Virago, 1984.

— *Irish Stories.* Dublin: Poolbeg, 1978.

Connolly, Sybil and Helen Dillon. *In an Irish Garden.* London: Weidenfeld and Nicolson, 1986.

Hayden, Ruth. *Mrs. Delany and Her Flower Collages.* London: British Museum Press, 1980.

Sheehy, Jeanne. *Walter Osborne 1859-1903.* Dublin: Town House and The National Gallery of Ireland, 1991.

Waterman, D. M. "Tully Castle." *Ulster Journal of Archaeology* 22 (1959).

Westropp, T. J. "Leameneagh Castle." *Journal Royal Society Antiquarians of Ireland* 30 (1900).

Looking Out, Looking In: Nautical Paintings by MacGonigal, Yeats and Keating

Kristin Morrison

As full-time literary scholar and part-time sailor, I find myself surprised by the marine paintings in the Brian Burns collection. They are all so tranquil and firmly land based — although Ireland is a country surrounded by dangerous waters rich with dramatic imagery. Yet, not only here, but in most Irish paintings of the late-nineteenth and early-twentieth centuries, the gentleness of the sea, the static visual details of its strands and harbors, occupy the painters' attention rather than the life-threatening perils of a powerful Atlantic. Jack Yeats (nos. 40-46), Seán Keating (nos. 17-19) and Maurice MacGonigal (nos. 15, 16) — the first, one of the finest painters of this century and the other two important in their time — all were drawn to the west of Ireland. They contemplated its imagery and painted its scenes from first-hand experience, yet, for the most part, rendered their studies of sea and boats in surprisingly mild terms.

This choice is all the more puzzling in light of the three artists' commitment to Irish nationalism. Keating devoted himself to the creation of a visual identity for the new Irish Free State (Marshall 90);[1] MacGonigal believed that "well-observed landscapes could assist the establishment of a national identity" (Kennedy, *Irish*

Painting 36), and Jack Yeats provided the nation with heroic images of its native people.[2] Yet these painters for the most part avoid rendering the real turbulence of that ocean in the midst of which they lived and whose power they had witnessed directly. At best they present scenes of moderate struggle, such as Yeats's *Dinish Ferryman* (1905) and *Off the Donegal Coast* (1922); but even in Yeats's *Many Ferries* (1948), whose choppy brushstrokes evoke a more dangerous sea, the artist positions his viewer and himself on the highest point of the island, safely distant, well inland.

Jack Yeats's watercolor *The Lookout* (c. 1911) (no. 45) provides a useful focus for my further speculations about this puzzling matter. The most striking element in this painting is the fact that the titular figure looks in toward the land, not out toward the sea. At the extreme left, the dark shingled edge of the house, occupying a vertical strip almost as wide as a quarter of the canvas, bespeaks fixity and solidity. In the right half of the composition, the sea, the ships, the lighthouse seem mistily remote. Between these two parts, the figure himself moves with all his body toward the sea and toward his task: his weight begins to shift forward, his arms hold the binoculars poised for use; only his head

---

[1] Brian P. Kennedy writes that Keating "was, to an extent, the official artist of the Irish Free State" (*Ireland, Art into History* 147).

[2] From June 3 to July 3, 1905, Yeats toured Connemara and Mayo with J. M. Synge, who was commissioned to write a series of 12 fact-finding essays about the Congested Districts for the *Manchester Guardian*; Yeats supplied the illustrations. For a fuller discussion of this matter, see Dalsimer (201-230). Keating's visits to the west coast and Aran began around 1913; MacGonigal's during the 1930's (S. B. Kennedy 170, 178).

and his eyes turn back. He stands arrested between two states of matter, solidity and fluidity, two forms of color and light, heavy darkness and glowing blues, two ways to live, in safety or in danger, with the known or with the unknown. For the viewer of the painting, two particular unknowns add to the sense of mystery: what has the figure seen through his binoculars (or what does he intend to look for)? and what has caught his attention in the house behind? Both are off the canvas; only the figure knows and sees. He gazes, and the spectator gazes at him. Both he and the spectator look *in*. Even the boats head in toward the land. There seems, at first glance, to be no "out" in this picture despite its title.[3]

This inward orientation of Yeats's *The Lookout* prompts me to see afresh other paintings of harbors and boats in the Brian Burns Collection. Such marine subjects, of course, have always been popular with painters. Graceful curves of hulls contrasting with upright masts and rigging, reflections in the water (like the painting itself, a second world that does — and does not — resemble its original), bright colors, shimmering light, cobblestones, piers, clinkerbuilt dinghies, ropes and nets, indistinct weathered faces and forms, abundant variety in line and texture: all this imagery, no doubt, presented interesting technical challenges to the artists and probably sold better than "still life with fruit." MacGonigal's *Fishing Boats at Clogherhead* (c. 1943) (no.15) and Keating's *The Port Authority* (c. 1940s) (no.18) may simply be competent if rather tame manifestations of a pleasant and popular marine genre. Even so, they share with the more subtle Yeats a similar slant on people in their paintings. And this I begin to find significant.

Although MacGonigal has made his figures less important than the scene, he, too, like Yeats and Keating, has sketched all the figures as men; furthermore, all three artists have given these eighteen men identical hats, the mark it would seem of a common confraternity. Here, at least in these particular paintings, Yeats, Keating, and MacGonigal present an exclusively male world. All their men are busy, full of purpose, but except for Yeats's lookout, none, not even Keating's striding authority, seems aware of anything remote, anything or anyone

"out there," anything "other." Like their boats, the men are either headed in or securely moored in their masculine ports.

Were there no women in the actual nautical world of the western counties that Yeats, MacGonigal, and Keating visited? No Irish equivalents of the actual Scottish fishwives who carried their menfolk on their backs through the water to the boats and who themselves controlled the economy of the port? Was there no Irish Grace Darling, famous for rowing out in a storm off the Northumberland coast to rescue survivors from the wrecked steam ship Forfarshire in 1838? Workers or heroines, where are the women?[4] An historian can supply the factual answer for Connaught and Galway in the late-nineteenth and early-twentieth centuries. What is clear in the imaginary world of Irish marine painting for that same place and time, as represented by these paintings, is that women are absent. As, indeed, is that mightiest of others, the challenging turbulent sea.

By contrast, literature of this period contains several important instances of weather-racked waters and courageous women. J. M. Synge, who visited the Aran Islands often, and who accompanied Yeats on his tour of Connemara and Mayo, has rendered the sea as the most powerful presence pitted against the chief female character in his elegant one-act drama, *Riders to the Sea* (1904). Even as late as 1955, Peadar O'Donnell, in *The Big Windows,* uses island life, with its vital open-mindedness (a gift of the sea, embodied in Brigid, the main character), to present a critique of conservative Irish rural life in the glens. And, to take a particularly long and vivid example, Emily Lawless in her novel *Grania. The Story of an Island* (1892) presents the violent and destructive imagery of the sea as none of these Irish painters have. Her titular character is a genuine lookout who knowingly, heroically braves the sea and whose story demonstrates, by contrast, how very land-based and even timid are any corresponding marine paintings supposedly concerned with "national identity."

By phrasing her title *Grania. The Story of an Island*, Lawless has equated principal character with scene. Grania's is not "an island story,"

---

[3] In Yeats's *Misty Morning* (c. 1943) (no. 45) the main figure exhibits a similar "divided stance," resembling a view of this lookout from the back; here, too, the only boat presented seems inbound, very close to shore, ready to land (or so the first impression of the painting suggests: closer examination, however, reveals that oarlocks and rowers are oddly positioned, too far forward for effective rowing, though perhaps the mist distorts the scene). This man on shore also gives his attention to what is apparently headed in, not out.

[4] MacGonigal's portrait of a peasant woman (no. 16) shows her land-based and idle, flanked by haying equipment that looks as if it has never been used, her hands passive in her lap.

nor *a* story *about* the island: instead, her story and the island's are one and the same. In embodying her island, Grania takes on mythic status in her own right, quite apart from the associations of her name.[5] Her personal history thus stands for more than its starkly tragic events; Grania's life and even her death offer a positive emblem of national identity.

The plot — the mere skeleton of a story — is simple enough. Grania, a girl of Inishmaan, in Galway Bay, grows up loving a handsome island boy named Murdough, who, though a fisherman, proves physically and morally weaker than she. Attracted to her greater wealth (that is, by island standards), he agrees to marry her eventually. When Grania's sister is dying, Murdough refuses her request that he row, through blinding fog and rough sea, to Aranmore to summon the priest.[6] So Grania goes herself — and perishes — but only after ensuring that the priest will reach her sister in time. Such a reduction of story to plot suggests —albeit minimally — how scenic elements support narrative and serve as analogues for Grania's character. Inescapably, ocean and weather are chief among these scenic elements, realistically bracketing the novel, beginning and end.

Boldly, Lawless begins her novel with two one-sentence paragraphs, the first chastely declarative, the second as nuanced in structure as what it describes:

> A mild September afternoon, thirty years ago, in the middle of Galway Bay.

> Clouds over the whole expanse of sky, nowhere showing any immediate disposition to fall as rain, yet nowhere allowing the sky to appear decidedly, nowhere even becoming themselves decided, keeping everywhere a broad indefinable wash of greyness, a grey so dim, uniform, and all-pervasive, that it defied observation, floating and melting away into a dimly blotted horizon, an horizon which, whether at any given point to call sea or sky, land or water, it was all but impossible to decide. (I, 1f)

After this gentle opening, appropriate to Grania's simple and untroubled childhood, there

follows a very long segment describing the challenge that proves her character. Thus the last 96 pages of the novel describe in eerie vividness the heavy fog that makes even the island itself dangerously slippery, the final 25 pages recounting Grania's heroic venture through treacherous waters, "exactly like trying to row blindfold" (II, 277). Here Lawless sustains the sense of peril generated in the land-fog passages, intensified now by rocks and tide, while at the same time conveying the admirable calmness and bravery of Grania's resolve:

> Greenish points were rising dimly in every direction, some of them within an inch or two of the surface, and beyond these again were other and larger masses, formless as the very fog itself, but which could be nothing but rocks, the barnacle-coated knife-edged rocks of Portacurra, a touch from one of which would tear a hole in the curragh's canvas sides and sink it like a stone.

> Backing cautiously, she managed to escape without any contact. Only just in time, however; another stroke of the oars, two seconds' more delay, and Phelim's warning would have come too late.

> They were now out in Gregory's Sound, and the only serious danger therefore was of missing the great island altogether, and rowing straight away into the Atlantic. (II, 278f)

Between these two scenic brackets of opening mild afternoon and concluding nighttime fog, with the ultimate and absolute danger of being lost at sea, the novel unwinds its story, showing the kinds of choices Grania must make. Thus throughout the novel Lawless uses vivid descriptions of rocks and tides to literalize the terms of Grania's — and the island's — life … or death, as in this picture of "bare sea-washed sheets of limestone" (II, 54).

> Ledge above ledge, layer above layer, these last rose; straight, horizontal, clean cut as if laid by some builder's hands, a mass of crude, uncompromising masonry. Under that lowering sky it was about as cold and as menacing a prospect as could well be imagined—a prospect, too, that had a

---

[5] The Grainne of Celtic myth is Finn's "affianced wife," who elopes with Diarmuid. See "The Pursuit of Diarmuid and Grainne" in Cross and Slover's *Ancient Irish Tales* (370-421).

[6] Lawless herself knew these waters very well. Sichel's lengthy memoir and tribute, written on the occasion of Lawless's death, discusses Lawless's childhood in Galway, her adventurous explorations of the coast, her love of the water, her skill in rowing and sailing, her visit to the Aran Isles when preparing *Grania*, and offers the supplementary observation that "the real hero of *Grania* and *Hurrish* is The Atlantic," other *dramatis personae* being "the winds and the storms—the rocks—the weather" (90).

suggestion somehow about it of cruelty. "Look well at me," it seemed to say, "you have only to choose. Life up there on those stones! death down here upon these—there, you see, where the surf is licking the mussels! Choose—choose carefully—take your time— only choose!" (II, 54f).

Throughout the novel, land is associated with propriety and fixity; the sea, with dangerous passion. In a long, detailed, and strangely erotic drowning scene (II, 292-300), Lawless weaves together the strands of Grania's story. She sinks into deep water, caught by the fast-running tide, the seemingly gentle swell, engulfed "by the big lonely Atlantic" (II, 295). After vigorous efforts to save herself, she finally ceases to struggle (II, 297); she gives herself up to the water and seaweed as if to an embrace with her beloved:

> … she let her head fall back upon the seaweed, her cheek resting upon it as if upon his shoulder, her eyes at the same time closing with a long-drawn sigh of satisfaction, and so resting and so sighing she sank slowly, insensibly, and without a struggle into the great folds of the laminaria, which, after supporting her in that position for perhaps a minute, began gently to loosen its long sashlike strands, floating presently away by degrees over the hardly undulating surface, returning again and again, and sweeping back, though in a less compact mass, now under, now over, now round her, the great brown ribbons swaying in easy serpentine curves about the floating form, the two getting to be hardly distinguishable in the all-pervading dreaminess, a dreaminess of which the very fog itself seemed to be but a part; a dream too deep and apparently too satisfactory to be ever again disturbed or broken in upon by anything from without. (II, 299f)

By accurate physical and psychological description, Lawless avoids sentimentality: her phrasing and sentence rhythms suggest the actual movements of seaweed; the phenomenon of a mass of laminaria briefly supporting a tired swimmer is not unknown; and the dreaminess that lulls Grania is caused, not by romantic idealization of Murdough, but by the coldness of the water — a cold that numbs her to the physical horror of her imminent drowning and fills her with a kind of delight.

Grania has done what no one else in the novel would do, risked all to save another, and her death is presented as triumphant consummation, not delusion. She has dared to leave the safety of land, the certainties of custom and traditional role, to face the perils of the sea. Such movement is not a matter of geography, but of character and psychology. Though rowing toward the "mainland" of Aranmore, she opens herself to the unknown. Rowing blindly, she faces *out*, heroically, as indeed so must her island, if, as Lawless implies, it is to live fully.

Where does all this leave us with regard to images of "a national identity"? What might Keating, MacGonigal, and even Yeats have learned from Lawless? This "deeply patriotic Irishwoman" (Wolff, I, xiii) shies away from what is to become the traditional republican rhetoric of blood sacrifice. Death, here, is involuntary, simply the conclusion of an act undertaken without concern for peril. What matters is the life, the act itself. And herein lies the interesting paradox of *Grania: The Story of an Island*. Solid and self-contained, islands are surrounded by waters that move and change. Which direction will the islander face, in or out? What mode will the islander develop, insular or adventurous, passive or dynamic? Lawless suggests through her plot, through her protagonist, and through her imagery of the sea that the fearlessness of an adventurous islander is preferable to the conservative self-protection of those who cling to land. Grania may die, but she is not destroyed. She achieves her goal, and in *that*, she lives — heroically.

Lawless's novel leads me to further speculation. Since some islands face other smaller islands, what really constitutes a "mainland"? Aranmore is an island of Ireland. But Ireland is itself an island, rising out of the water close to yet another, larger island, which stands off an even larger land mass. The waters between are both barrier and road. When Grania rows from Inishmaan to Aranmore, what sort of mainland does she seek? Aran Islanders, who go to Galway for trade, seek yet a larger mainland. Is the affinity that makes particular islanders perceive a given land mass as the mainland merely a matter of geographical proximity, or is there more at stake? Certainly in *Grania*, the sense of the "other" and the "out there" is a relative geographic concept. For example, Grania's mother was from Galway, but the women of Inishmaan called her a "'Black stranger,' a 'Foreigner,' a girl 'from the Continent'" (I, 40). For these women to consider Ireland a continent is to shrink their world; to think of Ireland as "the Continent" is to magnify greatly its global status. Lawless presents this brief vignette of peasant awe and prejudice comically, but, in the context of the novel, the scene highlights the social and cultural limitations of insularity of any kind, no matter how small the island or how large. Look *out*, reach *out*, venture *out* is clearly her unstated imperative. Risk the unknown, the uncertain. Turn "out there;" face what is "other;" dare to ride the dangerous sea.

Why did Emily Lawless, writing in the 1890s, propose so brave a model of national identity while artists, working amidst the political turbulence of independence and early statehood, present such timid and landlocked imagery? The example of J. M. W. Turner makes clear that the answer lies beyond differences of genre.[7] The commonplace (and also erroneous) opinion that, despite localized fishing, the Irish are not a sea-going people begs the question, since it is the local experience of the sea that is at issue here. Gender difference — the female novelist with her passionate heroine, in contrast to the three painters with their stolid male figures — also seems too limited an explanation.

But that a troubled new state might want images of what is settled and definite seems to accord with the actual historical moment in which Keating and MacGonigal found them-selves.[8] The fluidity and unpredictability of the sea does not, perhaps, provide apt imagery for men whose newly independent nation soon found itself torn by a civil war with hatreds carrying well into the following decades. But even so, it is difficult to see how sketchy figures subordinated to a static harbor scene, or even more fully realized fishermen on land with their backs to the sea, can provide the vitality a new state would surely need. Even Yeats's later painting *Men of Destiny* (1916), showing fishermen whose "faces and bodies are aflame

with more than the glow of the setting sun," despite its positive elements depicts those men walking inland "after securing their hooker" (Pyle 157).[9] Their direction — in, not out— is entirely opposite to the one Lawless proposes. I know how comforting it is at the end of a hard sail to have secured one's boat, to be home safe; and such imagery may indeed have its political usefulness in establishing and consolidating a sense of national identity. But there is no avoiding the fact that these images are inward turning and perhaps even timid.

In light of Lawless's challenge in *Grania*, we can read Yeats's *The Lookout* with new eyes. Although the figure is caught between two directions, his grip on the binoculars (tighter than their weight requires) suggests his determi-nation to scan the sea: the boat to his left may be headed in, but he knows there is more to be seen beyond. His posture suggests that whatever calls him back and causes him to turn his eyes inland, engages him less than what is "out there." After Lawless's descriptions of sea and weather, Yeats's house seems altogether too solid for the painting, too much a mere dark panel. What is visually interesting in the scene, besides the figure itself, is the sea, with its intrusion on the land, its distant lighthouse (an acknowledgment of danger), its traffic of boats, one of which is faint and half off the canvas, suggesting the "more" out there which the title also indicates. Yeats's very medium itself gives a fluidity to the work, liquid sky, water, and weather dominating. This sea may not be visibly turbulent, but the painting acknowledges its dangers, nonetheless. And the figure, though temporarily looking back, now seems ready to face the unknown, the sea out there, disposed to fulfill his essential function of look out.

---

[7] The greatest nineteenth-century British painter, J. M. W. Turner, may have been unusual in having himself strapped to the mast in order to observe a storm at first hand, but his oeuvre certainly stands out as a prime example of the artistic usefulness of sea and ship scenes, both the turbulent and the tranquil. Even his harbor scenes tend to play down the solidity and fixity of land; for example, his *The Sun of Venice Going to Sea* shows water and weather-filled sky supporting the ghosting ship as it heads out, the magnificence of Venice a mere blur in the background.

[8] Brian Kennedy argues in his essay on the images of the Irish Free State that "[m]ale artists painted and sculpted subject matter that was bold, vigorous and in keeping with a state founded on physical struggle" (152), but he does not consider marine painting as such or speculate on its peculiar timidity of subject.

[9] This painting, not part of the Burns collection, is in the National Gallery of Ireland. It is instructive to compare it with Keating's painting *Economic Pressure* (c. 1930), in the Crawford Municipal Art Gallery, Cork, which provides a negative image of Irish identity, showing the reluctant departure of an emigrant. Here the proposed direction of activity is out to sea, not in toward the land; but interestingly enough, Keating, too, has composed his painting so that land dominates: the ocean horizon is obliterated by a large rock, occupying the center of the canvas and extending almost to the top, in the foreground of which the grieving couple embrace; and although the scene contains two boats, the curagh at the shore is cut in half by the figure of the man who will row it out to the waiting vessel — and that ship itself is anchored half off the canvas. Once again, despite the painting's different attitude and subject matter, sea and ships are minimized; land and its solidity emphasized. Even a painting such as Paul Henry's *Launching the Curragh* (National Gallery of Ireland), though depicting an action which is vigorously outward bound, also positions its straining men on the sand, not actually in the water.

Despite good intentions, Keating and MacGonigal may have unwittingly presented images of the sea that were counter-productive, like some of the extreme "nativist" illustrations published by the Department of Education in the early decades of the new nation and described by Brian P. Kennedy as charming and quaint, but also lethargic. Kennedy cites the *Saorstat Eireann Official Handbook* (1932), to which both Keating and MacGonigal contributed illustrations, as a fine example of "the type of painting that was politically acceptable" in the Free State, with its "Celtic-style cover" and its emphasis on, among other things, "the importance of the Irish heritage" (*The Irish Free State* 146). But Ireland has more than the Book of Kells. There is a certain irony to invoking an ancient tradition, but neglecting one of its great images, the powerful sea, to which another art, early Irish poetry, made frequent tribute. Calm waters, safe harbors, moored boats: such static and inward-turning images do not vivify a nation or render its Celtic tradition as well as do images of "the coiling surface of the sea" and "the fierce cry of the wave/ Whipped by the wintry wind."[10]

Great energy is needed, not fixity but movement. The powerful sea, the surging ocean provides one of the best and most appropriate images for an island artist, pictorial or verbal. Thus of all the marine paintings in the Burns Collection, Yeats's "The Lookout," comes closest to presenting a realistic and salutary image, worthy to shape and challenge an islander's sense of national identity: turning, like Grania, from what is merely insular, facing those waters, the "other," bravely outward looking.

---

[10] These instances and many more can be found in Montague 63, 66f, 74 : "the coiling surface of the sea," "the waves, crest on crest/ of the great shining ocean, composing/ a hymn to the creator, without rest," *Colmcille*; "All those far seas and shores that must be crossed,/ They terrify me," [yet may] "Hope of our life, Lord of the sounding sea,/ Of wind and waters Lord,/ Give thee safe passage on the wrinkled sea,/ Himself thy pilot stand,/ Bring thee through mist and foam to thy desire,/ Again to Irish land," *Colman*; "I hear the fierce cry of the wave/ Whipped by the wintry wind" and many similar references throughout *The Hag of Beare*.

Works Cited

Cross, Tom Peete and Clark Harris Slover, eds. *Ancient Irish Tales.* Totowa, New Jersey: Barnes & Noble Books, 1981

Dalsimer, Adele. ed. *Visualizing Ireland: National Identity and the Pictorial Tradition.* Winchester, MA: Faber and Faber, 1993.

Kennedy, Brian P. "The Irish Free State 1922-49: A Visual Perspective." *Ireland, Art into History.* Ed. Raymond Gillespie and Brian P. Kennedy. Dublin: Townhouse, 1994.

— *Irish Painting.* Dublin: Townhouse, 1993.

Kennedy, S. B. *Irish Art and Modernism: 1880-1950.* Belfast: The Institute of Irish Studies, The Queen's University of Belfast, 1991.

Lawless, Emily. *Grania: The Story of an Island.* 2 vols. New York: Garland Publishing, Inc., 1979.

Marshall, Catherine. *Irish Art Masterpieces.* China: Hugh Lauter Levin Associates, 1994.

Montague, John, ed. *The Faber Book of Irish Verse.* London: Faber and Faber, 1978.

Pyle, Hilary. "The National Gallery of Ireland's Collection of Paintings by Jack B. Yeats." *Art Is My Life: A Tribute to James White.* Dublin: The National Gallery of Ireland, 1991.

Sichel, Edith. "Emily Lawless." *The Nineteenth Century.* 1914: vol. LXXVI, no. 449.

Wolff, Robert Lee. Introduction. *Grania.* By Emily Lawless. New York: Garland Publishing Inc., 1979.

Artist and Artisan:
James Brenan as Art Educator

Peter Murray

The career of the nineteenth-century Irish artist James Brenan, whose four decades as head-master of two prominent art schools enabled him to exert a lasting influence on art education in Ireland, has remained curiously undocumented. Brenan was also a talented artist whose narrative paintings were directly inspired by contemporary theories on art and technical education. In 1860, at the age of twenty-three, he was appointed headmaster of the Cork School of Art, and thirty years later went on to become headmaster at the Metropolitan School of Art in Dublin. He had strong and determined views on the relationship between art training and the development of economic self-reliance, particu-larly in rural areas, and he helped introduce to Ireland many of the concepts underlying the Arts and Crafts movement, which flourished at that time in Britain and the United States.

Born in Dublin in 1837, Brenan enrolled in the Drawings Schools of the Dublin Society and studied at the at the Royal Hibernian Academy as well. He received at least two medals during his time at the Dublin Society's schools (Strickland 77). Moving to London, Brenan participated in the designing of the Crystal Palace, the gigantic pre-fabricated glass and iron building that became the centerpiece of the 1851 Great Exhibition in London. Even by the standards of the day he must have been some-thing of a prodigy, for according to the dates of his birth in Strickland's biographical data, he would have been a mere fourteen years of age. According to Strickland's *A Dictionary of Irish Artists*, Brenan assisted the designer Owen

Jones and also Matthew Digby Wyatt, who was later to become the first Slade Professor of Fine Art at Oxford, in the decoration of the Pompeian and Roman Courts at the Crystal Palace.

Brenan's future philosophy of art education was profoundly influenced by The Great Exhibition of 1851. Drawing more than six million visitors during its six-month run, the exhibition gener-ated funds to purchase a large site in South Kensington for the construction of the Museum of Ornamental Manufactures (the present Victoria and Albert Museum). Its first director was Sir Henry Cole, the organizer of the 1851 event. Celebrating a new concept of culture, which encompassed mechanical developments ranging from lavatories to steam-threshing machines, the exhibiton, however, also high-lighted the poverty of technical education in Britain. Duly awakened, the British government established the new Department of Science and Art to support a growing network of art schools throughout Britain and Ireland. An amendment to the Public Libraries Act, in 1855, also provided public money for the support of the new institutions (which included the Cork School of Art).

Returning to Dublin, Brenan taught for a period at the Dublin Society's Schools and, in 1855, was admitted to the National Art Training School at Marlborough House, London. In the years following, Brenan continued to study and teach, working for short periods at Liverpool, Taunton and Yarmouth, before his appointment as headmaster of the Cork School of Art in 1860.

The curriculum he inagurated, and particularly his highly successful introduction of lace-making and embroidery classes there, reflected his interest in art and industry as inspired by the Great Exhibition (Stickland 77).[1]

As an artist, Brenan was extremely prolific. Between 1861 and 1906, he exhibited more than one hundred paintings at the Royal Hibernian Academy. Several are now in the permanent collection of the Crawford Municipal Art Gallery in Cork, notably *The Prayer of the Penitent* (1863), *News from America* — now titled *Letter from America* (1875), (fig.4), *Patchwork* (1892), and *Committee of Inspection*, (fig.5), exhibited at the R.H.A. in 1878. This last painting is typical of Brenan's work in that it shows the interior of a cottage in county Cork, complete with authentic detail of fittings, country furniture and utensils. In the background an old man works at a handloom. In the foreground, a man and woman, probably buyers from a city department store, inspect a piece of homespun cloth. The gloomy expressions on the faces of the other women in the cottage tell their own stories. The cloth they wove on their cottage loom could ill compete with the cheap factory cottons which Ireland was importing in great quantities from England.

In France, particularly in Lyon, government-funded schools of design worked closely with the textile industry, ensuring that their mass-produced fabrics were well designed and well made. In 1801, when the Jacquard loom was exhibited at the French National Exhibition, the French government promptly bought the rights and put the machinery into production. England, however, lacked such a relationship between industry and education, and clothing manufacturers rejected the cottons produced in mills of Lancashire in favor of the far more fashionable French fabrics. The unwanted English cotton was then dumped on markets around the world, including Ireland, destroying in each the indigenous hand-weaving tradition and economy. The British government acknowledged this problem, which had been highlighted at The Great Exhibition, and set up a network of schools of design in Britain and Ireland to rival the French system. Old habits die hard, however, and in each new school the artists, teachers and students demonstrated their social prejudice against industrial design and in favor of fine art. As an educator, Brenan was to spend the greater part of his life searching for ways to turn his most talented students, usually the offspring of middle-class professional families, who had little interest in working directly with industry, into trained artisans, industrial designers and craft workers.

Most of Brenan's paintings have a strong narrative quality and were directly inspired by his awareness of social and economic issues. His concern with education and literacy is evident from at least two paintings. *Letter from America*, in the Crawford Gallery collection, and *The Village Scribe* (no. 13), reveal the depth of Brenan's desire to improve literacy and education. The former shows a cottage interior in which a young girl reads a letter to her parents, who are probably illiterate. The letter may be from a relative who has emigrated to the United States, and the child is probably the first member of this family who has learned to read and write — perhaps at one of the National Schools set up throughout Ireland in the 1860s. *The Village Scribe* poignantly illustrates the disadvantages caused by illiteracy. Brenan's other painting in the present exhibition, *The School-room* (no. 14), like *Letter from America*, derives much of its narrative strength from an awareness of the sorry state of education at the time. The desk of the absent schoolmaster, its stool leaning askew, and the open door suggest a message or moral, which Brenan generally sought to impart through his painting. Here he affirms, perhaps, his belief that the primary work of the educationalist begins in the classroom. The furniture, floorboards, wall maps, and other details of the schoolroom probably represent Brenan's actual observations of classrooms in county Cork schools.

Students and teachers of the Cork School of Art who, since 1830, had been housed in the former customs house, must have welcomed Brenan's appointment in 1890. According to contemporary accounts, the roof of the early eighteenth-

---

[1] Tracing Brenan's career as an artist in Cork can be difficult as Strickland records at least two other artists of the same surname working in the city. In the earlier part of the century, the competent but uninspiring landscape painter John Brenan exhibited at the annual exhibitions organized by the Society for Promoting the Fine Art in Cork, while his son James Butler Brenan, equally competent but even duller, spent the greater part of his life producing half-length portraits of local merchants and matrons. James Butler Brenan and James Brenan both worked in Cork and both exhibited at the Royal Hibernian Academy, which has caused confusion. The name Brenan is less common in Ireland than Brennan, and may indicate a Scottish rather than a Gaelic Irish, origin. Even so, this rather fine distinction was lost on several nineteenth century journalists, and so the name appears in accounts in the *Cork Examiner* and *The Cork Constitution* spelt both ways. Even the scrupulous Walter Strickland is guilty of incorrectly attributing the painting *A Committee of Inspection* to James Butler Brenan rather than James Brenan.

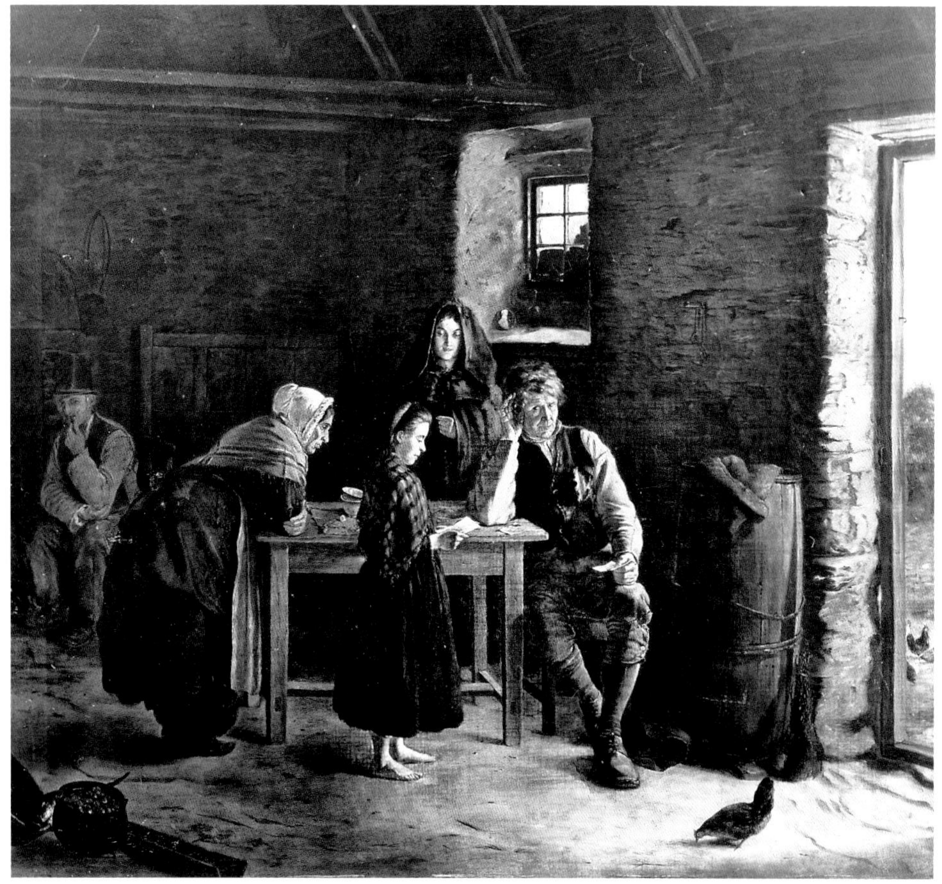

fig 4

Letter from America,
James Brenan,
oil on canvas,
Courtesy of
the Crawford
Municipal
Gallery, Cork

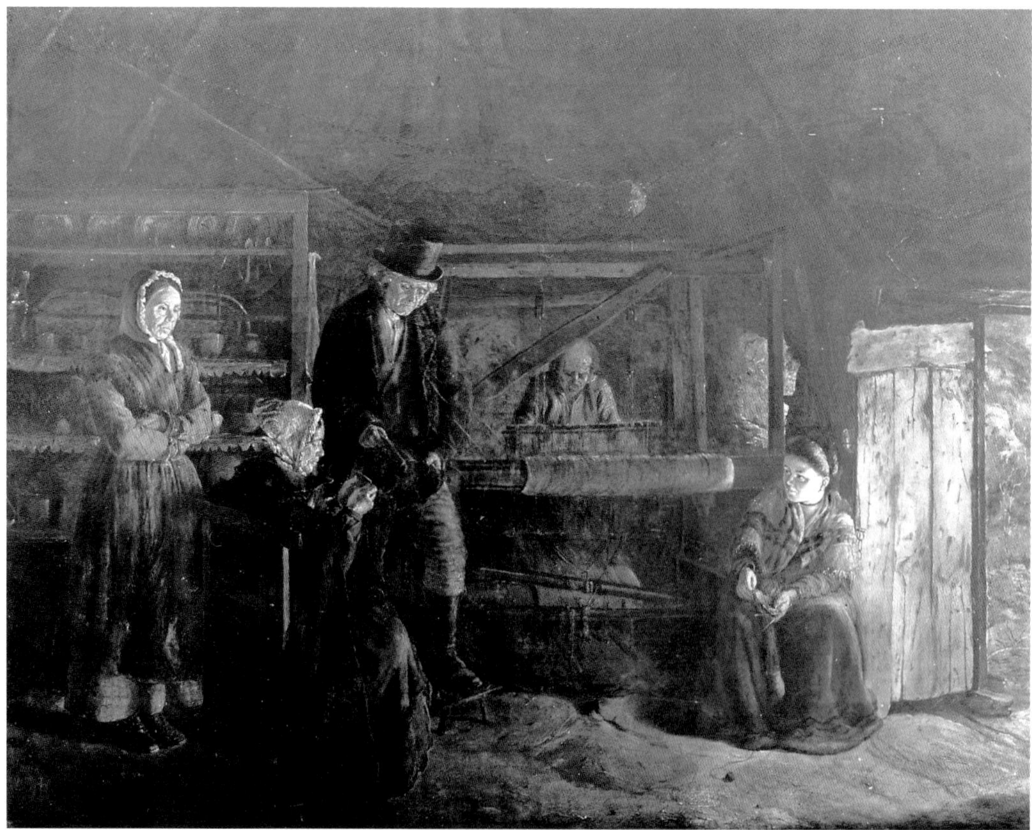

fig 5

Committee of Inspection,
James Brenan,
oil on canvas,
Courtesy of the
Crawford Municipal
Gallery, Cork

century building leaked constantly, the old staircase creaked, and the students' studios and workshops lacked proper lighting. Students and teachers were particularly frustrated by the absence of a gallery in which to display the school's excellent Greek and Roman sculpture cast collection. While the Cork school had been founded in 1819, and incorporated into the Government Schools of Design system in 1850, it was not until 1876, by which time students numbered more than 250, that a committee was established to examine how to integrate it into the South Kensington system. Brenan, and Cork architect Arthur Hill, were the honorary secretaries. Their report, presented in January 1878, unsurprisingly took as its starting point the differences, highlighted by the Great Exhibition of 1851, in technical education among Ireland, Britain and other industrialized nations. They pointed out that goods manufactured in Britain and Ireland all too often showed a "poverty of design, inelegance of form and glaring contrasts of colour." They also dwelled at length on the deficiencies of the School of Art:

> The building in which the school is conducted, and which is held from the Royal Cork Institution at a rent of £60 a year, was built for a custom house in the last century, and is badly adapted for art teaching. The class rooms are not spacious enough for the large classes now attending, and the light from the windows is so defective that the pupils, especially the advanced ones, labour under serious disadvantages. Add to this that the premises are very much out of repair. (*Cork Examiner* 26 Jan. 1878: 5, qtd. in Murray 245)

Brenan found a generous benefactor in William Horatio Crawford, of the Cork brewing firm Beamish and Crawford, who contributed £20,000 toward the construction of a magnificent addition to the art school. The 1884 extension more than doubled the size of the building, providing two enormous sculpture galleries, a life-drawing room, and workshops on the ground floor, while on the floor above were five large studios for the teaching of painting and other activities. Three galleries for exhibiting paintings were also provided, as well as a library. The wrought-iron gates at its entrance bear the date 1884, the year the work was completed, but the official ceremony was delayed until April 1885, when the Prince of Wales (later King Edward VII) formally opened the building. A report in *The Cork Examiner*,

April 16,1885, gives a graphic account of the event, which highlighted the growing political divisions between nationalists and Loyalists at the time:

> … The Princess of Wales led the procession through the building, leaning on the arm of Mr. James Brenan. The male students of the school cheered the Royal party as they visited the old portion of the building, while the lady students were also cordial in their demonstration of welcome, and at one period of the visit they sang "God Save the Queen." The crowd in the street kept hissing all the time, except when they varied the sibilant expressions of disapproval by cheering for Parnell and singing "God save Ireland". (3, qtd. in Murray 250)

Brenan participated in various educational initiatives in Cork. In 1883, he had been in charge of the Fine Art section of the Cork Industrial and Fine Art Exhibition, which was modeled along the lines of the Great Exhibition of 1851 and which attracted over ten thousand visitors (*Cork Examiner* 7 June 1883: 2, qtd. in Murray 248). Along with works by other artists, Brenan showed several of his own paintings, including *One of the Band*, *The Beleaguered Fortress*, *The Young Housewife*, and *The Spinning Lesson*, the titles of the last two indicating his continued efforts to improve the position of women in Irish society, and his advocacy of home industry as a source of income for women in rural areas.

At Brenan's invitation, Alan S. Cole, the son of Henry Cole (the organizer of the Great Exhibition of 1851), lectured at the 1893 Cork Exhibition, where lacework from most of the convents of Munster was displayed along with a collection of antique lace borrowed from the South Kensington museum (the catalogue for which Cole had written). Cole had to agree with Brenan that, while the craftsmanship of the lace produced in the convents of Munster met the highest standards, much of it lacked any real design sense. In the spring of 1884, Brenan and Cole visited a number of the convents around county Cork where lace-making was taught, and persuaded the nuns to affiliate with the Cork School of Art. As Brenan wrote,

> The Science and Art Department approved of this scheme, and the first class was commenced at the Convent of Mercy, Kinsale, followed immediately by a class at the Convent of Poor Clares, Kenmare. Before two years had elapsed there were classes

in operation at Killarney, Tralee, Youghal, Thurles, Skibbereen, and St. Vincent's and Blackrock Convents, Cork. My idea was that a class of designers should be formed in each centre, with the work-room in close proximity, so that it would be possible to make trial pieces from the designs. It is absolutely necessary in order to judge of the effect of a piece of lace. I have been informed by M. Lefebure, the great lace manufacturer in Paris, that he has sometimes had as many as five trial pieces made from a design before the result could be considered satisfactory. This ideal of mine was realised in some instances, notably at Kenmare and Kinsale. (*The Modern Lace Industry* 424)

Having received a grant of £200 each from the Cork Exhibition committee and the Department of Science and Art, Brenan purchased examples of antique lace, which he circulated among the various convents as teaching aids. (Many of these framed samples are preserved in the collection of the Crawford Municipal Art Gallery in Cork). He established a lace class in the new school building to supply designs to convents unable to generate their own, and tapped a few advanced students at the Cork School to copy the laces in the loan collection at the Cork Exhibition. At the same time, they learned the techniques of lace-making and transformed their own designs into actual lace. Brenan found that,

> Like the poet, a good designer cannot be made… I remember two ladies, sisters, who had studied together; both drew equally well from the cast and from nature and had passed through all the elementary work creditably. They informed me that they wished to learn designing for lace. I set them, for about a month, to make working drawings from photos of old lace, restoring the good drawing, and studying the construction of the pattern. At the expiration of that time, I gave them a space of two inches wide between two horizontal lines, and told them to make a design for a border for needle-point lace, using any arrangement they pleased. One sister had a very good design made in a few hours; the other sat, day after day, over the paper for nearly a month without producing anything. At the end of that time, she told me she thought it would be well for her give up the idea of designing—a conclusion in which I thoroughly concurred. (*The Modern Lace Industry* 424)

As well as improving lace design facilities, Brenan worked tirelessly to enhance the School of Art industrial and technical design courses, but with limited success. In his annual report for 1885, he notes with dismay that, of 235 male students, only nineteen were in the "Science Classes," and only two took the construction-trade examination.

> It is true that close study and earnest work are required by those who do attend, but when the utility of these subjects is considered, it cannot but appear strange that in a city like Cork, where technical education is so much spoken of, such subjects as descriptive geometry, machine drawing, etc., which form the foundation of a great deal of technical knowledge, should not attract more than 19 students, of whom only five or six attended to the end of the course. (*Cork Examiner* 24 Feb. 1885, qtd. in Murray 251)

In contrast, women students eagerly attended the lace-design classes, on which Brenan increasingly focused his attention. By 1887, the Cork School of Art coordinated lace-design classes taught at the Convent of the Poor Clares in Kenmare, the Presentation Convents in Killarney, Tralee and Youghal, the Convent of Mercy in Kinsale, St. Vincent's Convent in Cork and the Ursuline Convent in the Cork suburb of Blackrock. Many students at the Cork School and its branches won the competitions sponsored by South Kensington. Brenan applauded the training these classes provided and was particularly gratified students were hired to prepare designs for professional firms in London and Ireland.

By the end of the decade, the 300 workers associated with the various lace schools in Cork and Kerry were earning respectable livelihoods. James Brenan, however, would leave Cork on the eve of their success. The *Cork Examiner* of March 30, 1889, records the "gloom over the entire establishment" when Brenan departed to take up his new post as headmaster at the Metropolitan School of Art in Dublin. Holding theories similar to those of Ruskin and William Morris, he "believed firmly," according to the newspaper report, that the educational system could "do nothing better than add art to industry;" in going to Dublin, he hoped to continue carrying out the principles that had guided him in Cork (qtd. in Murray 254).

At the Dublin Metropolitan School of Art, Brenan continued to monitor the progress of lace classes in Munster, but he also introduced himself to the active and successful lace classes in Carrickmacross and Crossmaglen, in the north of Ireland, as well as the lace classes at the Ursuline Convent, in Thurles, and the Dominican Convents, at Dun Laoghaire, and Wicklow.[2] Within the Dublin School of Art, itself, he emphasized the importance of design, and within a year had instituted a successful lace and embroidery design class. As in Cork, Brenan also set up branch classes in lace-making at nearby convents.[3]

The London Arts and Crafts Exhibition of 1896 showed lace from the Irish convents to great advantage, while the patronage of Lady Aberdeen, the wife of the Lord Lieutenant of Ireland at the time, immeasurably fostered the Arts and Crafts movement and the Celtic Revival throughout Ireland. By 1900, the Dublin lace design class, now highly and widely acclaimed, was headed by Alice Jacob, once its most brilliant students (Turpin 178). The capital city was, however, less receptive than was Cork to Brenan's efforts to develop his design classes. His frustration became obvious by the turn of the century:

> I quite agree with the remarks made by Mr. [Joseph] Chamberlain [Secretary for the Colonies 1895-1903] ... that the province of schools of art was to give a sound education in all the branches of art which might be allied to industry, and not to the production of tenth-rate artists of which, I am sorry to say, there are too many. (qtd. in Turpin 178)

Brenan's views on art education had fallen out of step with the prevailing fashion in Ireland of "art for art's sake" and the wide popularity of the Art Nouveau movement. He was beginning to sound embattled and embittered when, in 1900, he attacked "the extravagances which are frequently exhibited in the decoration of what are called art objects ...." (*Dublin Metropolitan School of Art Report 1900,* qtd. in Turpin 173). On a trip to the continent six years earlier, Brenan had visited art schools in Hamburg, Stockholm, Vienna and Berlin and found a sophisticated approach to the application of art to industrial design. On his return to Dublin, he lamented the lack of a similar commitment to design education there. "Until a series of technical classes in those subjects with which art is more immediately connected are (sic) established in the school, and which will allow the students to embody their ideas in the material," Brenan wrote, "the work of the School cannot be considered to be complete" (*Art Instruction in Ireland* 101).

By the end of the century, the South Kensington system had largely failed in its ideal of uniting art and industry and, in 1900, the Department of Science and Art was merged into the new Board of Education, signaling the end of a chapter in British and Irish art history. In Ireland, the passing of the new Local Government (Ireland) Act of 1898 began a new phase in art education, that established technical schools throughout the country. The co-operative movement, founded by Horace Plunkett (and inspired by co-operatives in the United States) provided another source of state support of technical and art education.

Brenan retired from the Dublin Metropolitan School of Art in 1904, after having spent a half century in the active and enthusiastic promotion of the philosophies that had inspired the Great Exhibition of 1851. Although he was practical in his methods as an arts educator, his aesthetic views did not advance markedly throughout his career. His own paintings show the influence of the Realist movement and the straightforward narrative genre paintings of William Mulready and others, which formed the staple diet of nineteenth-century art in Europe and North America. Brenan's fixed views restricted the mark he might have left on the art world. Insisting that the observation of nature and the art of preceding eras provided the best course of study, he ignored the new aesthetic that mechanized production had inspired in the industrialized centers of Europe. Ultimately, his most enduring contribution was, through his consistent and excellent administration, the development of the two most important art schools in Ireland, schools that even today, still retain their pre-eminent position in art education.

---

[2] 38th Report of the Science and Art Department (1891) 373., Turpin, 178.

[3] 37th Report of the Department of Science and Art (1890) 320, Turpin, 181.

Works Cited

Brenan, James. "The Modern Irish Lace Industry." *Ireland, Industrial and Agricultural.* Ed. William P. Coyne. Dublin: Department of Agriculture and Technical Instruction 1901: 420-32

— "Art Instruction in Ireland." *Ireland.* Coyne. 146-48.

Murray, Peter. "A Chronology of Art in Nineteenth Century Cork." *Illustrated Summary Catalogue of the Crawford Art Gallery.* Cork: Vocational Educational Committee, 1991.

Strickland, W. G. *A Dictionary of Irish Artists.* Dublin: Maunsell & Co., 1913.

Turpin, J. *A School* of Art *in Dublin since the Eighteenth Century.* Dublin: Gill & Macmillan,1995.

Putting on Airs: Cultural Nationalism as Consumer Commodity in the Irish Free State

Philip O'Leary

Despite its title, Jack B. Yeats's painting *Patriotic Airs*, (no. 42) completed in 1923, is haunted by ironic silences. In the early years of Saorstát Éireann (the Irish Free State), as his brother William Butler Yeats championed the cause of the former Anglo-Irish ascendancy,[1] the country's most original and accomplished painter subtly suggests a quite different agenda. If our immediate attention is focussed on the comfortable, middle-class audience enjoying instrumental renderings of, doubtless, well-known tunes from the extensive nationalist repertoire before, or in the interval of a theatrical performance at Dublin's Gaiety Theatre, Yeats challenges us to question what might be missing from this picture — whom we do not see and what we do not hear.

The two figures in military uniform standing at the rear of the stalls should remind us that 1923 was a very violent year in Ireland. Throughout the first quarter of the year, Free State forces moved inexorably against what remained of Republican resistance in Munster. In April, they killed Republican chief of staff Liam Lynch in the Knockmealdown Mountains of Tipperary, and, by May, had forced Éamon de Valera to issue his famous dump arms order to the "Soldiers of the Republic, Legion of the Rearguard." The rest of the year saw the rounding up and internment of defeated and often embittered Republicans, and the

entrenchment of Free State authority under the leadership of what Kevin O'Higgins, one of its most influential and uncompromising ministers and a hero to W. B. Yeats, called "probably the most conservative-minded revolutionaries that ever put through a successful revolution" (qtd. in White 145).[2] Thus, whether Yeats painted *Patriotic Airs* before or after de Valera's order brought the Civil War to an anti-climactic suspension in May, this was a year when both the canon and the custodianship of the nation's ballad treasury were contested far more passionately than one would ever imagine from looking at this picture without reference to its historical and cultural contexts.

Those Southerners of Unionist background, who had between 6 December 1921 and 22 March 1923 seen the burning by nationalists of 192 of the "Big Houses" owned by people who shared their political views (Brown 86), would have heard nothing but sedition glorified in a performance like that pictured here. But, for others in the audience, the rebel sentiments may not have been fiery enough. These musicians could hardly have presented songs like those Ernie O'Malley tells us Republican prisoners composed in the internment camp on the Curragh of Kildare (O'Malley 281) — not to mention *Take It Down from the Mast, Irish Traitors* — as innocuous, uplifting incidental

---

[1] As in his famous divorce speech to the Free State Senate in 1925.

[2] See Yeats's poem "Death," written after O'Higgin's assassination in 1927. In "Ireland after the Revolution" from *On the Boiler* (1938), O'Higgins was the only Catholic whom Yeats included in a list of what he hailed as "the true Irish people" (Yeats 242).

entertainment in the Dublin of 1923. Yet, in one of the many ironies the painting so neatly evokes, given that Republicans in the time-honored tradition often simply changed words or added verses to appropriate familiar melodies for their cause, the orchestra in the Gaiety might well have been playing selections carrying very different sets of lyrics to the minds, and emotions, of listeners depending on their political allegiance. Nonetheless, whatever seditious personal concerts are playing in their heads, even the "diehard" Republican members of this audience, perhaps aware of the uniformed figures behind them, seem able to control any visible signs of political fervor.

A second silence in the painting centers on social class. In 1923, what Joseph Lee has called "a rash of industrial disputes which resulted in the loss of 1.2 million working days" plagued the new state (Lee 95). Other economic challenges facing the government included a growing unemployment soon to be exacerbated by the demobilization of Free State soldiers and the endemic poverty of much of the country. Both of these problems were particularly acute in Dublin, and, in response, the government, again in Lee's words, "substituted for what the Democratic Programme called 'the present odious, degrading and foreign poor law system,' an odious, degrading and native system" (Lee 124). And, of course, it was also in 1923 that Sean O'Casey introduced Abbey Theatre patrons to the plight of Dublin's slumdwellers with *The Shadow of a Gunman*, the first of his Dublin trilogy that was also to include *Juno and the Paycock* (1924) and *The Plough and the Stars* (1926). The stolid and well-dressed folk Yeats depicts in *Patriotic Airs* probably would have attended *The Shadow of a Gunman*, been moved by *Juno*, and maybe even been outraged by the "scurrilous insinuation" that provoked national-ist protest on the production of the *Plough*.[3] None, however, were likely to have gone home to, or even crossed the threshold of a Northside tenement, except in the service of the St. Vincent de Paul Society. The men and women

Yeats shows us here are of the solid burgher class, comfortable consumers of the goods and services so prominently advertized on the fire curtain that dominates the entire left side of the painting.

The third silence in *Patriotic Airs* is perhaps the most intriguing, both in itself and in that, in many ways, it unites the other thematic elements in the painting. Unlike his poet brother, towards whom the Gaelic movement had long been ambivalent at best and who, by the 1920s, was regarded as actively anti-Gaelic for various stands he took as a Free State senator,[4] Jack Yeats was always held in high esteem by Irish Irelanders. In part, of course, the nature of his medium facilitated this acceptance. In their own minds, language activists could not imagine Jack's sturdily independent western peasants speaking anything but Irish. With their own ears they heard W. B.'s stage representations of western country folk speaking what they regarded as a distressing brand of English. Yet Gaelic respect for the painter transcended this accidental aspect of his work. Jack Yeats's active involvement with the language cause began no later than 1899, when he designed a program cover for the "Irish Ball" sponsored by the Gaelic League of London (Ó Súilleabháin 19). Moreover, between 1902 and 1906 he illus-trated a series of Gaelic League instructional booklets, *Ceachta Beaga Gaedhilge* (Little lessons in Irish) by Norma Borthwick (Pyle 177).[5] And although Hilary Pyle overstates the case when she writes, "He entered the Gaelic Revival movement his brother was engaged in and became the artist of a cause which had never had an artist before" (Pyle 43), Jack Yeats's willingness to study Irish in some depth (Pyle 118) had to impress Gaelic activists weary of so many Irish artists and intellectuals paying lip service to the language, among them W. B. Yeats himself.

More practical indication of his support for the movement is Jack Yeats's regular participation in the art exhibitions held from 1905 on under

---

[3] This characterization is from a letter to the *Irish Independent* from Sean O'Shea, quoted by Robert G. Lowery in *A Whirlwind in Dublin: The Plough and the Stars Riots* (Westport, Ct.: Greenwood, 1984), 62.

[4] For example, as early as 1923, Pádric O Domhnalláin, the editor of *Fáinne an Lae*, was warning of a Yeatsian legislative agenda: "A little while ago another Senator, W. Yeats, opposed the saying of any prayer in Irish on the commencement of business in the Senate. No one would expect anything different from him, for it is clear from his poetry that he adheres more to paganism than to Christianity." (Tamall beag ó shoin ann chuir Seanadóir eile W. Yeats i gcoinne aon phaidir a rádh as Gaedhilg ar dhlúthas a bheith dhá chur le hobair an tSeanaid. Ni bheadh aoinne ag súil le'n a mhalairt uaidh-sean óir is iontuigthe ó'n a chuid filíochta gur mó a chlaoidheas sé le págántacht ná le Críostaidheacht.) (O Domhnalláin, FL 22 December , 1922)

[5] Yeats also illustrated Séamus O Beirn's *Páistidheacht* (Childishness) in 1910 and Tomás O Faoláin's translation of Máirín Cregan's *Sean-Eoin* (Old John) for the Free State's Irish language publishing agency, An Gúm, in 1938.

the auspices of the Gaelic League's annual national cultural festival, An t-Oireachtas. In 1906, the League's journal, *An Claidheamh Soluis*, reported "Jack B. Yeats has designed some striking posters for the Oireachtas Art Exhibition" (Pearse, 4 August, 1906). However, in a review of that year's show in the same journal, Patrick Pearse wrote: "Jack B. Yeats is not, we think, seen at his best in this exhibition" (Pearse, 11 August, 1906). In 1911 it was Yeats along with the president of the Royal Hibernian Academy who arranged the Oireachtas art exhibition for the Gaelic League (Mac Giollarnáth, 5 August, 1911). Even negative comment on his work had its roots in Irish Irelanders' high expectations. Thus, in an editorial review of the 1911 Oireachtas show, Seán Mac Giollarnáth, Pearse's successor at *An Claidheamh Soluis*, wrote: "Jack B. Yeats exhibits five watercolors … none of which represents the enormous advance he displayed at his last exhibition in the Molesworth Hall (Mac Giollarnáth, 5 August, 1911).

Most significant, unlike W. B., Jack was always recognized by the Gaelic movement not just for his "highly individualized talent" (Mac Giollarnáth, 29 July, 1911), but also for the ineffable "Irishness" of his art. Attempting to describe, if not define, this quality in his discussion of the new Irish art on exhibit at the 1906 Oireachtas, Pearse wrote, with W. B. clearly in mind as a foil for his brother:

> It will be characterized by a complete absence of what has come to be known as the 'Celtic note,' — which is in reality an Anglo-German note … It will concern itself with life and not with dreams (or nightmares); with elemental impulses and not with cults. It will bear to English art and to recent Anglo-Irish art respectively the same relation that a Middle-Irish nature poem bears on the one hand to a story in the *Family Herald*, and on the other to one of the sicklier plays at the Abbey Theatre.[6] (Pearse, 5 May, 1906)

It was doubtless with similar criteria in mind that Seán Mac Giollarnáth wrote in 1911, "There is no question of the Irish appeal in Sheppard, Duffy, Osborne, Russell, and Yeats" (Mac Giollarnáth, 29 July, 1911). The language movement's approval stood the test of time. For instance, in April 1924, the reviewer for the League journal, under its new title, *Fáinne*

an Lae, praised Yeats's exhibition *Pictures of Life in the West of Ireland* at the Engineers' Hall on Dawson Street, observing that some artists were already "trying to put the beautiful places and the varied people of this country on canvas in a Gaelic manner. It is Yeats who is the most adept of them: and he has a particular style of his own to do that." ("ag iarra áiteacha áilne agus aosa éagsamhla na tíre seo a chur go Gaedhealach ar chonabhás. Atá an Yéatsach ar an duine is paitionta díobh siod: agus modh ar leith dá chuid féin aige le sin a dhéana.") ("Pictiúirí," *FL* 5 April, 1924). In October of the following year a reviewer for the monthly *An Sguab* wrote of another exhibition of Yeats's work at the same venue, "There is a special magic in connection with Jack B. Yeats that lures people to his pictures. Whatever it is, I spent a lovely afternoon looking at them." ("Tá draoidheacht fé leith ag baint le Seán B. a mheallann daoine le na chuid pictiúirí. Pé'r domhan de ba aoibhinn an tráthnóna a chaith mé féin ag féachaint orra.") ("Séamas"). The author of the *Fáinne an Lae* column "I mBaile is i gCéin" (At home and abroad), probably the editor Pádraig O Domhnalláin, was more explicit about the source of this bewitching charm: "We don't have any painter who is as Gaelic as Jack B. Yeats. He has the gift of putting people and images and views and characteristics before you very naturally." ("N'íl aon ghaisdidhe linn atá cho Gaedhealach le Iac Yeats. Atá de bhuaidh aige daoine agus samhla agus radharcanna agus airdheana a chur os do chomhair go rí-nádúrtha.") ("I mBaile," *FL* 24 October, 1925).

To many Gaelic Leaguers, Yeats's success, aesthetic and national, came as no surprise. He had long been a kindred spirit, who, in his work, was merely honoring the inspiration that had saved him from provincial mediocrity. In his 1905 editorial "O'Growney and the Revival of Art," Pearse had traced virtually all of the cultural ferment in the Ireland of his time to the Gaelic revival, symbolized by the series of little language texts *Simple Lessons in Irish*, written by Father Eugene O'Growney. Pearse wrote:

> The instant the nine men who founded the Gaelic League came together in their back room in O'Connell Street, the whole series of activities, potencies, and aspirations which we summarize as "Irish Ireland" became inevitable. Remembering this, we shall see

[6] In a 1905 letter to Thomas Flannery, Pearse stated that all unsigned material in *ACS* during his editorship was from his pen. See To Thomas Flannery, *The Letters of P. H. Pearse*, ed. Séamus O Buachalla (Gerrards Cross: Colin Smythe, 1980), 98.

nothing bizarre in the contention that an Irish Art Revival has sprung from the study — not of old or of modern masters, not of anything that has been achieved in art, or taught about art, or written about art, but from the study of O'Growney. If the *Simple Lessons* or some such book had not been put into the hands of Young Ireland thirteen years ago we might have sought in vain for evidences of a national consciousness in the recent show of the Hibernian Academy.

Pearse continued that without O'Growney and his primers "there would be no Dún Emer, no Túr Gloine, no Irish Art Companions. Jack B. Yeats would be illustrating English comic papers ...." (Pearse, 14 July, 1906).[7] Instead, one of his creations, *The Man that Buried Raftery*, was to grace Sgoil Éanna (St. Enda's), Pearse's own Irish-Ireland school for boys.[8]

Jack Yeats's involvement with the Gaelic movement was, then, both long and active. Therefore he can hardly have been unaware of the significance of the Gaiety Theatre in its literary history, particularly in light of his friendship and artistic collaboration with John Millington Synge (Dalsimer 201-30). In October 1901 W. B. Yeats's Irish Literary Theatre included a play in Irish, Douglas Hyde's *Casadh an tSúgáin* (The twisting of the rope), on its bill at the Gaiety, along with with *Diarmuid and Grania* by Yeats and George Moore. This Gaelic play, directed by Willie Fay with the dubious assistance of Moore,[9] was the first play in the language staged in a Dublin theatre. The effect was immediate and electrifying. The critic for *An Claidheamh Soluis* predicted: "The Gaelic drama will drive the English drama out of the country, and Irish-speakers will control the Irish stage. We think English will be driven from the stage altogether within a few more years." ("Buailfidh an dráma Gaedhealach an ceann Sasanach amach as an tír, agus beidh stáitse na hÉireann ag na Gaedhilgeoiribh. Díbreofar is dóigh liom an Béarla de'n stáitse go léir i gceann beagán bliadhanta eile.") ("Casadh," *FL* 26 October, 1901)

By far the most memorable account of the evening is Synge's, written, perhaps appropriately, in French for the Paris magazine *L'Europeen*. After commenting on the singing of folk songs in Irish by young enthusiasts in the balcony during the interval of *Diarmuid and Grania*, Synge continued, in lyrical terms that echo the Gaelic movement's creed that only through Irish could Ireland be properly understood, "Then the curtain rose, and the play began again in the midst of a vital emotion. One had just felt the soul of a people hovering in the room for an instant." ("Puis le rideau se leva, la piece recommenca au milieu d'une vive émotion. On venait de sentir flotter un instant dans la salle l'ame d'un peuple.") (Synge 381-382)

This marvelous promise would never be realized; Gaelic drama would languish in parish halls and rented rooms for decades. It is yet another irony that the plays for the 1923 Oireachtas were staged in the Gaiety Theatre. The critic for *Fáinne an Lae* pronounced attendance at these performances "shameful" (*náireach*) ("Mícheál na Téide"). Éamonn Mac Giolla Iasachta (Edward Mac Lysaght), the editor of *An Sguab* agreed entirely, saying, "It does not matter what excuse is given for it, the way the Gaiety was neglected that week is a source of shame, not a source of satisfaction." ("Is cuma pé leathsgeul a ghabhtar 'na thaobh ní cúrsaí sástachta ach cúrsaí náire an slighe a righneadh faillighe ar an 'Gaiety' an tseachtain úd.") (Mac Giolla Iasachta). Strapped by debt, the Oirechtas was to shut down after the 1924 festival not to return until 1939.

Whatever else might, then, be hovering over the sedate audience of *Patriotic Airs*, it is not the Gaelic soul of a Gaelic people Synge had detected in 1901. Unlike the rambunctious young Gaels of Synge's account, Yeats's audience members sit passively in the best orchestra seats, indulging in a gentrified brand of bourgeois patriotism stripped of the guttural,

---

[7] An Túr Gloine ("The Glass Tower") was a school for the production of native Irish stained glass. The Dún Emer Guild was a crafts workshop established by Elizabeth and Susan Mary Yeats. See Jeanne Sheehy, *The Rediscovery of Ireland's Past: The Celtic Revival, 1830-1930* (London: Thames and Hudson, 1980).

[8] In her biography of the painter, Pyle informs us that Pearse bought one of Yeats's works (47). Séamus O Buachalla identifies and reproduces the picture in *Pádraig Mac Piarais agus Éire lena Linn* (Patrick Pearse and the Ireland of his time) (Baile Atha Cliath: Cló Mercier, 1979), 47.

[9] See the comic account of one of the actors, "Duine Acu," in "Casadh an tSúgáin," *Banba* 1, no. 1 (December, 1901), 7-8.

if not downright alien, vitality of the Irish songs of twenty years before. Synge's heroes were spontaneous, unselfconsciously amateur performers of real national airs. The Irish people of *Patriotic Airs* are merely listeners and consumers, this time of a packaged and institutionalized "national" culture. This is the provincial world of second-rate, would-be professional, and thoroughly Anglicized "artistes" dissected with such scrupulous meanness by James Joyce in "The Mother" from his story collection *Dubliners* (1914). Indeed, one can imagine some of them as guests at the cultural soiree hosted by the Free State's "Minister for Arts and Crafts," his social-climbing wife, and his woefully inept vocalist daughter in Denis Johnston's 1929 play *The Old Lady Says "No!"*. The Minister sets the tone for the evening as he welcomes his guests, saying, "But mind you, I do say this. Talent is what the country wants. Politics may be all OK in their way, but what I say to *An Taoiseach* is this, until we have Talent and Art in the country we have no National Dignity. We must have Talent and Art." Tellingly, he is supported by Lady Trimmer "of the old regime" who, without opposition, defines the appropriate ethos and audience for that art. "Quite," she says. "And cultivated people of taste. You mustn't forget them, Mr. Minister. Art cannot live, you know, by taking in its own washing — if I may put it that way" (Johnston 54-55).

At the graveside of Jeremiah O'Donovan Rossa in August 1915, Pearse had called for an Ireland "not free merely, but Gaelic as well; not Gaelic merely, but free as well" (Pearse, "O'Donovan Rossa" 135). In this painting Jack Yeats offers a subtly satiric comment on how distant that dream remained even after the foundation of the native state whose creation had, through the ages, inspired so many patriotic airs.

Works Cited

(Abbreviatons: ACS = *An Claidheamh Soluis*, FL = *Fáinne an Lae*)

Brown, Terence. *Ireland: A Social and Cultural History, 1922 to the Present.* Ithaca: Cornell University Press, 1985.

"Casadh an tSúgáin." *ACS* 26 October 1901: 564.

Dalsimer, Adele. "The Irish Peasant Had All His Heart. J. M. Synge in *The Country Shop.*" *Visualizing Ireland: National Identity and the Pictorial Tradition.* Ed. Adele M. Dalsimer. Winchester: Faber and Faber, 1993: 181-230.

"I mBaile is i gCéin." *FL*, 24 October, 1925: 1.

Johnston, Denis. "The Old Lady Says 'No!': A Romantic Play in Two Parts with Choral Interludes." *The Old Lady Says "No!" and Other Plays.* Boston: Little, Brown and Co., 1959.

Lee, J. J. *Ireland, 1922-1985: Politics and Society.* Cambridge: Cambridge University Press, 1989.

Mac Giolla Iosachta, Éamonn. "Aithnightear Cara i gCruadhtan" (One knows a friend when times are hard). Editorial. *An Sguab* September 1923: 227.

Mac Giollarnáth, Seán. "Art at the Oireachtas." *ACS* 29 July 1911: 6.

— "The Oireachtas." Editorial. *ACS* 5 August 1911: 7.

"Mícheál na Téide." "Drámaíocht" (Drama). *FL*, 10 November 1923.

Ó Domhnalláin, Pádraig. "Caingean Ghallda" (A foreign dispute). Editorial. *FL* 22 December 1923: 2.

O'Malley, Ernie. *The Singing Flame.* Dublin: Anvil, 1978.

O Súilleabháin, Donncha. *Conradh na Gaeilge i Londain, 1894-1917* (The Gaelic League in London, 1894-1917). Baile Atha Cliath: Conradh na Gaeilge, 1989.

Pearse, Patrick. "The Art Revival." *ACS* 5 May 1906: 6.

— "Brusgar" (Odds and ends). *ACS* 4 August 1906: 7.

— "The National Salon." *ACS*, 11 August 1906 Duilleachán an Oireachtais: 2.

— "O'Donovan Rossa / Graveside Panegyric." *Collected Works of Padraic H. Pearse: Political Writings and Speeches.* Dublin: Phoenix, n.d.

— "O'Growney and the Revival Movement." Editorial. *ACS* 14 July 1906: 6.

"Pictiúirí" (Pictures). *FL* 5 April, 1924: 1.

Pyle, Hilary. *Jack B. Yeats: A Biography.* London: Routledge and Kegan Paul, 1970.

"Séamas." "Pictiúirí." *An Sguab* November 1925: 474.

Synge John Millington. "Le Mouvement intellectuel Irlandais." *Collected Works,* vol. 2. Ed. Alan Price. London: Oxford, 1966.

White, Terence de Vere. *Kevin O'Higgins.* Tralee: Anvil, 1966.

Yeats, William Butler. "Ireland after the Revolution." *The Collected Works of W. B. Yeats: Later Essays* (vol. 5). Ed. William H. O'Donnell with assistance from Elizabeth Bergmann Loizeaux. New York: Charles Scribner's Sons, 1994.

The King O'Toole and Other Relics of Old Decency

Timothy O'Neill

James Plunkett popularized the story of The King O'Toole in *The Gems She Wore — A Book of Irish Places* (1972). The tale, which the author heard from his friend Conor Hogan, whose family lived in Glencree, has been part of the folklore of Enniskerry, County Wicklow, for generations.

Around the turn of the century, in a side valley of Glencree known as the Raven's Glen, an old man lived alone in a shack he had made for himself. He owned but a few mountain sheep, which he drove down to Enniskerry once or twice a year to sell. Like the other shepherds, he would have a few drinks after market, but, when the drink worked in him, it stirred up a deep bitterness, a sense of wrong, which, after the pubs had closed, sent him marching up the avenue to Powerscourt House.[1] On reaching the entrance he would lift up his stick and hammer on the door, shouting, "Leave my house, youse usurpers and impostors."

His shouting would continue until the police came to take him away. Next day, the magistrate, who was, of course, Lord Powerscourt himself, would fine the old man a shilling and order him to keep the peace. Here, the matter would rest until the next fair in Enniskerry, when the old man could be relied on to stage a repeat performance. His name was O'Toole, and the people of the district always referred to him as The King O'Toole.

The Ua Tuathail, as the O'Tooles were called in ancient times, were powerful folk in Wicklow around 1000 A.D. Keeping a tight control over the monastery of Glendalough, they provided a succession of abbots, the most famous of whom was St. Lawrence O'Toole, Archbishop of Dublin in 1170, at the time of the Norman attack on the city. The family controlled the valleys around Enniskerry throughout the middle ages. Even though Felim, O'Toole's lands at Powerscourt, were confiscated in 1589 and granted to Richard Wingfield in 1603, the O'Tooles continued to dominate the region well into the seventeenth century (Smith 54–56). In Keating's painting, the landscape, typical of a Wicklow glen, is recognizable as Glencree with Knockree mountain in the background. The King O'Toole, empty pipe in hand, leans on a granite stone wall and gazes eastwards toward the rising sun — the direction of Powerscourt House. His expression is proud and sadly defiant, yet somewhat hopeful in the summer morning light.

In the painting *King O'Toole* (no. 19) Keating expresses the patriotic romanticism which inspired him throughout his career. More than any other twentieth-century Irish painter, Keating's work embodies the nationalism of the Irish Free State and its pride in the achievements of past heroic Celtic figures. O'Toole is a visual expression of the ideals of de Valera's nationalism, fully articulated ten years after this painting was executed:

---

[1] The beautifully situated Powerscourt House, built about 1730, was enlarged and landscaped in the nineteenth century by Viscount Powerscourt. The house was destroyed by fire in 1974, but the Slazenger family, who now own the property, have plans to restore it in the near future.

The Ireland which we dreamed of would be the home of a people who value material wealth only as a basis of right living, of a people who were satisfied with frugal comfort and devoted their leisure to things of the spirit…a land whose countryside would be bright with cosy homesteads, whose fields and villages would be joyous with the sounds of industry, with the rompings of sturdy children, the contests of athletic youths and the laughter of comely maidens, whose firesides would be forums for the wisdom of serene old age. (Eamon de Valera, St Patrick's Day Address, 1943)

The O'Tooles were the subjects of considerable historical research in the late nineteenth century. In 1890, Reverend P. L. O'Toole published his monumental *History of the Clan O'Toole and Other Leinster Septs.* In his introduction, the author states that he aims to trace the fortunes and vicissitudes of the clan and to give an authentic pedigree and sketch of the most prominent characters now "reduced to the position of toilers on the broad freeholds of their forefathers." In the final paragraphs of the work he mentions that "a junior branch of the Powerscourt family appears to have been suffered to remain in Glencree and Enniskerry as tenants to the new proprietors." He cites records of 1695 and 1768 and concludes that the families of George and John O'Toole of Ballyreagh, Glencree, are their descendants, living there "in obscurity to the present day" (531). Maybe the king was a representative of another branch of the clan, or, perhaps, these families moved away soon after the history was published, leaving behind the one man who became known as The King O'Toole. We will likely never know the true story, but the tale illustrates Dáithí Ó hÓgáin's observation that, although historical reality often differs widely from folkloric suggestion, there is always some connection between the two (2).

Ironically enough, as Keating worked on the painting in the 1930s, many members of Ascendancy families were becoming accustomed to the drips of leaking roofs and to the whiff of dry rot. Most of their political power had been lost fifty years earlier when the Land League and the tenant-right movement undermined the economic base of their huge estates. Mark Bence Jones recounts how Lord Emly, rarely without his cigar, moved from one room to the next as the rains came into Tervoe House, his family mansion in County Limerick. Across the Shannon, in Lismohane, County Clare, old Colonel George O'Callaghan Westropp lived with threadbare carpets and peeling wallpaper,

"surrounded by a pack of mangy terriers clothed in old vests to stop them scratching." The colonel, a Protestant and an aide-de-camp to King George, loved Ireland and took pride in his O'Callaghan ancestry. In the eighteenth century, members of the old Gaelic and Anglo-Norman families frequently turned Protestant in order to hold on to ancestral lands. To confirm his belief that he was the O'Callaghan chief, the colonel resolved to have members of the clan (sept) living in the ancestral territory in County Cork proclaim him so in the Gaelic fashion. One day in 1937, a large crowd responding to his newspaper advertisement assembled at a hotel in Mallow, and, having been liberally entertained with whiskey and beer, unanimously elected him chief. Although, as it turned out, there were fewer than a dozen O'Callaghans in the crowd, he persuaded the newly established Irish Genealogical Office to recognize his claim when they set about verifying the Chiefs of the Name (descendants of the ancient Irish Chiefs). Later, it seems, authorities were unable to document the accuracy of his pedigree, but, in deference to the colonel's eighty years, Chief Herald Edward MacLysaght allowed him to keep the title for the rest of his life (Bence-Jones 261–62). The list of officially approved "Chiefs of Name" published in *Iris Oifigiuil* in December 1944, included O'Toole. An amended roster, published in 1976, lists The O'Toole of Fer Tire as "dormant since 1965" (MacLysaght *Chieftainries* 50).

The relentless warfare waged by the forces of Queen Elizabeth in Ireland in the last decade of the sixteenth century, and the following colonization of Ulster, brought about the collapse of the Gaelic world and ended the power and independence of the native Irish and Gaelicised Anglo-Norman chiefs. Many emigrated following the "Flight of the Earls" in 1607, and those who remained in Ireland lived in greatly reduced circumstances. The respect and honor accorded the old chiefs by the native population, however, vexed the planters and new landlords. In the words of an Act of Charles II, they numbered the chiefs among the large class of idlers who walked "up and down the country with one or more greyhounds coshering or lodging or cessing themselves, their followers and their greyhounds upon the inhabitants" (Maxwell 320).

The poets, in particular, lamented the decline and fall of the chiefs who were their patrons. From earliest times, poets and bards had enjoyed a privileged position in royal households and were honored for their poems and songs of praise, but universally feared for their satires. Aristocratic and haughty characters like the

Limerick poet Dáibhí Ó Bruadair (c. 1623–1698) despised the peasantry; his contempt deepened as they sneered at his misfortune and poverty. Through their writing, the poets — Ó Bruadair, Aodhagán Ó Raithaille and others — managed to keep alive some vestige of the old order in the years after Cromwell. But even that trace faded away with defeat at the battle of the Boyne in 1690 and the disasters at Aughrim and Limerick which soon followed. When hundreds of the defeated Irish soldiers and their officers sailed for France in the autumn of 1691, Ó Bruadair, for one, turned inward in his bitterness, showing showed little regard for the harmless survivors of the old Gaelic families. Ironically, these soon became not the subjects of bardic poetry, but instead, objects of curiosity — fodder for English diarists and other travelers from abroad.

One such traveler was bookseller John Dunton who, during his visit to Connemara in 1699, met "O'Flaghertie, the most considerable man in the territory." The chief entertained Dunton in his summer quarters, a house consisting entirely of one "room with a fire in the middle and a vent for smoke in the roof. The walls were hurdles plastered with dung and clay." Dunton enjoyed a day's hunting with O'Flaherty and his grey-hounds and, that night, in the house, sat down to at a feast of venison, boiled beef and oat cakes, which they washed down with ale (Maxwell 121).

In *A Tour in Ireland 1776–1779*, English agriculturist Arthur Young discusses farming methods and land use among the wealthy landlords with whom he stayed on his travels. Occasionally, his hosts mentioned the descen-dants of ancient Irish nobles who still lived in the neighborhood. He tells of Mc Dermot "Prince of Coolavin" who, despite his income of but £ 100 per annum, had such an idea of his own impor-tance that he forbade his children to sit down in his presence. Young also reports on old Mc Dermot's visit from Lord Kingsborough, Mr. Ponsonby, Mr. O'Hara, Mr. Sandford and others. When they arrived at the door of his house, he addressed them as follows: "O'Hara, you are welcome, Sandford, I am glad to see your mother's son [his mother was an O'Brien], as to the rest of ye, come in as ye can."

Young recounts that on a visit to Roscommon, one Mr. O'Conor of Clonalis received a tribute of cattle and gifts from his tenants. "They consider him," Young says, "the prince of a people involved in one common ruin," and wished to enhance his income. Even poorer was his neighbor and kinsman Charles O'Conor of Belanagare. A well-educated antiquary and musician, who owned a priceless collection of Irish manuscripts, he farmed a tiny portion of his ancestral lands. O'Conor would say to his sons as they helped him with the plowing, "Boys, you must not be impudent to the poor. I am the son of a gentleman, but ye are the children of a ploughman" (219).

The loss of ancient land-rights and the conse-quent poverty may have been less irksome among those of lineage long and pure. Almost every surviving medieval Gaelic manuscript contains a genealogical section tracing its patron's ancestry, often as far back as Adam. Not just the nobles, but the nation as a whole, seemed to engage in the obsession. Richard Head observed in 1674 that the Irish,

> … are great admirers of their pedigrees, and have got their genealogy so exactly learnt that though it would be two hours work for them to repeat the names only from whence they are descended lineally, yet, will they not omit one word in half a dozen repetitions…Their greatest zeal is in keeping sacred some old sayings of their great grandsires, an preserving sacred some old relics of their grandmothers. (MacLysaght 20)

The two O'Conors were lineal descendants of the last high-king of Ireland, Rory (Ruaidri Ua Conchobair), who reigned over much of the country as the Anglo-Normans approached, but their lifestyle was far removed from that of twelfth century royalty. Instead, they appear much closer in material wealth to their noble eighth century ancestors, who, according to archaeologists and Celtic historians, ruled a rural, pastoral society divided into a multitude of small kingdoms, where,

> The royal roads were cow paths.
> The queen mother hunkered on a stool
> and played the harpstrings of milk
> into a wooden pail.
> With seasoned sticks the nobles
> lorded it over the hindquarters of cattle.
> (Seamus Heaney, *The First Kingdom* 101)

The popular quest for roots suggests that pride of race and ancestry lives on, and contemporary historians and political leaders see more in the past than the "backward rote of names and mishaps/bad harvests, fires, unfair settlements" (Heaney 101), which it was for Ó Bruadair, O'Conor and O'Toole. Today, the dawn light of Seán Keating's *The King O'Toole* may indicate a brighter future for all — Celt, Anglo-Norman or Planter who have come to share the land of Ireland.

Works Cited

Bence-Jones, Mark. *Twilight of the Ascendency.* London: Constable, 1987.

Hartnett, Michael. *Ó Bruadair: Translations from the Irish.* Dublin: The Gallery Press, 1985.

Heaney, Seamus. *Station Island.* London: Faber and Faber, 1984.

MacLysaght, Edward. *Irish Life in the Seventeenth Century.* Dublin: Irish Academic Press, 1979.

— "The Irish Chieftainries." *Burke's Irish Family Records.* London: Burke's Peerage Ltd., 1976.

Maxwell, Constantia. *The Stranger in Ireland.* Dublin: Gill and Macmillan, 1979.

Ó hÓgáin, Dáithí. *The Hero in Irish Folk History.* Dublin: Gill and Macmillan, 1985.

O'Toole, Rev. P. L. *The History of the Clan O'Toole and Other Leinster Septs.* Dublin: 1890.

Plunkett, James. *The Gems She Wore: A Book of Irish Places.* London: Hutchinson and Co., 1972.

Smyth, Alfred P. *Celtic Leinster: Towards an Historical Geography of Early Irish Civilization A.D. 500–1600.* Dublin: Irish Academic Press, 1982.

Young, Arthur. *A Tour of Ireland 1776–1779.* Shannon: Irish University Press, 1970.

Immoral Economy: Interpreting Erskine Nicol's *The Tenant*

Kevin Whelan

The British responded to the famine in ways profoundly informed by their prevalent Protestant religious sensibility. They understood the phenomenon of famine — saturated in biblical resonances — in essentially religious terms, as a form of providentialism — God's personal intervention in the natural world. The evangelical wing of British opinion stressed the consequent necessity to allow the unrestricted operation of the natural moral law, thereby encouraging a minimalist reaction. This marriage of malthusian pessimism and a strident eschatological emphasis emphasized the inevitability of the famine and its function as a retributive sign. At its most extreme, it could interpret the famine as a direct divine punishment of Irish Catholics for remaining stubbornly steeped in the superstitious stupor of popery. Martha Cox, from the evangelical landlord family at Dunmanway in Cork, wrote to her daughter in Binghamstown, New York,

> Ireland is under the curse of God and will be till she is delivered from the curse of Popery and the crying sins of the Protestant Church. God has now manifested his continued wrath against us by completely destroying the potato crop. Never was there a greater quantity planted- never was a more glorious promise of plenty. We were all hoping to lift our heads again and that, after this year, rents would be well paid again, when a blight showed itself and the crop is all gone again. It is said to be worse than the first year. On that I can make no comment but that, as a nation, we have

done everything to provoke God's wrath. Never was Ireland so bloody, so wicked in every possible way of sinning as she has been since His arm was bared to destroy. And the way the priests are hounding on the people to every kind of murderous and blasphemous outrage in the late elections reminds you of what we are told of the Jews at the destruction of Jerusalem. (Cox MS 28 April 1847)

This Christian providentialism was crucial to the easy government acceptance of laissez-faire economic policies, arguing against interference with free market forces; it affirmed the destruction of the potato as a good thing in itself because the potato could be construed as the literal root of all Irish evil — a lazy root, grown in lazy beds, by an incorrigibly lazy people. One Irish commentator caricatured the dominant British stereotype,

> [The potato] has done incalculable mischief, and has raised and supported a miserable population, who depend on him alone for subsistence, and who, should he fail them, have nothing else to look to- they must have potatoes or perish. By his pernicious influence, a brave manly people have been brought down to the lowest level of mere existence. At one time, he copiously supplied them with food, and encouraged extravagance and waste - at another, he has disappointed their hopes, and sent famine through the land, and caused shrieks of despair to be heard on every side … The people who subsist on this detestable root are standing on

the last rung of the ladder of human life, below which they cannot go.
(Connery 22-3)

The Lord Lieutenant Clarendon callously commented: "The wretched people seem to be human potatoes, a sort of emanation from the root; they have lived by it and will die with it" (Gray 36). The potato was an inferior food, pinning the backward and degenerate Irish poor to the pit of civilization. Its destruction could therefore be welcomed. Thomas Carlyle asserted that: "It is really a tremendous epoch we have come to, if the potato will not return … all revolutions are but small to this if the potato will but stay *away*" (Gavan Duffy 25)!

The blight would allow the pernicious potato to be replaced as a food source by a higher form like grain, and this change in itself would force the feckless Irish up the ladder of civilization. The famine would then be a harbinger of the future, a short term loss for a long term gain. It would teach the Irish poor the immutable laws of political economy, encouraging them to exercise moral and religious restraint; by eliminating the potato, which underpinned their monstrous overpopulation, it would give them "room to become civilized" (Donnelly 33), mercifully obliterating the archaic, anarchic culture, and slovenly society which the promiscuous potato had permitted. In Charles Trevelyan's words, the Famine would thereby produce "permanent good out of transient evil" (68).

These attitudes influenced the government's decision to import maize (Indian corn) as the preferred relief food (Gray, 1995). Maize could not be grown in Ireland and therefore would have to become a purchased food. This policy by itself would eliminate the potato wage which sustained the cottier system (the farmers' source of cheap labor), curtailing agrarian modernization. Farmers would then have to pay their laborers in cash rather than in kind (potatoes), and perforce become more efficient. Eliminating the potato would also liquidate the western micro-farmer, another pool of endemic poverty and overpopulation. The result would be a modern, efficient agricultural sector, with large-scale farmers and a wage earning sector- a lumpen rather than a lumper proletariat. These changes would generate a healthier social structure, more closely approximating the English and Scottish models. The famine's long term effect, then, would be as an accelerator of agrarian anglicization in Ireland, thereby copperfastening the Union. The promotion of social engineering of this type, rather than relief or saving lives *per se*, dominated the British administrative and political response to the famine.

As well as eliminating the potato, and with it the cottier laborer, the view also developed that it was necessary to wipe out the whole system of social and agrarian organization in the west of Ireland, based on collective settlement and infield-outfield cultivation. Writing from one such area- Gweedore in northwest Donegal,- the parish priest Hugh McFaden described the inhabitants as

> almost all on an equality. The great majority hold but a cow's grass, as it is termed, which average one acre of tilled ground. These scrapholders, who mainly lived and depended upon the potato from the facility of producing that root by sea manure, are, now that the potato is gone, reduced to the greatest extremity of destitution (Donegal Relief Committee, N.A.2/441/36).

But these "scrapholders" - the western rundale farmers- received little sympathy. Palmerston, a Sligo landowner and cabinet minister, opined,

> It was useless to disguise the truth that any great improvement in the social system of Ireland must be founded upon an extensive change in the present state of agrarian occupation, and that this change necessarily implies a long continued and systematic ejectment of smallholders and of squatting cottiers (Donnelly 163).

Clarendon, the Lord Lieutenant, depicted "depletion" (wholesale emigration) as the only cure for the condition of Connaught,

> I would sweep Connacht clean and turn in upon it new men and English money just as one would to Australia or any freshly discovered Colony- the nearer one can get to that the more probable will be the solution to the 'Irish Problem' (Kerr 333).

Thomas Carlyle blamed Irish poverty on the character defects of the Irish people, "a people of holed breeches, dirty faces, ill-roofed huts- a people of impetuosity and of levity- of vehemence, impatience, imperfect, fitful industry, imperfect, fitful *veracity*" (Gavan Duffy 14).

Behind these conceptions lay the utopian ideal of *tabula rasa*- a clean Irish slate on which the new English values could be legibly inscribed, deleting the chaotic scrawl which the Irish had scribbled all over their dishevelled landscape.

That whole agrarian mess should now be swept away as so much junk, the tangible embodiment of the arrears column in the double entry bookkeeping utilized in the landlords' rentals. The policy arms to this scenario were the £4 rating clause (which made landlords responsible for the rates on all holdings valued at under £4- in effect, the majority of western small holdings), and the Gregory quarter-acre clause, which refused relief to anyone holding more than that amount. By legally rendering the small farmers of the west a parasitic encumbrance on landlord property, these two clauses together became a clearance charter, leading to massive eviction in the west of Ireland, especially in the poorest counties of Mayo, Galway and Clare. Almost a quarter million people were evicted between 1849 and 1854 alone (*after* the worst was over) and as many as a half million may have been affected. A western bishop reported that in 1850, "Melancholy starvation, heartless extermination, and unexampled emigration of our people to the shores of the United States of America have rendered this poor diocese (in common with the west of Ireland) a wilderness" (Kerr 169). *The Times* predicted that "In a few years a Celtic Irishman will be as rare in Connemara as a Red Indian on the shores of Manhattan" (qtd. in Kerr 297) while *Punch* gloated,

> The old Irish cry of 'Ireland for the Irish' will soon be ... heard no more; for if emigration keeps up its present enormous rate, there will soon not be a single Irishman in Ireland, and the cry must be changed to 'Ireland for the English.' (no. 21, [1851]:167)

Clarendon was equally chauvinistic: "Priests and patriots howl over the 'Exodus' but the departure of thousands of papist Celts must be a blessing to the country they quit ... Some English and Scots settlers have arrived and...they encourage others to come" (Kerr 299).

This remark alerts us to the increasing exploitation of a racist discourse during the Famine. Between 1840 and 1880, the simianized version of "Paddy" appears, a more viciously "scientific" version of the Irish as "white negroes," a race of apelike Connemara Calibans. The first half of the nineteenth century witnessed the reorganization on a narrowly racial basis of the older English version of national character, inspired by the enlightenment model of Montesquieu, with its sophisticated and relatively sympathetic understanding of the interrelationship between geography, history and culture. The new science claimed that each country had an unique and unchanging racial destiny, genetically imprinting its national character. Ireland was obviously Celtic, a lower racial order, which accounted for the country's inferiority to Anglo-Saxon England. Celts were naturally lazy, feckless, violent and communitarian, lacking the sober integrity, sturdy individualism and self-reliance of the Anglo-Saxon. Combined with popery, racial defects determined Ireland's endemic poverty and violence. As the German Knut Clement argued in 1845, these defects also explained why Ireland should be subject to a political union,

> If ever the Irish should succeed in extricating themselves from the English clench, it is hardly likely that they will ever cast off their old Paddy habits and develop a completely new kind of person, for the Celt, the Slav and the Jew are unchangeable in their ancient ways. (Bourke n. pag.)

This racialist discourse solved a major difficulty for the post-Union British perspective on Ireland. Prior to the Union, Irish problems could be decisively attributed to the incompetence and corruption of its national legislature. It was axiomatically assumed in Britain that the self-evident virtues of an impartial imperial legislature would painlessly extend the manifold blessings of British civilization to Ireland. But Irish poverty and violence increased spectacularly rather than diminished after the Union, posing a severe conundrum: Why was Ireland not improving under the aegis of this marvellous empire — a civilized modern empire of trade and moral progress, not an ancient one of force and fear? As Horatio Townsend observed in 1810,

> It may seem a matter of just surprize, that a country, fertile and well situated, as this island, and which became a part of the British empire at a very early period, should still betray so many symptoms of poverty, rudeness and ignorance. (704)

That the imperial project itself could be problematic, that its civilizing mission could collapse so impotently on the shores of its nearest neighbor and oldest colony was unthinkable. The racial perspective squared this Irish circle: Irish problems were not socio-economic or political in character, but genetically rooted. Irish crime and poverty were endemic, irrational and "natural," and were therefore, irredeemably intransigent, impervious to moral or political suasion, amenable only to force and fear. In a paradoxical doubling, Irish poverty and disorder (whose obliteration was the initial justification for the

Union) now itself became the justification for the British presence, and a peculiarly minatory and repressive presence at that. And with this ideological somersault came a shift from sympathy to antipathy towards the Irish poor, and their interminable, nonsensical disputes. The intractable island must be held, not governed consensually.

This emerging "Celtic" discourse also fused with an existing religious one. Great Britain's self definition emerged essentially from heightened awareness of the imperial other: British identity was invented after 1700, consolidating around what Britons had in common, rather than what divided them. At the heart of this self definition was a robust Protestantism, which envisioned Britain as a beleaguered bastion, circled by a seething Catholic sea and constantly besieged by continental, especially French Catholicism. War and the threat of war with France unified Britons in an intensely shared hostility. In the nineteenth century, the aggressive British imperial mission again crystallized identity formation, bringing prolonged and pervasive awareness of an alien, recalcitrant empire. From this often anxious contact with a highly visible other, self definition clarified (Colley). Extending this argument into an Irish context, one can see how Catholicism became that highly insistent other, all the more visible because internalized in the state itself, against which British Protestant identity was defined. Irish Catholics joined the French as the negative signifier of British identity. They became the brutish barbarians against whom British civility could be measured (Whelan). In the 1790s and subsequently, Ireland assumed the French stereotypes — papist, republican, anti-monarchic — in both elite and popular British perceptions. Under the Union, it became the other within, whose poverty, violence, and surly separatism became a curiously comforting antithesis to British virtue, prosperity and stability.

Proto-disciplines like ethnology, phrenology and sociology gave a respectable scientific veneer to these prejudices. As science evolved a stadial model of civilization, race, religion and diet (paddy, popery and the potato) conspired to leave Ireland low on the ladder. By linking Celtic inferiority and the perverse popery of the Irish poor, Irish poverty could be re-interpreted as biological and moral in origin, reassuringly outside the remit of remedial political measures. These embryonic stereotypes stiffened during the famine, codified by organs of public opinion like *The Times* and *Punch. The Times* pontificated on 31 March, 1847, "We do not doubt,"

that, by the inscrutable but invariable laws of nature, the Celt is less energetic, less independent, less industrious than the Saxon. This is the archaic condition of his race … [Englishmen] can, therefore, afford to look with contemptuous pity on the Celtic cottier suckled in poverty which he is too callous to feel, or too supine to mend.

These viewpoints, shared by senior politicians, key administrators and influential journalists, encouraged an extreme reluctance to intervene decisively in Ireland during the famine. The British establishment could (and did) argue that it was only acting in accordance with God's obvious plan. In a society soaked in evangelical Protestantism, these arguments carried the dominant strand of public opinion with it in its view that Ireland should be allowed to starve — for its own good (Hilton). The government's role should primarily be moral — to force the feckless Irish to exert themselves into working for wages. This governing perspective derived from the providentialist view that God had personally intervened to permit this social revolution in Ireland. Hardline believers like Trevelyan and Wood were the dominant cabinet influences on Irish policy, as well as heavily influencing coverage in both *The Times* and *Punch. A Times* editorial hectored: "We help all those who help themselves but we do not like throwing money into a ditch" (qtd. in Campbell 8). Trevelyan and Wood agreed that "the right course was to do nothing for Ireland and leave things to the operation of natural causes" (Trevelyan 148). They envisaged public works as giant moral mechanisms to exert leverage on the Irish poor, and were described by a cabinet colleague as "sitting coolly, watching and applauding what they called 'the operation of natural causes,'" even as one million died (Kerr 197). Trevelyan described himself as "belonging to that class of reformed Cornish Celts who by long habits of intercourse with the Anglo-Saxon had learned at last to be practical men" (Hernon 17). There is little doubt that he extrapolated his familial odyssey as the desired trajectory for the Irish people as a whole.

A further fear infected British policy-makers: the Irish problem might spill over into Britain. To prevent this, Irish property alone must support Irish poverty, lest the enormous dead weight of Ireland drag England down to its own degraded level. Impoverishing England by relieving Irish famine would, in the words of Oxford economist Nassau Senior, culminate "in the ruin of all that makes England worth living in" (Ó Gráda, *Ireland Before* 113). And there was the nightmare prospect of an ever greater deluge of Irish emigrants flooding into England's industrial cities, multiplying the evils imagined by Thomas Carlyle in his venomous description of the pre-famine Irish in England,

> He is the sorest evil this country has to strive with. In his rags and laughing savagery, he is there to undertake all the work that can be done by mere strength of hand and back- for wages that will purchase him potatoes. He needs only salt for condiment, he lodges in any pig-hutch or dog-hutch, roosts in out-houses and wears a suit of tatters...There abides he, in his squalor and unreason, in his falsity and drunken violence, as the ready made nucleus of degradation and disorder. (Carlyle 28-9)

The cumulative result was to turn British opinion against Irish famine relief. Lord John Russell concluded in 1847 that "we have in the opinion of Great Britain done too much for Ireland and have lost the elections for doing so," while Charles Greville reported that "the English members and constituencies have become savage and hard hearted towards the Irish" (Greville 4: 274). These animosities deepened after the 1848 rebellion, seen in Britain as a sneaky stab in the back of empire. The dominant English feeling after it was "disgust at the state of Ireland and the incurable madness of the people" (3: 208). Russell was convinced that the real impediment to relieving Ireland was not so much high politics or cabinet dissensions but a popular prejudice against Ireland "which lies deep in the breast of British people" (Kerr 198).

That implacable hostility embraced not just the Irish poor but Irish landlords also. They were excoriated for having abdicated their responsibilities and for then selfishly expecting Britain to extricate them from their self-inflicted difficulties. Their own irresponsible greed had fuelled the notorious population increase, rackrenting to increase their rentals. Immorally enriched, many had become absentees, profligately spending their illgotten gains on living the high life in Bath, Rome, Paris, or other exotic watering holes. They had failed abysmally as a class to naturalize English rule in Ireland. English landlords, the oldest land-based capitalist class in the world, had become models of hegemonic rule, whose relationships with their tenants were based on custom, care and affection (Eagleton). This organic connection constituted the paternalistic loyalty at the core of British political stability. The Irish landed gentry were a scandalous rebuke to such considerations, a flagrant failure of their Gramscian hegemonic role. As a result, the British state had been forced to assume the role which the Irish gentry had abdicated. Thus, from a British perspective, the Irish gentry became progressively redundant, as the state became precociously interventionist. And as politicization hotted up, the British state in Ireland was tainted by the odor of Ascendancy, and taunted by Irish nationalist opinion for being so.

The danger for Irish landlords was that the British state was usurping their functions, precisely at the point when that liberalizing state in Britain also increasingly posed as a neutral arbitrator between classes, rather than as a mere partisan of an oligarchy. In these circumstances, the Irish landed class were doubly redundant; they had failed in their consensual role in civil society, just at the period when the state itself was abandoning unqualified support for them. Ireland had a centralized police force, maintaining order through coercion which the gentry should have overseen consensually. Similarly, Irish landlords had failed to sponsor education or a poor law system, again forcing the state to pick up their slack. While constantly insisting on their rights, they routinely renounced their duties. Idle, drunken, dissolute, they increasingly assumed in British eyes the wider negatives associated with the Irish poor. These fatal developments for them were accelerated by the famine, when British impatience with Irish landlordism reached a vituperative crescendo. The famine exposed their financial and moral bankruptcy in a peculiarly transparent way.

James Anthony Froude, the historian, typified prevalent English perceptions when he described an 1844 dinner in Cork to which local landlords had been invited,

> More than a hundred came, squires and squires' sons and brothers, large leaseholders, the Protestant chiefs of the district; there they sat, light-hearted, laughing, careless, the stuff out of whom had been made the Volunteers of 1782, but all changed now, with no thought of politics, with little serious thought at all; most of them in debt to their necks, but taking life lightly as it came, too wise to spoil the moment by troubling themselves about future possibilities. A Scotch grazier, come across on business, was sitting at my side. He said to me, 'You see

the gentry of the County of __. There is not more than one person here present who supposes that he was sent into the world for any purpose except to hunt, shoot, and fish, and enjoy himself. Poor fellows!- they will find before long that this was not what God Almighty intended with them at all.' They found it out even sooner than he could have expected. The next year the potato failed, and the social constitution of Ireland was shattered to pieces. (569-70)

British public and political opinion was hostile to Irish landlords, on the grounds that even though so many of them had abdicated their responsibilities, they now expected an indulgent Britain to bail them out. A newspaper reported sourly,

> It is but proper the English people should be told that the sons of a broken down gentry- a gentry full of beggarly pride but utterly destitute of the spirit of manly independence- are deriving the chief advantage from the present enormous expenditure of public money. (*Northern Whig*, 6 March 1847)

Even when landlords were physically attacked in Ireland, British opinion remained hostile. The Prime Minister John Russell observed,

> It is quite true that landlords in England would not like to be shot like hares and partridges. But neither does any landlord in England turn out fifty persons at once, and burn their houses over their heads, giving them no provision for the future. The murders are atrocious, so are the ejectments. (qtd. in Kerr 193)

In March 1848, he reiterated these views: "The murders of poor cottier tenants are too horrible to bear, and if we put down assassins, we ought to put down the lynch law of the landlord" (qtd. in. Donnelly 163). Thomas Carlyle wrote to Charles Gavan Duffy,

> Your Irish governing class are now actually brought to the Bar; arraigned before Heaven and Earth of misgoverning this Ireland, and no Lord John Russell, or 'Irish Party' in Palace Yard, and no man or combination of men can save them from their sentence, to govern it better, or to disappear and die. The sins of the fathers fall heavy on the children, if after *ten* generations. Surely, I think, of all the trades in the world that of Irish landlord at the moment is the frightfullest. The Skibereen peasant dies at once in a few days; but his landlord will have to perish by inches. (Gavan Duffy 25-26)

He contrasted the situation with that in England, drawing an ominous conclusion,

> We have already *another* aristocracy (that of wealth, nay, in some measure that of wisdom, piety, courage)- an aristocracy not at all of the 'chimerical' or 'do nothing' sort, though not yet recognized in the Heralds' books, or elsewhere well; but an aristocracy which does actually guide and govern the people, to such extent at least as that they do not by wholesale die of hunger. That you in Ireland, except in some fractions of Ulster, altogether want this, and have nothing but landlords, seems to me the fearful peculiarity of Ireland. To relieve Ireland from this; to at least render Ireland habitable for capitalists, if not for heroes; to invite capital, and industrious governors and guidance (from Lancashire, from Scotland, from the moon, and from the Ring of Saturn), what other salvation can one see for Ireland? (25-26)

By the 1840s, and in response to the perceived landlord failure, British opinion makers foresaw an utter transformation of the landowning system as being a necessary precursor to rebuilding the Irish economy. Middle class liberals from an industrial background argued that only free trade in Irish land would rejuvenate its economy. Useless encumbered proprietors should be swept away like their pauper peasantry to be replaced by a British yeoman class, who would introduce capital, entrepreneurial drive and the Anglo-Saxon virtues of persevering, relentless accumulation. By 1847, Russell could envisage with surprising equanimity "the displacement of one stratum of the social hierarchy of Ireland *viz* the Protestant gentry." (Kerr 93)

In these circumstances, Irish landlordism as a system came under pervasive challenge, and the British government insisted on their collectively shouldering the fiscal burden of the Famine. Hugh McFaden, the parish priest of Gweedore, wrote despairingly in December 1846: "The landlords leave us to the government and the government leaves us to the landlords and when they do so, they leave us to rest upon a broken reed" (Donegal Relief Committee, N.A. 2/ 441/36). The British establishment actually welcomed their bankruptcy; if financial difficulties forced them under, they could be painlessly replaced by a new breed of hard-headed English or Scottish owners, occupying freshly cleared estates for large-scale cattle or sheep ranching. The Encumbered Estates Acts of 1848 and 1849 were designed to facilitate this transition from

Irish to British owners, whose new managerial regime would transfuse the economy, modernize the society and anglicize the culture. The cumulative result would be the convergence of Ireland and Britain under a stable union settlement. Remarkably, the immediate post-famine period was followed by a surge of booster literature in Britain designed to attract these desirable new landlords to the west of Ireland in particular (Hooper).

> Land, of the best quality, to be had, to almost any extent, at a very moderate price; labor abundant and cheap; materials of all kinds almost always at hand, or to be procured at the most economical rates; communication to all parts certain and rapid, and markets either for the sale or purchase of goods as easily attainable as in most parts of Great Britain. (Webster 46)

This commentator also noted how the famine clearances would facilitate new owners,

> The disaffected and unthriving may be drafted from it [Ireland]; the industrious and well-intentioned, by having inducements offered them, may yet remain; while a most efficiently organised police force, combined with the numerous English and Scotch settlers, must quickly suppress any lingering system of intimidation that may yet remain. (5)

Thomas Miller noted the potential effects of the moral and physical convergence between the two islands,

> Every Englishman or Scotchman who settles in Ireland unites the sister kingdoms more closely together, and from twelve to sixteen hours of rail and steam will bring anyone from the heart of Ireland to the middle of England or Scotland. (Miller 10)

While the Encumbered Estates Court was very active — selling about 1,000 estates before 1853, and eventually passing one-eight of the country through its hands — it failed to attract new landowners. Only four per cent of the purchasers were non-Irish, and the bulk of the land was transferred between existing landed families. While there were a number of glamorous new settlers like Mitchell Henry at Kylemore and Allan Pollok in Galway, the overall effect was minuscule. By 1858, a total of 756 newcomers had settled in Ireland — 660 Scottish and 96 English (Miller 8). Friedrich Engels sneered at the post-famine landowning class,

> Their country seats are surrounded by enormous, amazingly beautiful parks, but all around is waste land … These fellows are droll enough to make your sides burst with laughing. Of mixed blood, mostly tall, strong handsome chaps, they all wear enormous moustaches under colossal Roman noses, give themselves the false military airs of retired colonels, travel around the country after all sorts of pleasures, and if one makes an inquiry, they haven't a penny, are laden with debts, and live in dread of the Encumbered Estates Court. (Carthy 4)

The Irish landowning class was extremely resentful of the British hostility. In 1851, Martha Cox of Dunmanway wrote to her New York relatives: "Almost everyone is ruined. Think of Lord Shannon's estate being brought to the hammer of the 'Encumbered Estates' Court.' This 'Encumbered Estates' Court' is one of Lord John Russell's plans to destroy the landed gentry of Ireland" (Cox MS, 23 August 1851).

If the poor and gentry were unlikely partners as the butts of British prejudice, the strong farmer became the preferred vector of a sustainable Irish future. In the long term, the strong farmer became the (unintended) beneficiary of the famine, in that it simultaneously removed the vexatious cottier class, while weakening the landlord's moral and political authority. The relatively untroubled transition to peasant proprietorship which ensued could not have occurred without the smoothing effect of the famine and large-scale emigration. In retrospect, the quietness of the social revolution in nineteenth-century Ireland was astonishing. The Land War cost remarkably little in lives or property (compare, for example, the turmoil in the later revolutions of eastern Europe). But in a counter-factual Ireland without the Famine, the Land War might have pitted the prosperous big-farm class against an alliance of the landless and the western small farmer. In such a confrontation, Davitt, not Parnell, might have been the uncrowned king of Ireland, spearheading a radicalism with rural roots, as in Italy. Indeed, the veteran Fenian and Land League organizer, Matthew Harris, cautioned against the alliance of grazier and small farmer- which he likened to the union between a shark and its prey. The Famine shattered the social formation on which such a scenario rested. Davitt's pleas for land nationalism fell on extremely stony ground: he would later claim that the Land War simply exchanged one form of inequality (landlord-tenant) for another (farmer-laborer). A deeply conservative politics gripped the newly empowered farming class. As Matthew Harris explained: "Farmers as a rule are a very selfish breed of men and are inclined to set the boundaries of the nation at the boundaries of their farm" (Bew 229). A police inspector made similar comments: "There is no-one more conservative than an Irish small farmer. The day of the paid politician and organizer in this country will be over when the people have the land in their hands" (Police Reports, C.O. 904/11/1).

That cautious conservatism emerged out of the Famine experience. With so many consigned to unmarked graves or scattered to the four winds, survivors had to be tough. James Fintan Lalor divined the message of the famine for the Irish farming class; they required a political project which would make them "secure as well as strong, based on a peasantry rooted like rocks in the soil of Ireland" (*The Nation*, 24 April 1847). That rooting acquired additional resonance precisely because it occurred in the midst of devastating deracination. The Irish sense of family emerged as an emotionally rooted island in a treacherous sea of breakdown and dispersal: the sense of place was shadowed by an all too pervasive displacement. In this sense, the Famine scarred its survivors. Malachi Horan observed that its main effect had not been to create poverty — "they were used to that" — but to make people "so sad in themselves" and make "many a one hard too" (Little 201). Edith Martin (the Galway half of the Somerville and Ross partnership) concluded that "the Famine yielded like the ice of the northern seas; it ran like melted snow in the veins of Ireland for many years afterwards" (Somerville and Ross 17). From Donegal, Hugh Dorrian described the aftermath,

> Years passed on, the same vicissitudes recurring, some few persons mounting a step higher in the scale of worldly comfort, some at a standstill, some drifting downwards in the face of all exertions, whilst self-preservation was the predominant thought with all men. Friendship was forgotten, men lived as if they dreaded each other, every one trying to do the best for himself alone. (N.L.I., MS 2047, ch.10)

Erskine Nicol's painting, *The Tenant* should be set against this complex Famine backdrop. He locates the tenant in an ambiguous, interstitial space, the landlord's hallway, where he sits warily, ill-at-ease, bolt-upright in an unaccus-tomed chair. Behind him on the wall are two potent symbols — the map of the landlord's property, underpinned by his blunderbuss, which points out towards the door. The map represents a legal landscape, an abstract, dehumanized world of numbers, valued in terms of property, power and money. The flesh-and-blood tenant disrupts this artifice, his head awkwardly breaking the map frame, embodying a moral and historical, rather than a legal, relationship between land and people. He inhabits a world of family, community and memory, in which invisible but powerful filaments of tradition, kinship and occupation link him to a living not a legal landscape. The landlord's "paper-and-parchment" landscape must bow to the tenant's prior moral claim, even when backed by the law and coercion- recalled here by the map and the gun. The landlord owns the land, an economic, political and legal category, but the tenant occupies the soil- an organic, moral and natural entity (Deane). As one Irish commentator aphorized, in the landlord's eye, the tenant was "nothing more than an instrument for converting soil into rent" (Connery 59). In the fissure between land and soil, in the gap between external and intrinsic value, the Famine fell between landlord and tenant, exposing the asymmetrical relationships between eight thousand landlords and eight million tenants.

That the landlord is viewed unsympathetically by Nicol is signalled by an explicit reference to *Castle Rackrent* — Maria Edgeworth's classic evocation of the notorious failings of the Irish landlord class — and an inaugurating moment in the history of the modern Irish novel. Edgeworth's text, published in the evocative year of 1800, had self-consciously consigned the ramshackle Rackrent family to history, claiming that since 1782, the Rackrents were extinct. And "for the instruction of the *ignorant* English reader," the preface asserts that the Irish landed gentry had since "acquired new habits and a new consciousness" because "nations as well as individuals lose attachment to their identity." By locating them in the past and erasing the distance between Ireland and Britain, Edgeworth makes a proleptic leap of faith in the new political arrangements: "When Ireland loses her identity by an Union with Great Britain, she will look back with a smile of good humored complacency on the Sir Kits and Sir Condys of her former existence." But it was precisely that "good humored complacency" which was lacking in post-Union Ireland, and the Famine in British eyes exposed a vicious proliferation of Sir Kits and Sir Condys. For contemporary observers of

Nicols painting, therefore, the historical reference could only be applicable to the current Irish landed class, the butt of so much savage criticism. The Scot Nicols points this out almost heavy handedly by assigning his Castle Rackrent to the stereotypically Irish "Th. O'Rafferty": the landed class is thereby aligned with prevalent racial stereotypes of the Irish poor as a whole, as well as being tarred with the rackrent brush — a return of the repressed. The gun behind the tenant's head then becomes an unambiguous image of the failure of the Irish landed gentry to attach their tenantry to them by consent rather than coercion. Only violence maintains them: their immoral economy has eclipsed any genuine moral economy between ruler and ruled.

The tenant's tatters becomes an implicit rebuke to the landlord (symbolically absent in the painting, as they were so often criticized for being in real life). The landlord's map depicts a massively subdivided property, whose tenants are literally spilling out into the bog referred to twice in his painting. The creased cóta mór, the careworn face, the battered boots become emblems of toil, the labor expropriated by an uncaring landlord. The ragged clothes of the Irish poor were a verbal and visual cliche by this time, as the German traveller J.G. Kohl explains,

> Irish rags and tatters have something special about them. For in no other land are they so worn-out, so riven, even down to the original threads and dissolving into dust on the body. At the elbows, and other angular parts of the body, the clothes disintegrate like the petals of a dying rose. The border of the jackets hang down in tresses. The outside is indistinguishable from the inside, the top from the bottom, the sleeves from the waist. In the end, the legs and arms no longer find their usual way into the garments. Every morning the costume is draped differently, and it could seem miraculous that such a heap of rags held together by threads can be arranged around the body if it were not all the same whether the trousers is used as a jacket or the jacket as trousers. (367)

Kohl specifically describes the incongruous top hats (which figure prominently in Nicol's painting): "comically collapsed and deformed silk top hats that had, God knows how often, dissolved to pap in the rain and had afterwards dried back into shape" (367). If clothes maketh the man, then the Irish poor were in bad shape. The social historian, Robert Scally, presents a penetrating perspective on the clothes of the pre-famine poor in County Roscommon,

> This haberdashery had never been manufactured locally; a generation out of fashion elsewhere, most had adorned more genteel heads years before and had finally been picked up for pennies near the end of their half-life from the itinerant peddlers of second-hand goods who plied the marketday crowds in towns like Strokestown. They were part of the flotsam and jetsam of the rag trade, flowing from east to west, circuitously seeking its lowest market, where the final drops of profit could be wrung out. Like leaves in the wind, there is no telling how far they had blown or what path they had followed before settling on the heads of Connor and McDermott, the commanding figures of Ballykilcline. Shoes travelled the same silent routes, along with sundry other manufactured and processed items from within the industrial core of western Europe, and some, like cotton cloth, tea, or tobacco, from distances beyond the cognisance of the townlanders. This was one of the markets of last resort in Europe, where commodities of the lowest and most exhausted quality found their last buyer. (32)

However, there is also something faintly sinister about that huge coat, incongruously worn indoors. *Castle Rackrent's* first paragraph, narrated by the ambivalent, doubled narrator, Thady Quirk, describes Thady's own coat in terms applicable to Nicol's painting,

> I wear a long green coat winter and summer which is very handy: as I never put my arms into the sleeves, they are as good as new, although come Holantide next, I've had it these seven years. It holds on by a single button round my neck, cloak fashion.

The linguistic and dress codes here are equally unstable, so Edgeworth inserts a long footnote alerting the English reader to the historical resonances that underpin this passage: "The cloak or mantle as described by Thady is of high antiquity." There then follows the celebrated passage from Spenser's *A view of the present state of Ireland*, written in 1596, in which he describes the mantle as "a fit house for an outlaw, a meet bed for a rebel, and an apt cloak for a thief,"

First, the outlaw being for his many crimes and villianies banished from the towns and houses of honest men, and wandering in waste places, far from danger of law, maketh his mantle his house, and under it covereth himself from the wrath of heaven, from the offense of the earth and from the sight of men. When it raineth, it is his penthouse; when it bloweth, it is his tent: when it freezeth, it is his tabernacle. In summer, he can wear it loose; in winter, he can wrap it close and at all times he can use it, never heavy, never cumbersome. Likewise for a rebel it is as serviceable; for in the war that he maketh, (if at least it deserves the name of war), when he still flieth from his foe, and lurketh in the thick woods, and straight passages waiting for his advantages, it is his bed, yea, and almost his household stuff. (76)

For Spenser, the mantle has become an intractably indigenous marker — an outward and visible sign of an inner refusal of English ways. Too easily nurturing the native, the mantle urgently needs reforming. Nicol's great-coated tenant has an ideological ancestry stretching behind the painting through Thady Quirk and beyond him to Spenser. Edgeworth updates Spenser by glossing "thick woods" with "black bogs," and Nicol's painting makes the same gesture. Thus, like Thady Quirk in *Castle Rackrent, The Tenant* inhabits an ambiguous territory: he may not be all that he seems. His red neckerchief draws explicit

attention to the recent year of Revolution in Europe. While his hat is doffed, there is something not entirely complaisant about his upright stance, his firm clench on his sturdy stick. The furrowed eyebrows and downcast mouth suggest distrust and unease. So Nicols' painting can also be firmly located within the age old colonial interrogation of the Irish — Who are these people? What do they want? Can we trust them?

It has become a lazy cliché to say that the sheer scale of the Famine horror overwhelmed existing systems of representation. Recent work has shown how anglo-centric and shallow this judgment is (Ó Gráda). Like literature, Nicol's painting, sensitively interpreted, can help us in the difficult task of grasping the famine at a human level. We must use every available resource while applying our fullest moral, intellectual and imaginative faculties if we are to reappropriate that buried experience. The frail Famine voices now faintly reach us across an aching void. We need to amplify that acoustic; in hearing them attentively, we might reclaim our Famine ghosts from their enforced silence and invisibility. In so doing, we can rescue them from the enormous cond-escension of posterity, paying them the respect which their lonely deaths so signally lacked. That very gesture of reconnection may alleviate a cultural loneliness we do not even know we have and liberate us into a fuller and more honest sense of ourselves, showing us how we got to be where we are, even as we leave it behind.

Works Cited

Bew, Paul. *Land and the National Question in Ireland 1852-82.* Dublin: Gill and MacMillan, 1979.

Bourke, Eoin. *German Perspectives on the Irish Question in the Nineteenth Century.* Unpublished Paper, 1995.

Campbell, Stephen. *The Great Irish Famine: Words and Images from the Famine Museum.* Strokestown: The Famine Museum, 1994.

Carlyle, Thomas. *Chartism.* London: 1839.

Carthy, James. *Ireland from the Great Famine to the Treaty of 1921.* Dublin: Fallon, 1965.

Colley, Linda. "Britishness and Otherness: An Argument." *Nations and Nationalisms: France, Britain, Ireland and the Eighteenth Century Context.* Eds. M. O'Dea and K. Whelan. Oxford: Voltaire Foundation, 1995.

Connery, James. *The Reformer or an Infallible Remedy to Prevent Pauperism.* 7th ed: London, 1836.

Curtis, L.P. *Apes and Angels. The Irish in Victorian Caricature.* Washington: Smithsonian Institute, 1971.

Deane, Seamus. "Land and Soil: A Territorial Rhetoric." *History Ireland,* II (1994): 31-4.

Donnelly, James. "Mass Eviction and the Great Famine: The Clearances Revisited." in Porteír, 1995.

Eagleton, Terry. *Heathcliff and the Great Hunger. Studies in Irish Culture.* New York: Verso, 1995.

Edgeworth, Maria. *Castle Rackrent.* Dublin: 1800.

Froude, J.A. *The English in Ireland in the Eighteenth Century.* vol. III. London: 1874.

Gavan Duffy, Charles. *Conversations with Carlyle.* London: 1892.

Gray, Peter. *The Irish Famine.* New York: Harry Abrams, 1995.

— "Ideology and the Famine." in Porteír, 1995: 86-103.

Greville, Charles. *A Journal of the Reign of Queen Victoria from 1837-1852.* 6 vols. London, 1885.

Hernon, James. "A Victorian Cromwell: Sir Charles Trevelyan, the Famine, and the Age of Improvement" *Éire - Ireland,* XXII (1987): 15-29.

Hooper, Glenn. *The Wastelands: Settler Opportunity in Post-Famine Ireland.* Unpublished Paper, 1995.

Kerr, Donald. *A Nation of Beggars? Priests, People and Politics in Famine Ireland 1846-1852.* Oxford: Clarendon Press, 1994.

Kohl, J.G. *Travels in Ireland.* London, 1844.

Little, George, ed. *Malachi Horan Remembers.* Dublin: Gill, 1943.

Miller, Thomas. *The Agricultural and Social State of Ireland in 1858, Being the Result of the Experience of Englishmen and Scotchmen Who have Settled in Ireland.* Dublin, 1858.

Ó Gráda, Cormac. *Ireland Before and After the Famine.* Manchester: University Press, 1988.

— *An Drochshaol. Beáloideas Agus Amhráin.* Dublin: Coiscéim, 1995.

Porteír, Cathal, ed. *The Great Irish Famine.* Cork: Mercier Press, 1995.

Scally, Robert. *The End of Hidden Ireland. Rebellion, Famine and Emigration.* New York: Oxford University Press, 1995.

Somerville and Ross. *Irish Memories.* New York: Longman, 1917.

Spenser, Edmund. *A View of the Present State of Ireland.* Ed. W. Renwick. Cambridge: University Press, 1934.

Townshend, Horatio. *Statistical Survey of the County of Cork.* Dublin: 1810.

Trevelyan, Charles. *The Irish Crisis.* London, 1848.

Webster, William. *Ireland Considered as a Field for Investment or Residence.* Dublin: 1852.

Whelan, Kevin. *The Tree of Liberty. Catholicism, Radicalism and the Construction of Irish Identity 1760-1830.* South Bend: Notre Dame University Press, 1996.

Manuscripts

Cox MS, Ts in possession of Desmond Fitzgerald, Knight of Glin, to whom I am grateful for permission to consult them.

Donegal Famine Relief Committees, Kilmacrenan Barony, incoming letters, National Archives of Ireland, 2/441/36-38. I am grateful to Breandán Mac Suibhne for these references.

Hugh Dorrian, "Donegal Sixty Years Ago - A True Historical Narrative." National Library of Ireland, MS 2047.

Police Reports, East Galway, Feb. 1920, Colonial Office (London) 904/11/1.

Catalogue

Nathaniel Hone, R.H.A.
(1831-1917)

Nathaniel Hone introduced nineteenth century French naturalism to Irish painting. Born in Fitzwilliam Place, Dublin, in 1831, Hone was the son of Brindley Hone, a merchant and director of the Midland Great Western Railway, and the great-grandnephew of the eighteenth century artist of the same name. In 1853, when he was twenty-one, Hone moved to Paris to study painting, primarily under Thomas Couture, one of the earliest exponents of realism. Hone also admired the Dutch painters of the Hague School (1860-1900) for their cloudy skies and subdued tones touched with pure color, and to whose work his seascapes, beach scenes, sand dunes, and fishing boats come particularly close.

While at Couture's atelier, Hone befriended Manet and most likely met Pissarro, Degas and Whistler. He became acquainted with the work of Corot and the Barbizon School at The World Fair of 1855 in Paris. About 1856, Hone moved to Barbizon where he painted with Millet, Daubigny, Harpignies and Corot. Hone was drawn to Corot's palette of rich greens, browns and earth tones. Much like English artist John Constable, Hone responded spiritually to the landscape and changing skies he painted. And like Constable, he often made pencil, then watercolor and then small oil sketches from which he painted his finished work.

Seven years after arriving in Barbizon, Hone moved to Bourron Marlotte. There he became acquainted with future Impressionists Monet, Renoir, Bazille, and Sisley, who, at that time, still worked in a tonal Barbizon style. He exhibited three times at the Salon in Paris between 1865 and 1869.

During his 17 years in France, Hone visited Ireland regularly. He moved back permanently in 1872. The paintings he completed during this period depict mainly the woodlands, pastures and coastline of North County Dublin, and maintain the mood, pensiveness and tonality typical of the Barbizon School.

From 1876 until he died in 1917, Hone exhibited his work almost yearly at the Royal Hibernian Academy where he was a full member in 1880, and appointed professor of painting in 1894. His joint exhibition with John B. Yeats (nos. 40-46) in 1901 was a watershed in the history of Irish art, for it convinced Hugh Lane that Dublin should have a modern art gallery. After Hone's death, his widow bequeathed his entire studio to the National Gallery of Ireland.

no. 1

Gathering Seaweed on the Strand, Malahide
Nathaniel Hone, R.H.A.
(1831-1917)
c. 1890
oil on canvas
25 in. x 36 in.

Signed lower right, with initials:
N H

Provenance:
John Quinn;
Christie's *Fine Irish Paintings and Drawings*, Dublin, June 28, 1995.

Exhibited:
This may be the painting entitled *Seaweed Gatherers,* exhibited at Ballymaclinton

Franco-British exhibition, London, lent by Sir George Brooke Bart, organized by Sir Hugh Lane in 1908, no. 24. The same painting was exhibited at the Royal Hibernian Academy, 1917, no. 18.

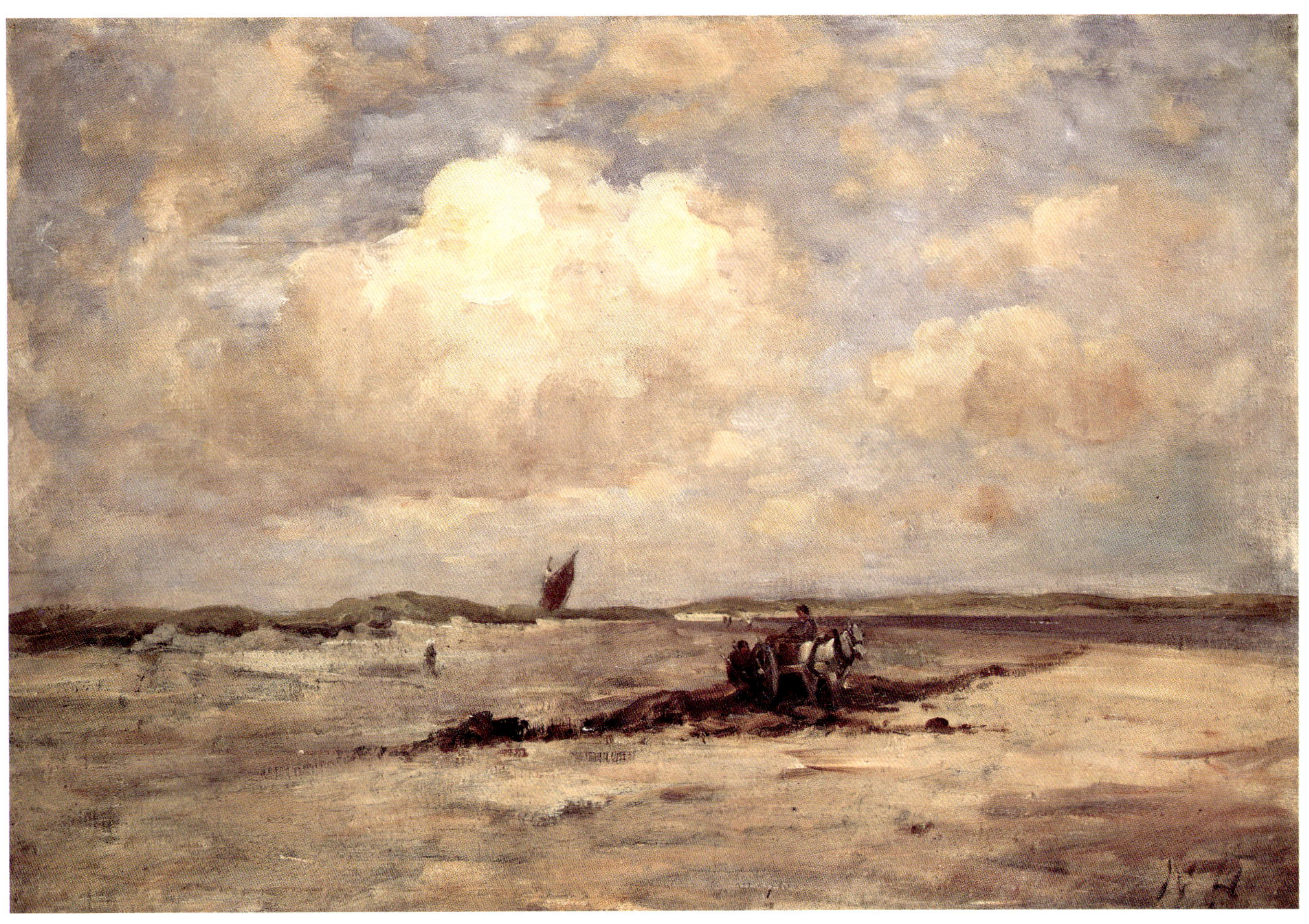

Here, as in most of his work, Hone gives as much value to sky and cloud as to land and sea. His great feeling for specific light, weather, and the play of light upon color — unique to the Irish landscape — are con-spicuous in this canvas.

Hone rarely dated his work; therefore, establishing a chronology is difficult, as is determining whether a view is Irish or French. Charting his stylistic development presents an equal challenge. Although his later paintings are looser in handling than his earlier work, all of his preparatory oil sketches demonstrate appealing spontaneity and freshness. Consistent throughout his career, however, are the muted earthy tones of his palette.

Although most of Hone's later works are pure landscapes, *Gathering Seaweed on the Strand, Malahide* shows a human presence. Hone painted many versions of this subject: *Donegal Coast: Seaweed Gatherers on Rock*; *Seaweed Gatherers with Two Groups of Donkeys*, and *Man, Horse and Cart, Load of Seaweed on Sands*. Seaweed gathering was also a popular subject among other Irish painters, such as Walter Osborne (nos. 34-35), Seán Keating (nos. 17-19) and Charles Lamb.

CK

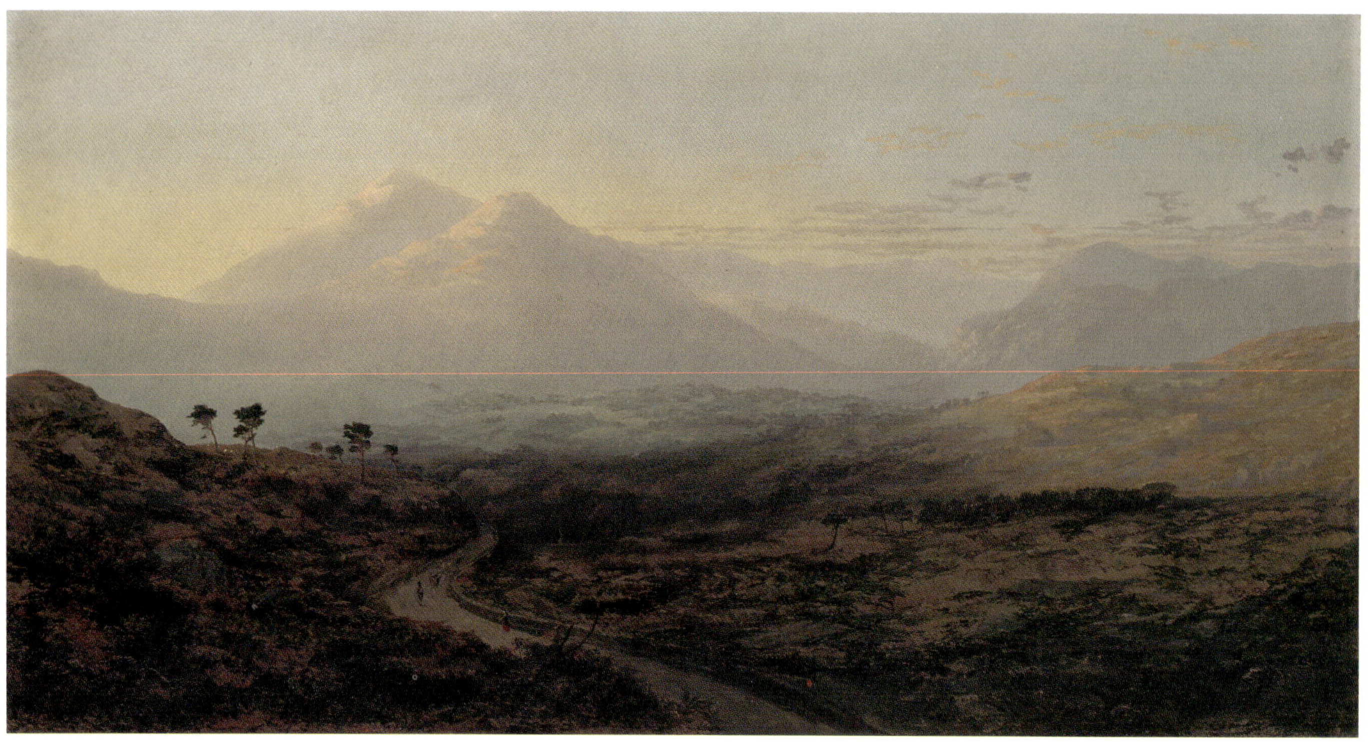

William McEvoy

(active 1858-1880)

An accomplished and sensitive landscape
painter, William McEvoy lived in Rathmines
in Dublin during the late 1850s and
early 1860s. From here he executed and
exhibited views of County Wicklow, made
popular by his more famous predecessor
James Arthur O'Connor (1792-1841).
Like his contemporaries, Patrick Vincent
Duffy and John Faulkner, McEvoy concentrated on the gentler, more nostalgic,
and atmospheric qualities of the landscape,
in contrast to the romantic dramas
that attracted O'Connor. His painting
A Country Funeral suggests that McEvoy
shared George Petrie's interest in folk
culture and ancient monuments. A view
of the ruins of Boyle Abbey, exhibited
at the Royal Hibernian Academy in 1860,
offers further evidence for this.

McEvoy moved to London in 1865, but
continued to send pictures to the
Academy exhibition in Dublin, many of
Irish locations. He chose as his subjects
remote scenic spots frequented by Victorian
travelers, particularly after the advent
of the railway. His work includes some
representations of London and of the Welsh
mountains, as well as those of Kerry,
West Cork, and Wicklow.

no. 2

***Glengariffe from
the Kenmare Road,
Evening***
(active 1858-1880)
1862
oil on canvas
28 in. x 52 in.

Signed and dated
in monogram:
WM 62

Provenance:
James Adams and
Sons, Dublin.

Exhibited:
Royal Hibernian
Academy
1863, no. 169.

Literature:
James Adam, *Sale
Catalogue*,
Wednesday, 16 June
1993, no. 70.

William McEvoy painted *Glengariffe from
the Kenmare Road, Evening* in 1862, before he
emigrated to London. The little coastal village,
at the head of Bantry Bay in the southwest
corner of Ireland, was already popular among
tourists at the time. Concentrating on the mood
of the landscape, McEvoy's panoramic, but
naturalistic, view of the area is reminiscent of
seventeenth-century Dutch and Flemish
painters. McEvoy is reluctant to engage in the
politics of landscape, refusing to comment on
the plight of the Beare Peninsula that was
separated from the rest of the country by the
Kenmare-Glengariff road (shown here) during
the Great Famine, just over a decade earlier.
The small group of figures on the road provides
a human scale against which to measure
the distant mountains, and suggests movement
in an otherwise quiet evening landscape.

CM

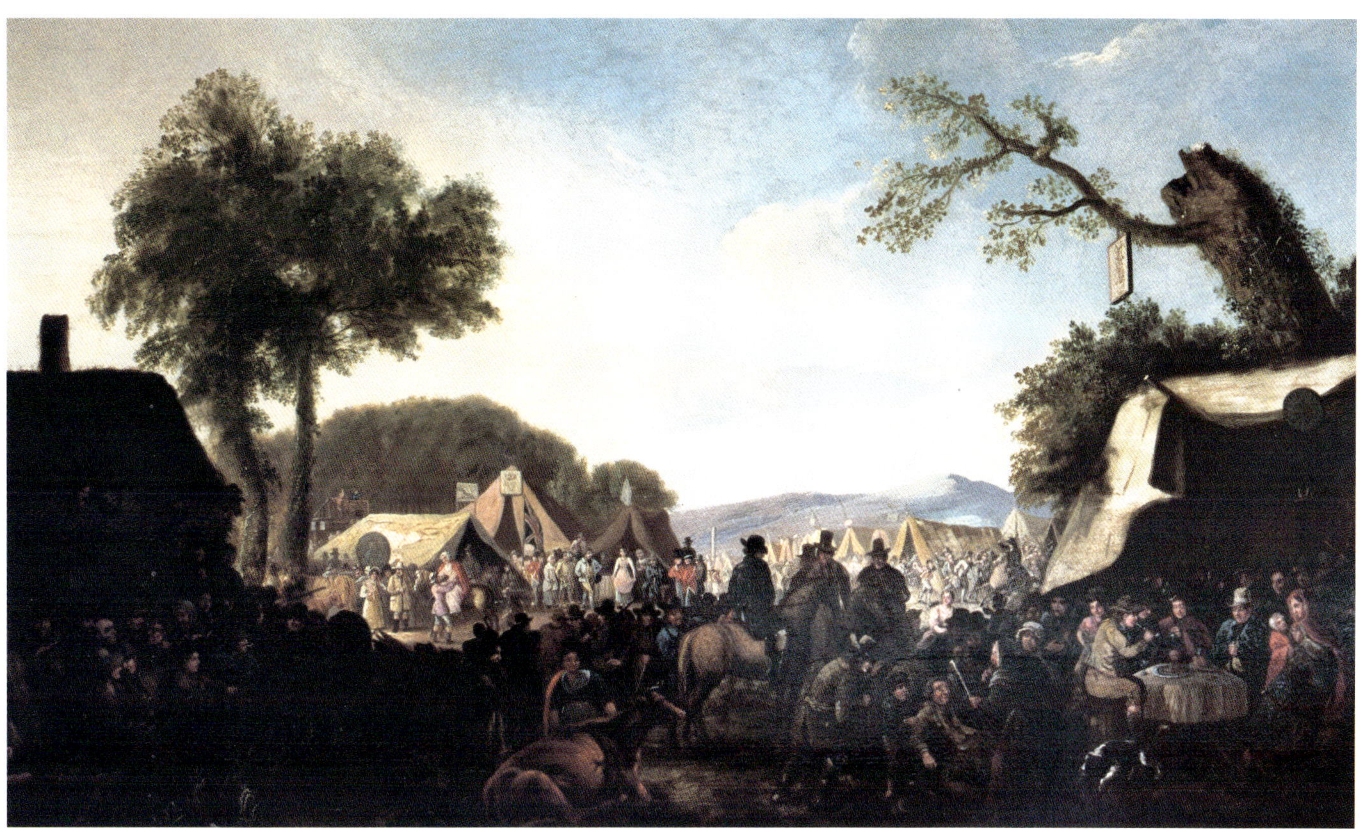

William C. Sadler II

(c. 1782-1839)

William C. Sadler was the son of an
artist of the same name who worked in
Dublin between 1765-1788. William Sadler
II specialized in landscapes and coastal
views. He also painted spectacular events,
such as fires and volcanic eruptions,
and a small number of Irish historical
subjects. Among the latter are depictions
of events that occurred during the
1798 republican uprising: *The Landing of
the French at Kilala* and *The Search
for Michael O'Dwyer*. Rare in Irish art, his
portrayals of the uprising were deemed
subversive.

Sadler is better known for his small views
of Dublin and its surroundings (such
as *Donneybrook Fair*), some of which he
exhibited at the Royal Hibernian Academy.

no. 3

Donneybrook Fair
William C. Sadler II
(c. 1782-1839)
oil on panel
21 1/4 in. x 35 3/4 in.

The horizontal format, dark foreground, and
coulisses on either side of this composition are
typical of Sadler, as is the stylized tree to the
right. Including many more figures than is usual
in his work, Sadler portrays the crowded
atmosphere of the fair with considerable vigor.
The faces are alive and expressive. Scenes
of wild disorder dominate the right side of the
picture: men and boys wield sticks and spill
their drink; mothers feed their babies; and in the
middle distance, a threatening crowd sets
upon a man on horseback. The left side, showing
the recruiting officer's tent behind the Union
Jack, a symbol of the political union with Britain,
is more peaceful, perhaps because of the
military presence nearby. Treated by many artists,

including the well-known English genre
painter Francis Wheatley in 1782, Donnybrook
is now a fashionable residential area in Dublin
City. In the eighteenth and early-nineteenth
centuries, however, it was still open country,
and the venue for an annual fair.

Sadler is known to have copied Dutch
genre pictures, and, in its range of color and
comic treatment of figures, *Donnybrook
Fair* clearly shows this influence. The treatment
of the crowd is similar to the crowd scenes in
William Hogarth's (1697-1764) *Election Series*.

CM

Sir John Lavery,
R.A., R.H.A., R.S.A.
(1856-1941)

Belfast-born John Lavery was one of
many Irish artists who studied in France in
the late nineteenth century. Orphaned at
an early age, and raised in Ireland and
Scotland, the teenaged Lavery used his
wages as a photographer's assistant to
support art classes in Glasgow. Determined
to become a painter, in 1881 he went
to Paris and then to the artists' colony
at Grez-sur-Loing. Like many of his Irish
colleagues, he was influenced by the
innovative *plein-air* techniques of the
French painter Jules-Bastien Lepage.
Unlike the French artist, however, Lavery
was more interested in portraying scenes
of leisure than of the peasantry at work.

After returning to Glasgow in 1885,
Lavery was selected to paint the portrait
of Queen Victoria at the 1888 International Exhibition — a commission
which launched his career as a fashionable
portraitist of international reputation.
His marriage, in 1909, to Hazel Trudeau,
the beautiful daughter of a Chicago
industrialist, confirmed his place at the
center of Edwardian society. He achieved
the height of his success when, in 1912, he
was commissioned to paint the Royal
Family for the National Portrait Gallery.

In the early years of their marriage, the
Laverys began alternating between London
and their winter retreat in Tangiers, where
the artist painted prolifically. After the
1916 Easter Rising, increasingly involved
in Irish political affairs, the Laverys used
their social connections, particularly their
friendship with Irish leader Michael
Collins, to facilitate negotiations between
Ireland and Britain. In his London studio,
during a period of safe conduct, Lavery
painted a series of portraits of Irish leaders,
including Eamon de Valera, Gavin Duffy,
Arthur Griffith and Michael Collins.
During the 1920s, the Laverys traveled
widely in France, Switzerland and America,
where the artist painted portraits of film
stars Shirley Temple, Maureen O'Hara and
Loretta Young.

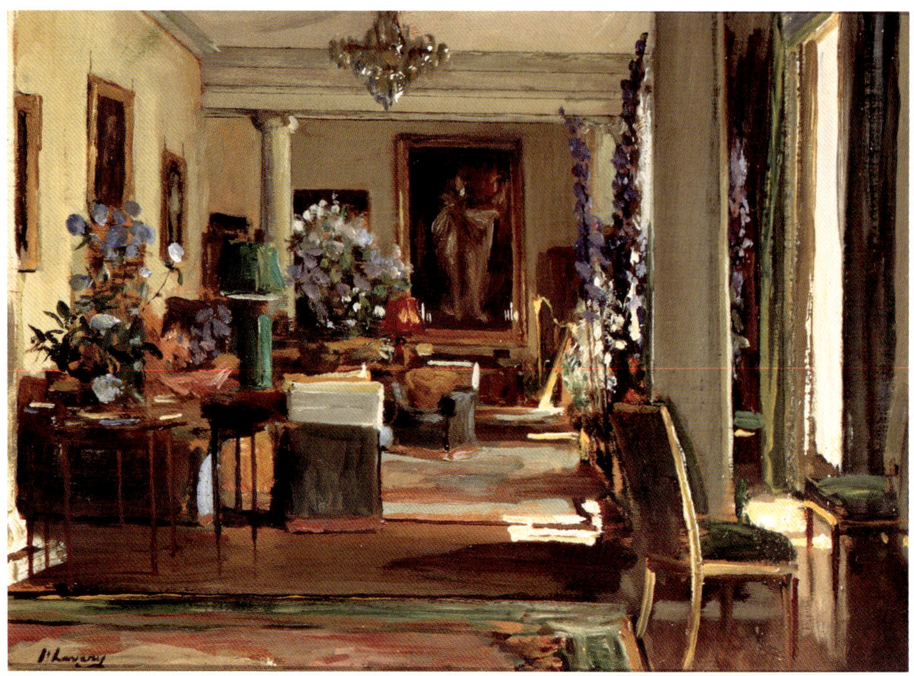

no. 4

*The Drawing Room
at Mount Stewart*
Sir John Lavery, R.A.,
R.H.A., R.S.A.
(1856-1941)
c. 1925
oil on canvas
10 in. x 14 in.

Signed, lower left:
J. Lavery

Provenance:
Dr. O. Cremin,
St. Stephen Green,
Dublin.

Exhibited:
Royal Hibernian
Academy,
1926, no. 20.

Mount Stewart, standing on the east shore
of Strangford Lough in County Down, was
the home of the Londonderry family. Begun in
the late-eighteenth century by the first
Marquess, the present house was completed
by the Irish architect William "Vitruvius"
Morrison in the early-nineteenth century.

Lavery painted his first portrait of the
seventh marquess, Charles, Lord Londonderry,
in 1919, forging a close friendship. After the
Marquess and his wife, Edith Lady Londonderry,
moved to their Irish home two years later, John
and Hazel Lavery were their frequent guests.
This rendering portrays the drawing room at
Mount Stewart c. 1925, a few years after
the seventh marquess of Londonderry had taken
up residence, and more than a decade before
that same Lord London-derry, eager to promote
Anglo-German relations, visited Hitler privately
in Germany and entertained Ribbentrop and
his wife at Mount Stewart.

Lord Londonderry helped Lavery to arrange
sittings with Unionist political leaders and

prominent churchmen. During his career, Lavery
painted numerous portraits of republican and
unionist figures and recorded a many occasions
of political and historical significance.

Lady Edith redecorated and refurnished much
of the interior of Mount Stewart during the
1920s. Her taste in furniture ran from
chinoiserie lacquer to English and Continental
eighteenth century gilt pieces. In the drawing
room she uses rich, luxurious velvets and
damasks in her favorite colors: rose, gold, jade
and dusky pink. The Mount Stewart "portrait
interior" is one of many related works of
this period in which Lavery subordinates figure
to setting, or simply omits human activity
altogether, to depict the apparent casualness
and informal chic of elegant interiors. Lavery
uses slashes of sunlight streaming in through
tall side windows to articulate space and
to depict the rich burnish and soft gleam of
the furniture, silver and silk damask.

CK

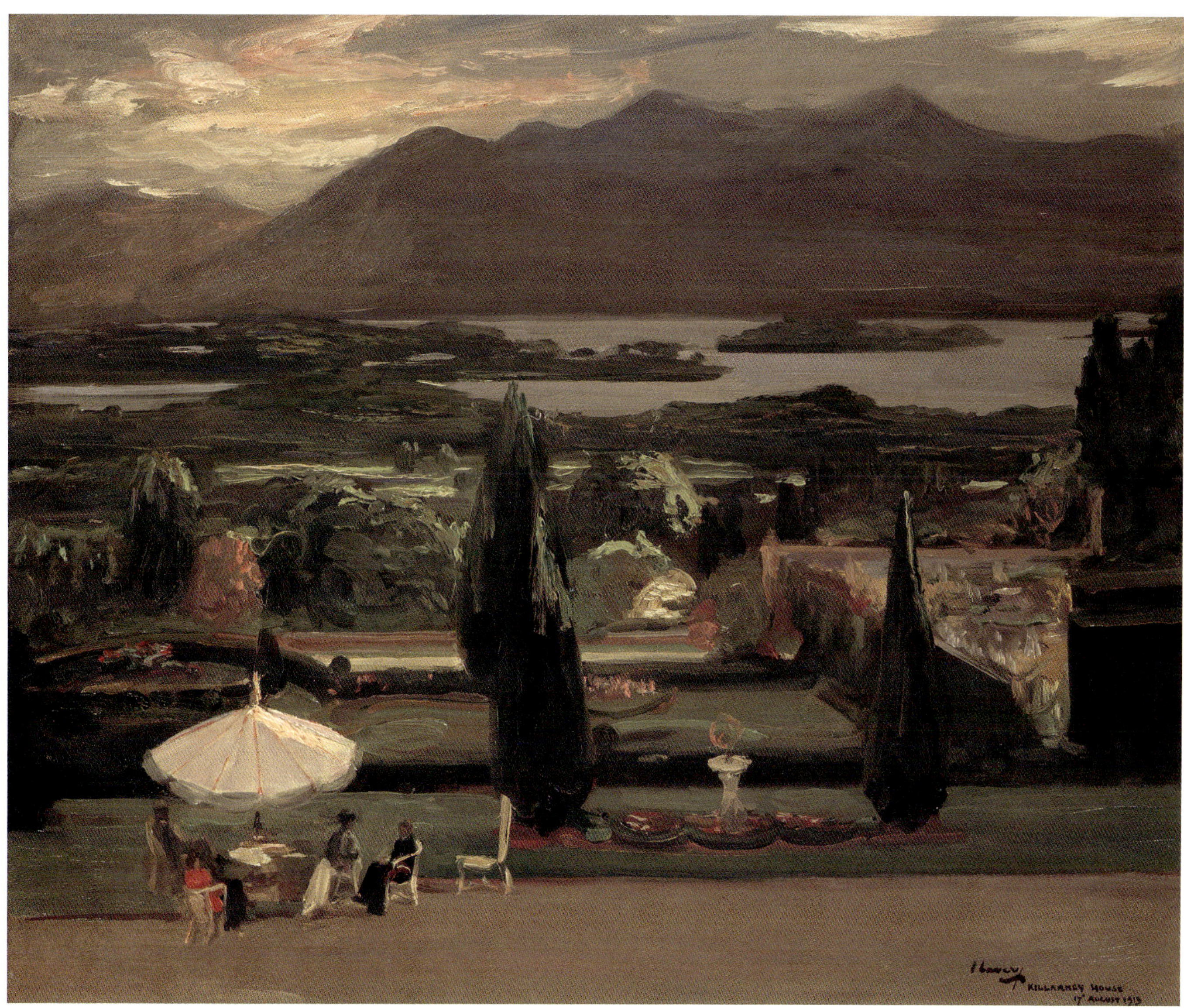

no. 5

*The Lakes of
Killarney*
Sir John Lavery,
R.A., R.H.A., R.S.A.
(1856-1941)
1913
oil on canvas
25 in. x 30 in.

Signed and
dated:
*Killarney House/
17th August 1913*

Signed and
dedicated on
reverse:
*To / The Countess
of Kenmare*

Provenance:
Elizabeth, 5th
Countess of
Kenmare, a gift
from the artist, and
then by family
descent to previous
owner; Sotheby's
The Irish Sale
London, 30th June
1995, lot 292.

Like *The Drawing Room at Mount Stewart*,
(no. 4), this painting is one of Lavery's
works depicting the houses and grounds of
wealthy patrons. The artist painted *The
Lakes of Killarney*, from an upstairs window of
Killarney House, also known as Kenmare
House. Two weeks later, on September 1, 1913,
the house was gutted by fire. Killarney House,
the residence of the 5th Earl of Kenmare,
was built in 1872 on 150,000 acres of land to
the northwest of Killarney. It commanded a
spectacular view of the lakes and surrounding
mountains, in an area which today comprises
part of the National Parklands. Lavery painted
this view of the house's formal gardens
and panorama of Killarney's famous lakes on
a late summer's day, while the Earl, presumably
Hazel Lavery, and a fourth figure sit beneath
a large sunshade and enjoy the view.

Painted from an upstairs window, the canvas
depicts a group of figures who are included
perhaps for scale. Beyond stretches the
breathtaking vista of the formal gardens of
Kenmare House, which gradually blend
with the shimmering greens and mauves of
the lakeland area. In the background, in
the hazy light of a late summer's afternoon,
soar the magnificent Macgillycuddy's Reeks.

Lavery was inspired by the visual drama
of mountain ranges and lakes after a visit to
Switzerland in 1912. A Scottish landscape,
of 1913, *Loch Katrine*, attests to this interest
as does the small study *The Madonna of
the Lakes* of the same year, in which Lavery
portrays Hazel against an almost identical
scenic backdrop.

CK

James Humbert Craig,
R.U.A., R.H.A.
(1878-1944)

Regarded as one of the premier landscape
painters in Northern Ireland, Belfast-
born James Humbert Craig spent his early
years in Ballyholme, County Down.
Craig was largely self-taught, turning
seriously to a profession as landscape artist
after the age of 35. Although frequently
sketching in Connemara, Sligo and Donegal,
Craig was particularly attracted to the
scenery of the Glens of Antrim, on
the northeast coast of Ireland. There he
purchased Tornamona Cottage at
Cushendun, which remained his home and
studio for the rest of his life. Craig
continued painting romantic landscapes of
rural Ireland, unlike contemporary artists
who were influenced by European
modernism. With Paul Henry (no. 7),
Frank McKelvey (no. 32), Charles Lamb
and Maurice McGonigal (nos. 15, 16),
Craig participates in an artistic tradition
once viewed as quintessentially Irish.

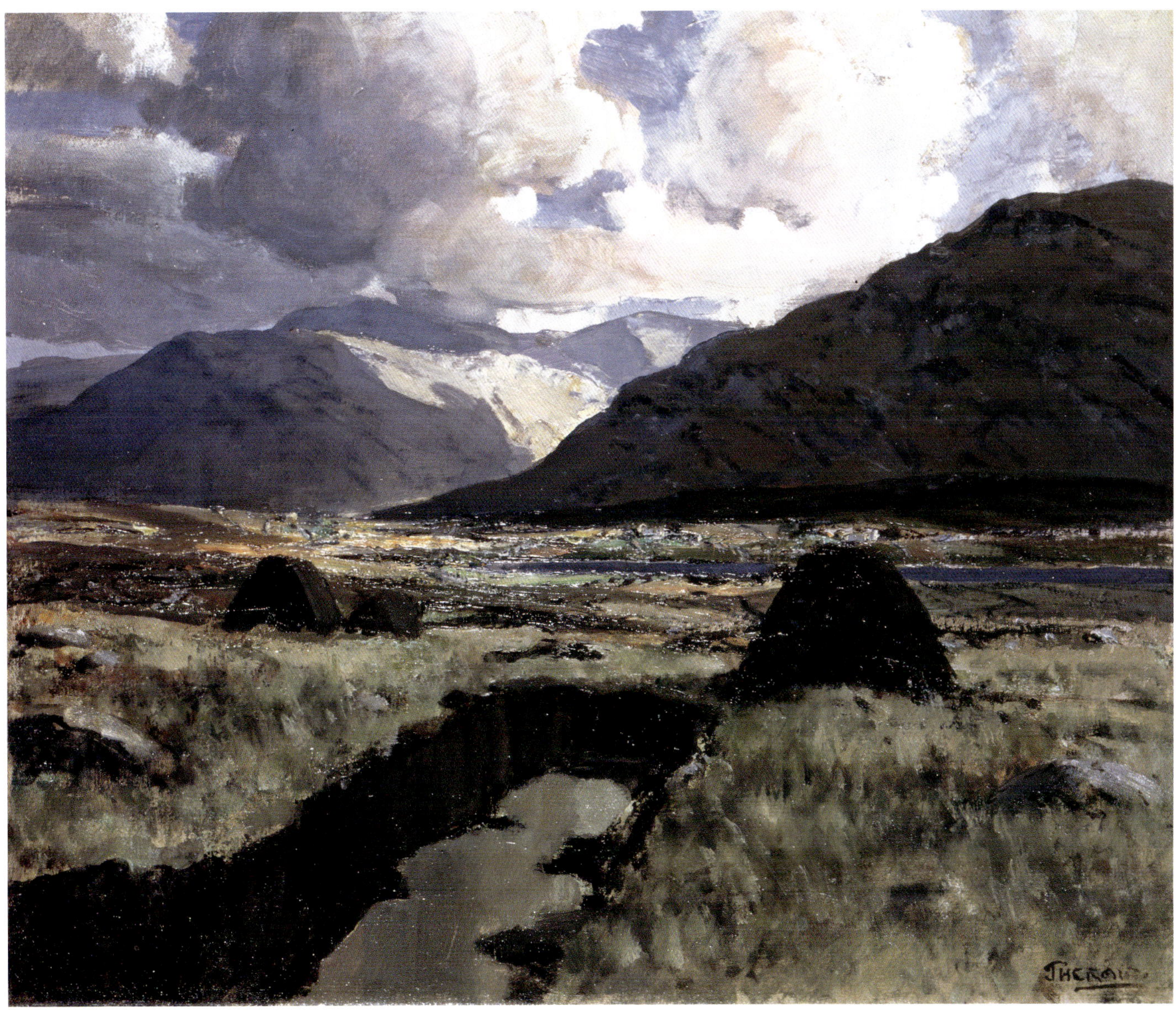

no. 6

*In County Mayo
(or Connemara Bog
and Mountain Scene)*
James Humbert Craig,
R.U.A., R.H.A.
(1878-1944)
oil on canvas
20 in. x 24 in.

Signed, lower right:
J.H. Craig

Provenance:
Dillon Antiques,
Dublin.

In County Mayo is a classic example of Craig's portrayal of the western countryside. Billowing cumulus clouds move across a gray-blue sky, while flickers of bright sunlight flash across broad mountain slopes and open moorlands. In a loosely impressionistic manner, with rich impasto technique, the artist captures a fugitive cloud formation, the gleam on the water, and shafts of bright light piercing dark shadows.

Visual drama emerges as sunlight and shadows restlessly sweep and fall across distant mountains, and momentarily illuminate the peatbog below. In the foreground, only the neatly stacked mounds of turf and sharply cut trench allude to a human presence in the landscape.

CK

Paul Henry, R.H.A.

(1876-1958)

Belfast-born Paul Henry is one of several painters who studied in France after an initial art education in Ireland at the Belfast School of Art. His early work reveals the effect of his continental apprenticeship, for he was influenced not only by the expressionist paintings of Van Gogh and the realist subject-matter of Millet, but also by Whistler's aesthetic of the superiority of tone over color. Subsequently, Henry worked as an illustrator in London for twelve years. In 1909, at the invitation of Sir Hugh Lane, he contributed some drawings to the Royal Hibernian Academy exhibition and, the following year, was allocated a wall to himself. But like many other Irish artist and writers at the turn of the twentieth century, he was most influenced by his discovery of the land-scape and life of the west of Ireland.

After reading J. M. Synge's play, *Riders to the Sea*, about life on an Aran Island, Henry visited Achill Island in County Mayo for a short holiday in 1912. He remained for seven years and painted its landscape for the rest of his life. Later, Henry explained that his decision to live on Achill was based on a purely emotional desire to identify himself fully with its life; he worked for a time as a paymaster in the Erris peninsula to supplement his income. The island provided him the subject matter he sought, and its peasant inhabitants reawakened his early interest in Millet and Van Gogh. His first Irish paintings depict the hard scrabble job of digging potatoes in hilly fields, as he paints Millet-like groups of workers in a rich expressionist palette. The islanders launch their boats against Atlantic breakers, fish, cut peat, or gather in small parties in dark cottage interiors. In his later works, figures occur less frequently; the social realism of Millet and expressionism of Van Gogh give way to a Whistlerian quiet. Henry painted mostly the landscape — mountains, still inland waterways, turf stacks, and boglands. Although describing a specific place, this landscape remains so simple in color and formthat it appears abstract.

Henry and his wife Grace, also a painter, moved to Dublin in 1920, where, with Jack B. Yeats (nos. 40-46), Mainie Jellett, and Letitia Hamilton (no. 8) among others, they founded the Society of Dublin Painters, an avant-garde group that represented all that was modernist in Irish painting of the day. By 1925, after exhibiting in group shows of Irish art in Paris and designing popular posters for the London Midland and Scottish Railroad, Henry's reputation had increased considerably. During this period, he developed his signature composition, bold and spare with but a few juxtaposed shapes and a severely limited palette. Now devoid of figures, these works, nonetheless tell of a human presence. Simple, majestic imagery, reducing the landscape to a few perfectly graduated forms and tones, came to represent the quintessential Paul Henry. In numerous variations on this characteristic painting, the artist explored the abstract properties of dark foregrounds and distant bays, or strongly contrasting white-wash and thatch against brooding hillsides.

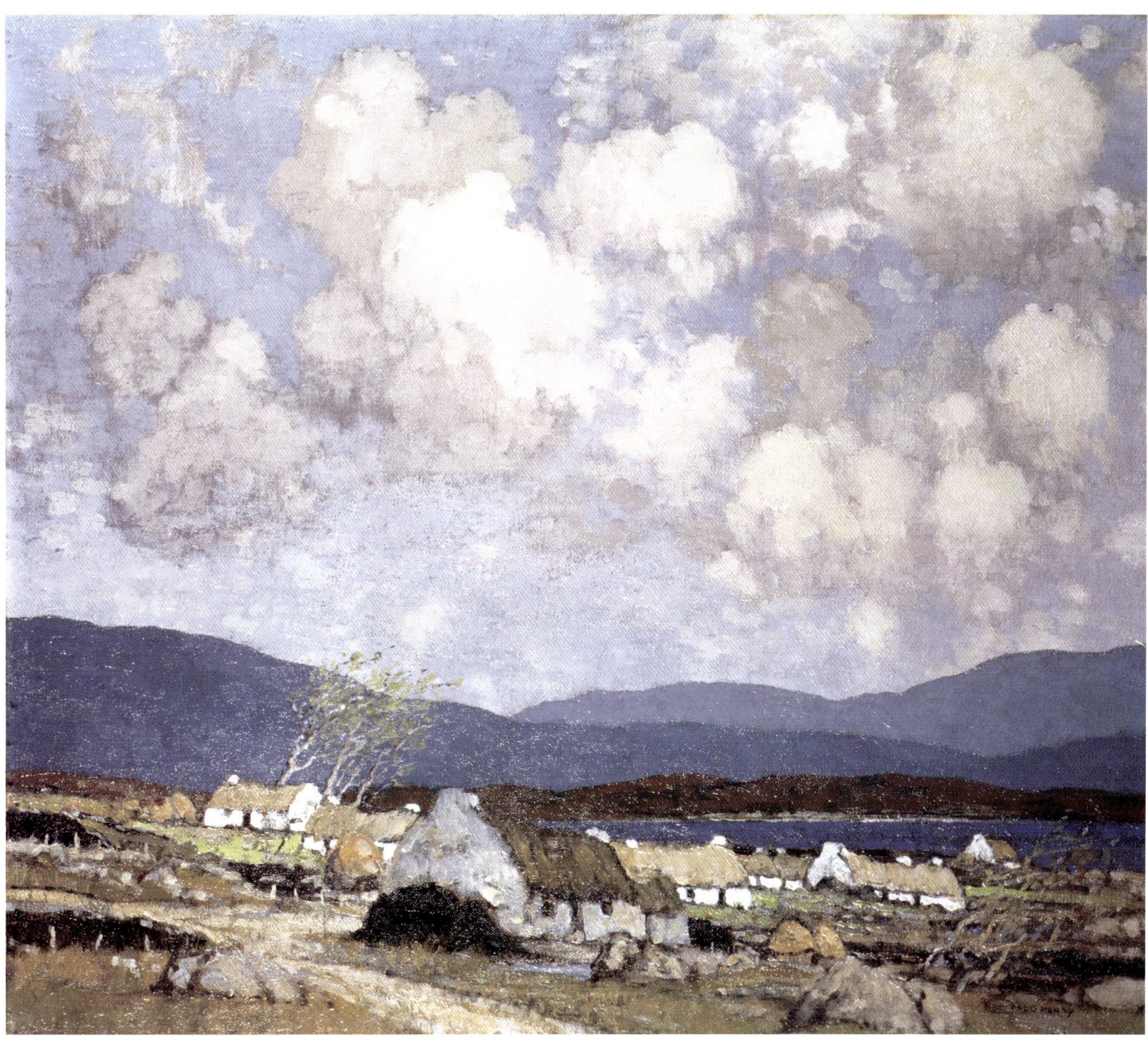

no. 7

Spring in Connemara
Paul Henry, R.H.A.
(1876-1958)
c.1930
oil on canvas-board
23 1/2 in. x 27 1/2 in.

Signed, lower right:
Paul Henry

Provenance:
James Adam and
Sons, 1989;
Dillon Antiques,
Dublin, 1989

Although he lived and worked on the east coast, in Wicklow, for the rest of his life, Henry remained faithful to his Achill experience and continued to paint the west. In the work shown here, painted after the artist had left Achill, Henry has captured, with characteristic effect, the calm omnipotence of the slate blue mountain range and the ever-present, heavy cumulonimbus clouds which sweep in from the Atlantic ocean. As usual, Henry has divided the composition into distinct parts: cloud formations dominate the upper portion, mountain and landscape the lower. Here, the small clusters of white-washed thatched cottages that dot the lakeside evoke human lives, although Henry shows no figures. The emphatic horizontal orientation of the composition accentuates the mood of pervasive stillness and tranquillity.

CK

Letitia Marion Hamilton, R.H.A.
(1878-1964)

Letitia Hamilton grew up in Hamwood
House, Dunboyne, County Meath, a member
of an artistic family. Her sister Eva was
also a painter of considerable talent, and her
cousin Rose Barton was a highly regarded
watercolorist. Studying at the Metropolitan
School of Art under Sir William Orpen (no. 26),
at the Chelsea College of Art, and in Belgium,
Hamilton's impressionistic work was largely
uninfluenced by her teachers' academic styles.
Instead, she adapted the reductive approach of
Paul Henry (no. 7), a contemporary Irish
artist. Henry rendered landscapes in flat,
simplified, outlined forms — intensifying the
impasto with a palette knife. Together with Jack
B. Yeats (nos. 40-46), Mainie Jellett, and Evie
Hone, Hamilton and Henry founded the
Dublin Painters Society. During the 1920s and
1930s, Hamilton exhibited almost annually, and
traveled widely in France, Italy and Yugoslavia,
where she painted mainly landscapes. In the
late 1930s, she worked in Venice and the Italian
lake district, using a gondola as her studio.
The pale tonalities she used to paint old Italian
masonry prevail even in her scenes of the
west of Ireland; in many of these Irish paintings
creams and beiges are broken only by black-
shawled women, their donkeys and carts.

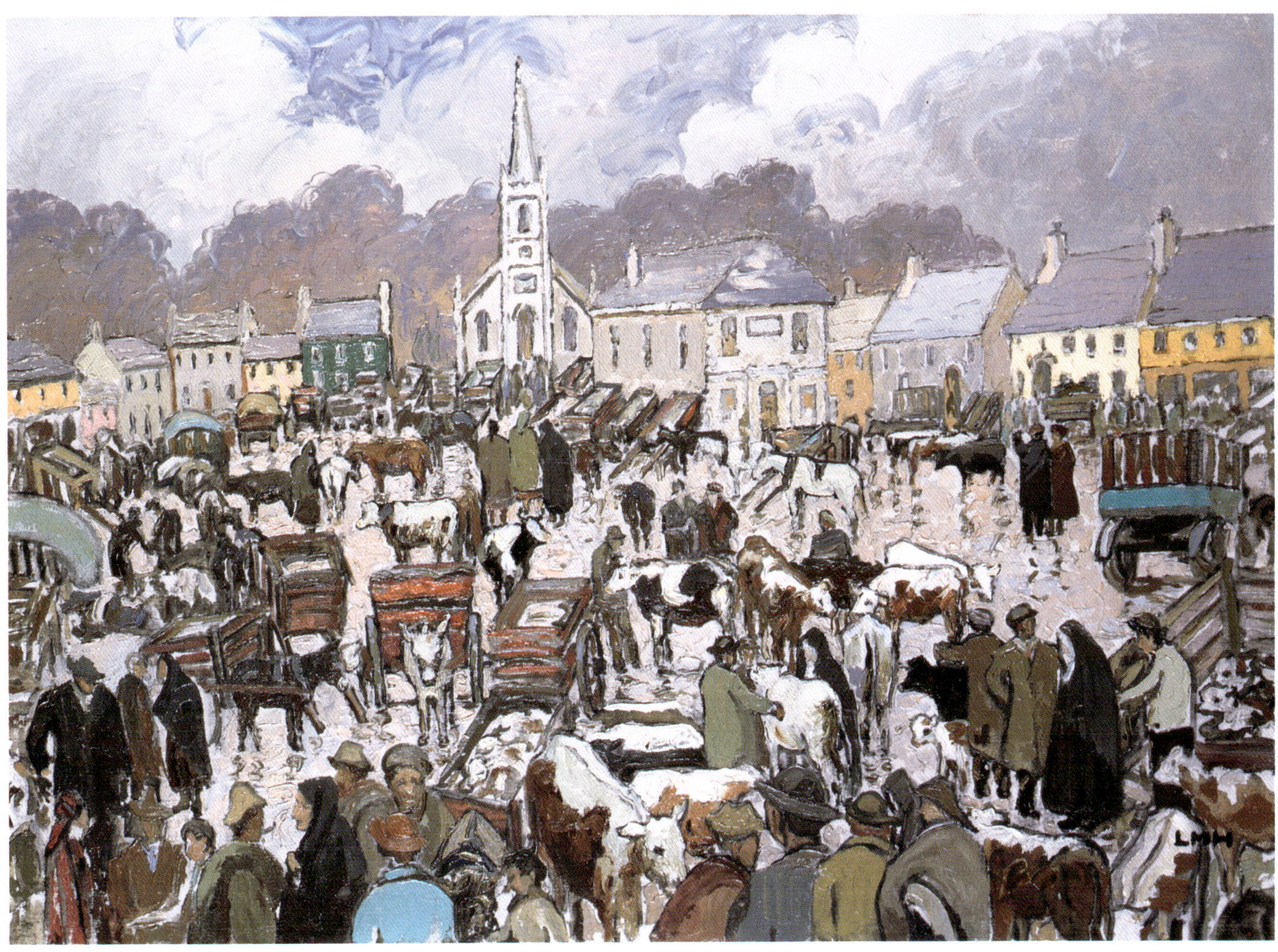

no. 8

*The Fair,
Castlepollard*
Letitia Marion
Hamilton, R.H.A.
(1878-1964)
c. 1948
oil on canvas
25 1/4 in. x 36 in.

Signed, lower
right, and verso,
with initials:
LMH

Provenance:
Dillon Antiques,
Dublin.

Exhibited:
Royal Hibernian
Academy,
Dublin, 1949,
no. 170;
*Exhibition
of Paintings by
Eva A. Hamilton
and Letitia
M. Hamilton*,
Dublin, May 7-21,
1949, no. 17.

Depicting the town square on the day
of a livestock market, market-goers, with their
donkeys, carts, cattle and calves, form a
dense pattern across the canvas. Their long
coats, caps and shawls imply a chilly, early
spring day. Painting from a first-floor window,
Hamilton captures character-types by shape
and pose. One or two nuns, wearing long black
habits, chat with the locals. Animals are
tethered or meander over the cobbles, tended
by their owners. Pale tones describe the square
and its buildings. Its shadowless, flat view
enhances the decorative quality of the painting.
Thick impasto defines the rolling clouds,
houses and the church that face the square.

CK

Lilian Lucy Davidson, A.R.H.A.

(1879-1954)

Lilian Lucy Davidson was born in Wicklow and studied at the Dublin Metropolitan School of Art. Although her relationship with the Royal Hibernian Academy lasted from 1914 until the year of her death, she was linked, nonetheless, with developments in Ireland that promoted modernism. In the early 1930s, she became a member of the Dublin Painters Society, the group Paul Henry (no. 7) established to provide exhibition space in Dublin for progressive art.

Davidson worked as a portrait painter, and her study of Jack B. Yeats, who greatly influenced her work, is now in the collection of the National Gallery of Ireland. Like Mainie Jellett and Norah McGuinness, Davidson was involved in theatre design, creating scenery and posters for the Dublin based Torch Theatre. To supplement her income, Davidson taught at her own studio and at a number of Dublin schools; the artist Anne Yeats was one of her many pupils.

Like many Irish artists of her generation, Davidson traveled in Europe. She exhibited scenes of Brussels and Bruges in the early 1920s, and later in that decade, spent time in France. Her subjects, exhibited at the Royal Hibernian Academy, reveal an affinity with rural areas such as Donegal, Mayo, Connemara, and her native Wicklow. Rather than focusing simply on the beauty of the landscape, Davidson's concern is with the lives of ordinary people, indicated through titles such as *Digging, Bait-Co. Dublin*, *Potato Harvest*, and *Fishermen-Rouen*.

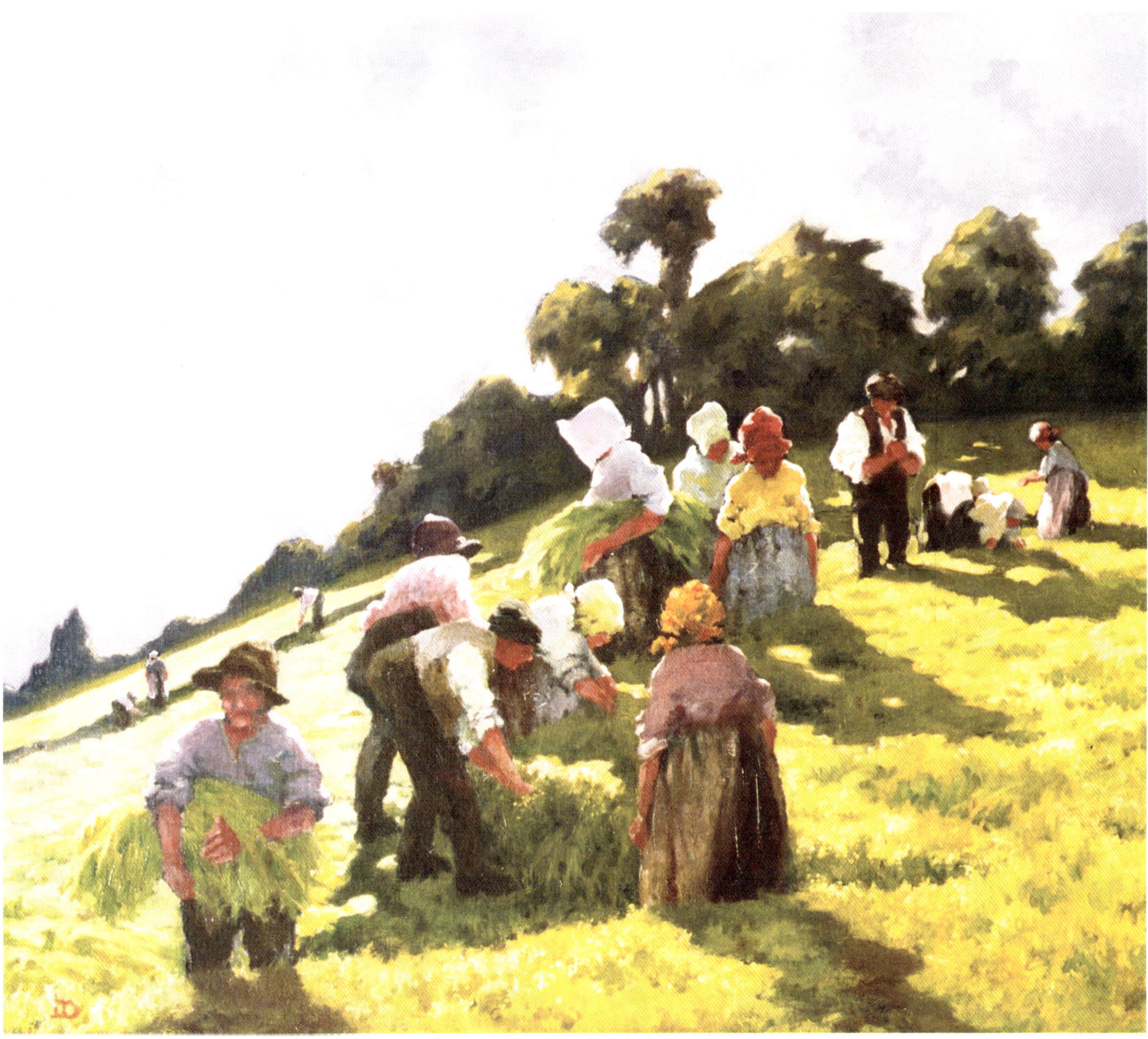

no. 9

The Flax Pullers
Lilian Lucy Davidson,
A.R.H.A.
(1879-1954)
oil on canvas
26 in. x 30 in.

Signed
with monogram,
lower left:
LLD

Exhibited:
Royal Hibernian
Academy,
1921, no. 58.

The Flax Pullers is typical of Davidson's rural scenes. It depicts a group of men and women working in the fields of County Tyrone gathering flax, used to make linen. The linen industry was focused in the north of Ireland. The number of northern scenes exhibited by Davidson in the early 1920s suggests that the artist spent some time in this region.

The bright sunlit colors of the composition reveal the artist's knowledge of French art. Despite a cloudy sky, the sun creates a halo-like effect around the figures, whose long dark shadows contrast with the yellow-green of the flax. Although Davidson's work has often been compared to the early work of Jack B Yeats, this painting is closer to Paul Henry's figure studies, especially *The Potato Diggers* (National Gallery of Ireland). Like Henry, Davidson reduces the figures to blocks of color; the male figure's simple black and white clothing contrasts with the red, yellow and blue worn by the women. The figures are not individual portrait studies; hats or bonnets obscure the faces, and the figures, both in the foreground and distance, are painted in the same broad manner. The composition slants sharply from left to right; background foliage rises from the low bushes on the left to the tall trees on the right, intensifing the slope of the field.

DO

Erskine Nicol, R.S.A., A.R.A.

(1825-1904)

Some of the most widely known images
of Ireland in mid-nineteenth century Britain
came from the popular and prolific brush
of the Scottish painter Erskine Nicol. Born in
Leith, Nicol was strongly influenced by
his compatriot Sir David Wilkie, who included
some Irish subjects among his popular
peasant genre scenes of the 1830s. In 1846,
Nicol came to Ireland to teach art for
the Department of Science and Art in Dublin.
He stayed until 1850. Although his visit
to Ireland corresponded exactly with the
Great Famine, his work shows only occasional
glimpses of the disaster that halved the
population of the country from eight to
four million in four years.

Nicol often intrudes racial stereotypes and
visual jokes about the Irish into his paintings,
which became widely known when they
were engraved to illustrate the nineteenth-
century book *Tales of Irish Life and Character
with Sixteen Reproductions by Erskne Nicol
R.S.A.* (Foulis, Edinburgh and London, 1909).
Nicol showed an altogether more sympathetic
view of the Irish plight in small pictures such
as *The Eviction* (National Gallery of Ireland)
and *The Merican Difficulty* (1862). The latter
portrays a bemused, elderly Irishwoman
struggling to read about the American Civil
War for news of her emigrant children.

By 1851 Nicol was back in Edinburgh, but he
continued to visit Ireland regularly and to
paint Irish scenes. He later moved to London,
where he exhibited at the Royal Academy,
but he returned to Scotland in 1885. His
portrayals of Irish peasant life, although often
marred by racist attitudes, offer a rare view
of social problems that native artists avoided
lest they be labeled as members of the Fenian
brotherhood, an organization dedicated
to the overthrow of British rule in Ireland.

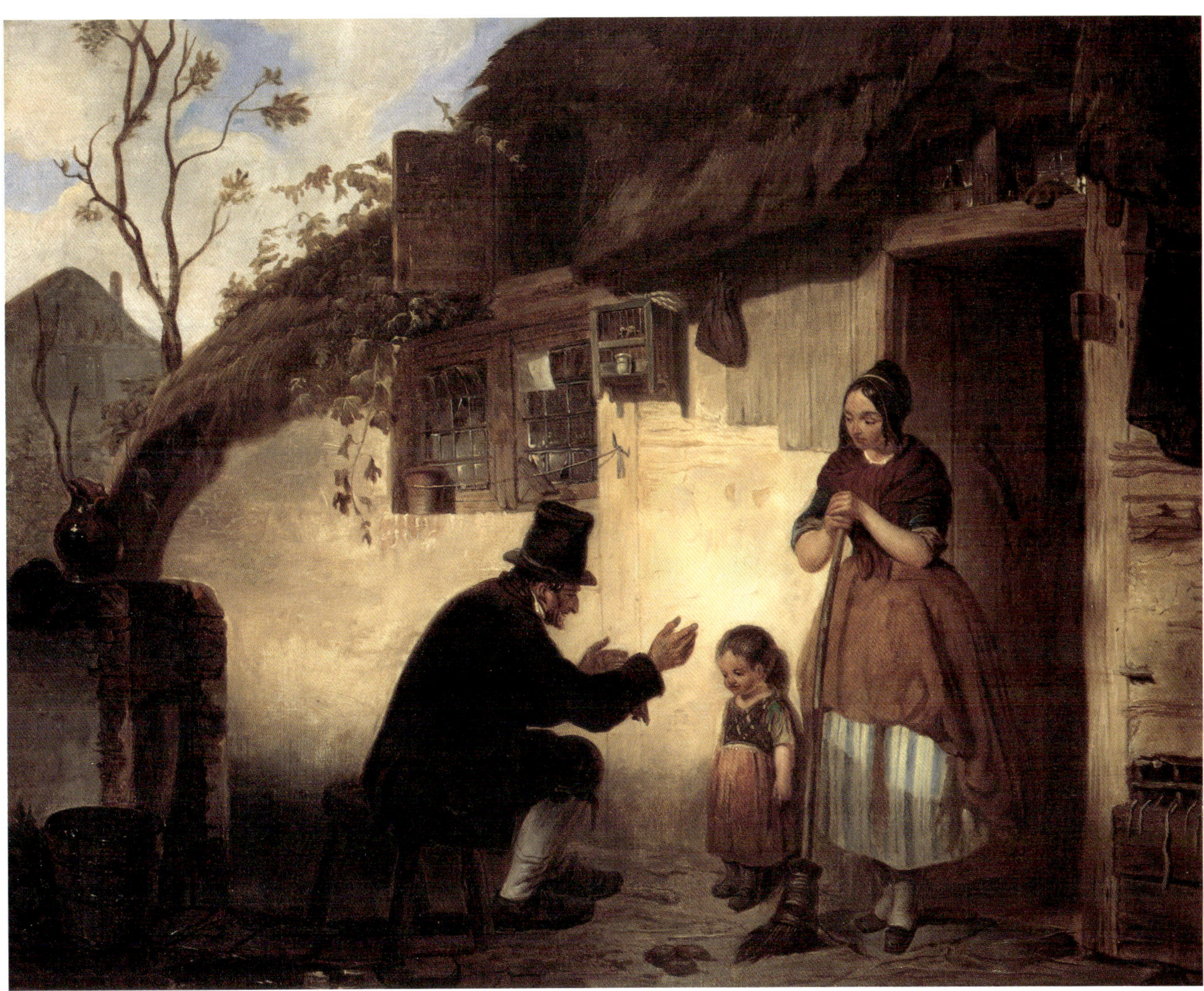

no. 10

The Seanchai
Erskine Nicol, R.S.A.,
A.R.A (1825-1904)
oil on canvas
18 1/2 in. x 23 1/2 in.

Provenance:
Dillon Antiques,
Dublin.

The seanchai, or storyteller, a highly esteemed member of Irish rural society, carried an ancient tradition into the twentieth century. Numerous accounts survive of the seanchai enthralling his audience, all of whom would have been sophisticated critics of his performance.

Nicol is at his best in his careful recording of the cottage: the still-life objects tucked into the shade of the thatch above the door, the "safe," or poorman's refrigerator, attached to the wall, and the glint of sunlight on the tiny, neatly glazed windowpanes. For all its poverty, this cottage appears more comfortable than those of the Irish rural poor that Nicol would have seen in the 1840s. The woman's striped skirt further suggests that this is a later work, painted after the artist returned to Scotland.

Nicol was influenced by Dutch genre painting of the seventeenth century. His work reveals a considerable debt to Jan Steen (c. 1625-1679), who painted a great number of tavern scenes and social gatherings. Steen invented a hunch-backed male figure who is the likely source for the man seated here. Often portrayed with a tall hat and very pointed features, his guises ranged from quack doctors and sham clerics to popular entertainers. He is almost always corrupt, an unhealthy influence on children and the innocent. The child here, his purity high-lighted by a golden halo of sunlight, confronts a moral dilemma. He must choose between the safe, if impoverished, environs of the cottage and the public world of the dark-hatted stranger.

CM

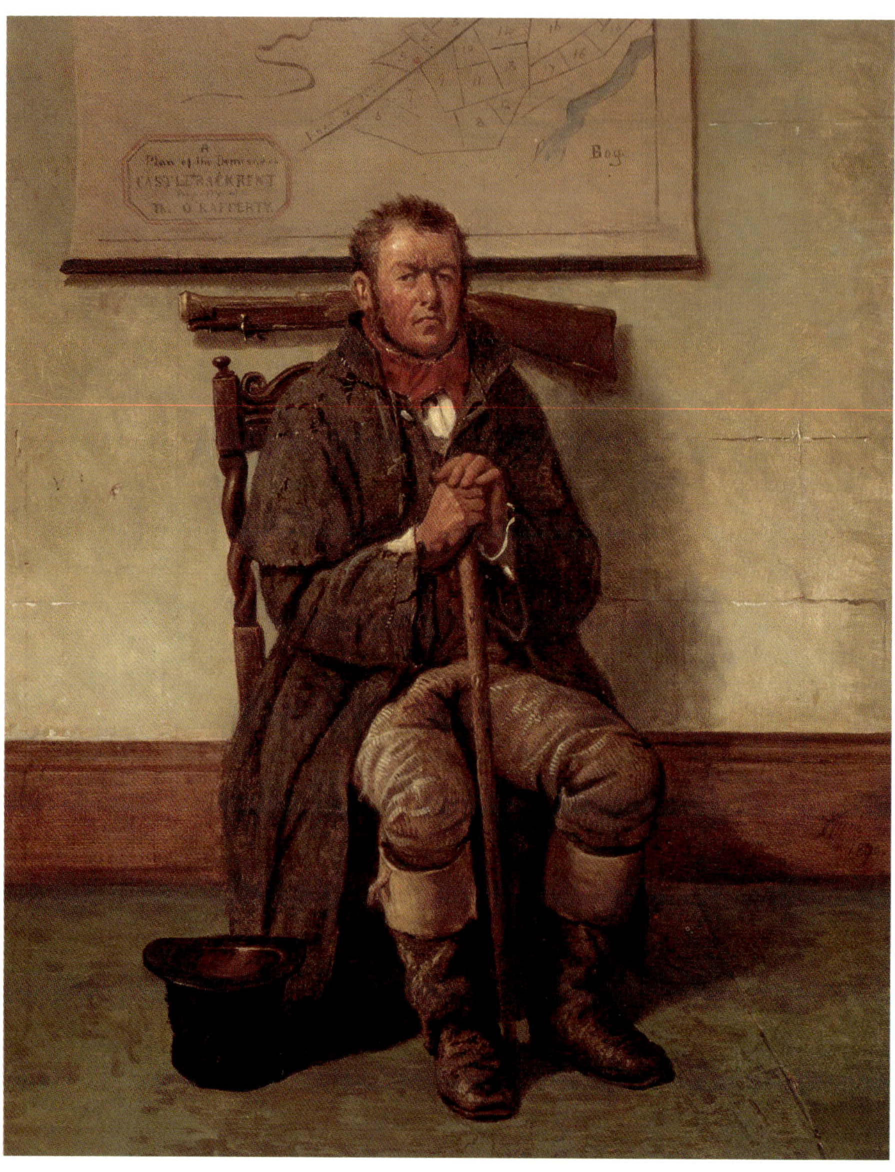

The title of this painting refers to the novel, *Castle Rackrent,* by the Irish writer Maria Edgeworth. Edgeworth advised Nicol's predecessor Sir David Wilkie about his Irish subject pictures. Although Nicol clearly was aware of her writing, there is no evidence that Edgeworth and Nicol ever met. *Castle Rackrent,* the novel, presents a scathing literary analysis of the failures of the Irish landlord class in eighteenth-century Ireland. The same criticism is implicit in Nicol's visual depiction of landlord-tenant relations in the mid-nineteenth century. Only the gun on the wall enables this landlord, Th. O'Rafferty, to maintain his proprietorship of the domain indicated on the map. The proliferation of small holdings, and their proximity to large areas of bog, suggest the desperate lot of a tenant on this estate. This painting mirrors the economic realities of rural Ireland during, and immediately after, the Great Famine.

Attracting attention through his considerable bulk and solidity, the tenant sits in his landlord's hallway; his level gaze and stalwart pose challenge the power relationship that the map and gun suggest. Although he is poorly dressed, his ruddy face proclaims health and good eating, perhaps reflecting the view, widely held in England, that the plight of the Irish peasant was less severe than some commentators alleged.

Setting aside his customary humor and condescension to confront a social reality, Nicol, here, is at his best. The fine draftsmanship that won him early recognition shows clearly in the sure articulation of the figure, while the artist's restricted palette perfectly fits the new tenant of Castle Rackrent.

CM

Leo Whelan

(1892-1956)

Leo Whelan, a leading academic artist of his generation, was born in Dublin in 1892. Educated at Belvedere College Dublin, he subsequently attended the Dublin Metropolitan School of Art with contemporaries Patrick Tuohy and Seán Keating (nos. 17-19). At the Metropolitain School, Whelan was taught by William Orpen (no. 26), whose influence is evident in much of his work. Whelan's skill was quickly recognized; in 1916 he was awarded the Taylor Prize by the Royal Dublin Society. Trained as an academic artist, Whelan exhibited for the first time at the Royal Hibernian Academy in 1911, and regularly thereafter until the year of his death. Established in 1823, the Royal Hibernian Academy emphasized tradition and artistic skill, remaining little influenced by the artistic developments of the twentieth century. Whelan established himself as one of the primary portrait painters in Dublin, producing likenesses of Michael Collins, Count John McCormack, and the first president of Ireland, Douglas Hyde.

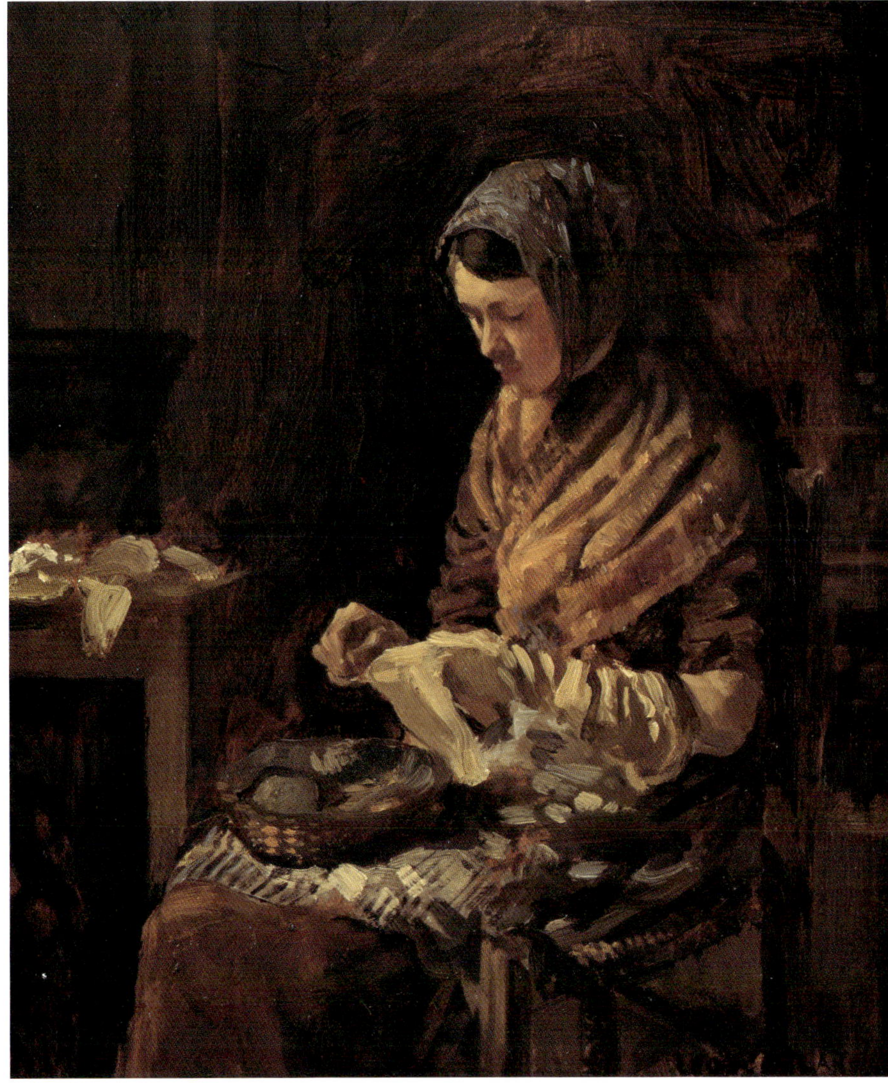

no. 12

The Artist's Niece
Lena, Sewing
Leo Whelan
(1892-1956)
c. 1940
oil on wood
12 in. x 10 1/4 in.

Signed,
lower right:
Leo Whelan

Provenance:
The artist's family
by descent.

When her uncle painted this portrait, Lena Murnaghan was a schoolgirl, staying with her grandmother at the Whelan family home at 65 Eccles Street, Dublin. Whelan provided Lena's costume; the plaid shawl, scarf and apron covering her skirt suggest an image from the nineteenth century, rather than the 1940s, the decade in which the work was actually painted. Lena, darning the heel of a sock, sits on a traditional sugán chair. Sugán chairs were made in rural Ireland, from ropes of twisted straw woven onto plain wooden frames.

Whelan suggests a simple kitchen scene. A table is placed in front of a fireplace, and to Lena's right, the suggestion of some wooden shelves. All of these elements, costume, sugán chair and basic room suggest a cottage in the west of Ireland, rather than a house in the center of a capital city. This evocation of rural life demonstrates Whelan's sympathy for the issue of national identity that had engaged so many artists in the years following political independence. Many regarded the west as the most "Irish" part of the country, where the Irish language and traditional way of life had survived relatively unchanged over the centuries.

As a result, artists who strove to create an Irish art, often concentrated on images of the west.

Despite his support for issues of national identity, Whelan's manner of painting is part of the European tradition of academicism. Whelan has used a narrow range of color in this work, predominantly blue and brown tones. Lena, placed at the center of the image, is illuminated by a light source outside the picture plane; this device focuses our attention on her face. In addition, Whelan has painted her features in some detail, which contrasts with his broad treatment of the background. His use of light and his choice of interior subject strongly recall *The Wash House* (National Gallery of Ireland) by his teacher, William Orpen. Whelan painted a number of kitchen interiors, emphasizing light and shade in each. However, he drew from sources other than Orpen. Studying the history of art, he grew to admire the work of Velazquez. This portrait of Lena reveals his debt to the Spanish artist who painted many kitchen scenes or *bodegones,* and the rich earth tones are reminiscent of the palette favoured by Velazquez.

DO

James Brenan, R.H.A.
(1837-1907)

One of the most popular figures in late nineteenth-century Irish art circles, Dublin-born James Brenan spent some years in England. He worked with the decorative painter Owen Jones before settling in Cork as Headmaster of the Cork School of Art, a position he occupied until 1889. Brenan was an important figure in the development of the lace industry in Ireland, bringing employment to impoverished rural areas. He set up classes in local convents near Cork, providing them with collections of old lace samples and visiting each at monthly intervals to offer support and monitor standards. Brenan continued to promote the lace industry when he moved back to Dublin in 1889 to serve as Headmaster of the Dublin Metropolitan School of Art, establishing design classes to facilitate this industry and other crafts. He became an Associate of the Royal Hibernian Academy in 1876, and a full member two years later.

Brenan's selfless encouragement of fellow artists and craft workers made him friends everywhere. One such friend was Joseph Stafford Gibson who, in gratitude for Brenan's help with his career, bequeathed his collection of Spanish ceramics and silverware, as well as a considerable sum of money for the purchase of paintings to the Cork School of Art.

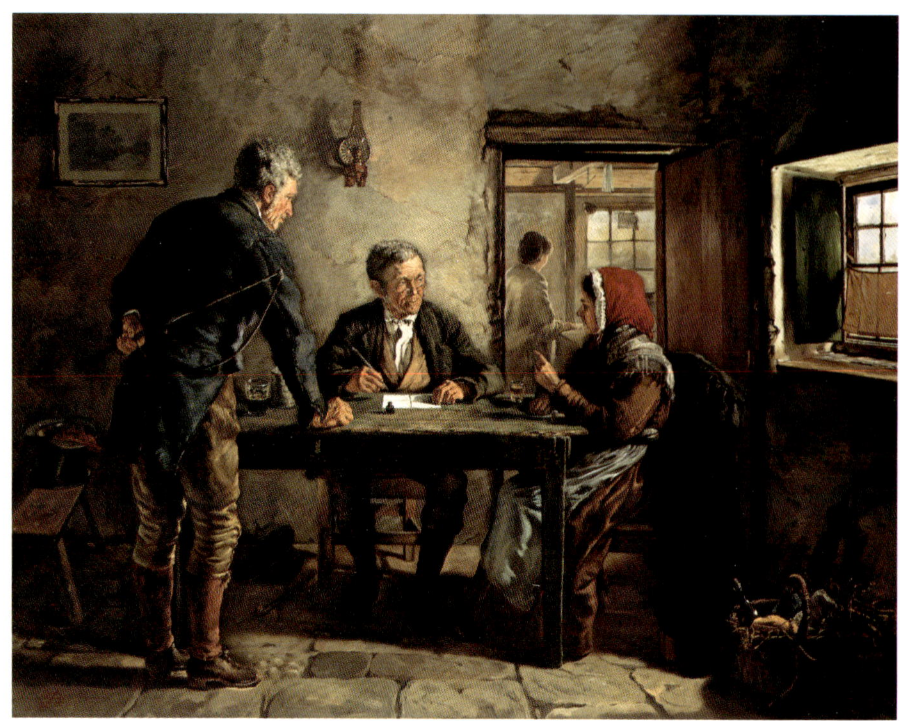

no. 13

The Village Scribe
(or The Rent Collector)
James Brenan,
R.H.A. (1837-1907)
1881
oil on canvas
11 1/2 in. x 9 1/2 in.

Signed and
dated in
monogram:
JB 81

Exhibited:
Royal Hibernian
Academy,
1882.

This painting has been alternatively entitled *The Rent Collector* and *The Village Scribe*. The latter title is more appropriate as rent transactions were not usually as friendly as the scene here suggests. The *Village Scribe* was exhibited in 1882, accompanied by the following short piece in the Irish language:

> Dubhairt an bhean-
> Tá lá fada geal agad
> Tá páipear breagh glan agad
> Tá do phagha ar do bhos agad
> Agus bidheadh do gnó a gceart agad.

A rough translation of this reads:

> The woman said-
> You have a long bright day
> You have fine clean paper
> You have your pay in your fist
> And may you get on with your job.

After the Great Famine (1845-1850), thousands fled rural Ireland to North America, Australia, and Britain in search of work, making letter-writing crucial to the emotional survival of the family. Along with news, emigrant children sent money home to supplement the family income. The relative prosperity of the couple dictating the letter here, indicated by the woman's fine Kinsale cloak and parasol, and the man's rather battered hard hat, suggests that they may well have received such aid. By 1881, a couple such as the one portrayed here, would ordinarily be literate in the Irish language; they might not, however, speak or write English. The village scribe (usually the schoolmaster) would be called upon to help. James Brenan understood the importance of the emigrant's letter. In 1875, he exhibited *News from America*, showing a peasant family excitedly listening to a reading of a letter from an absent relative. His painting *A Young Member of the Society for the Preservation of the Irish Language*, completed in 1880, the year before *The Village Scribe*, suggests that Brenan was also aware of the destructive effects of emigration on native culture, and particularly on the Irish language.

CM

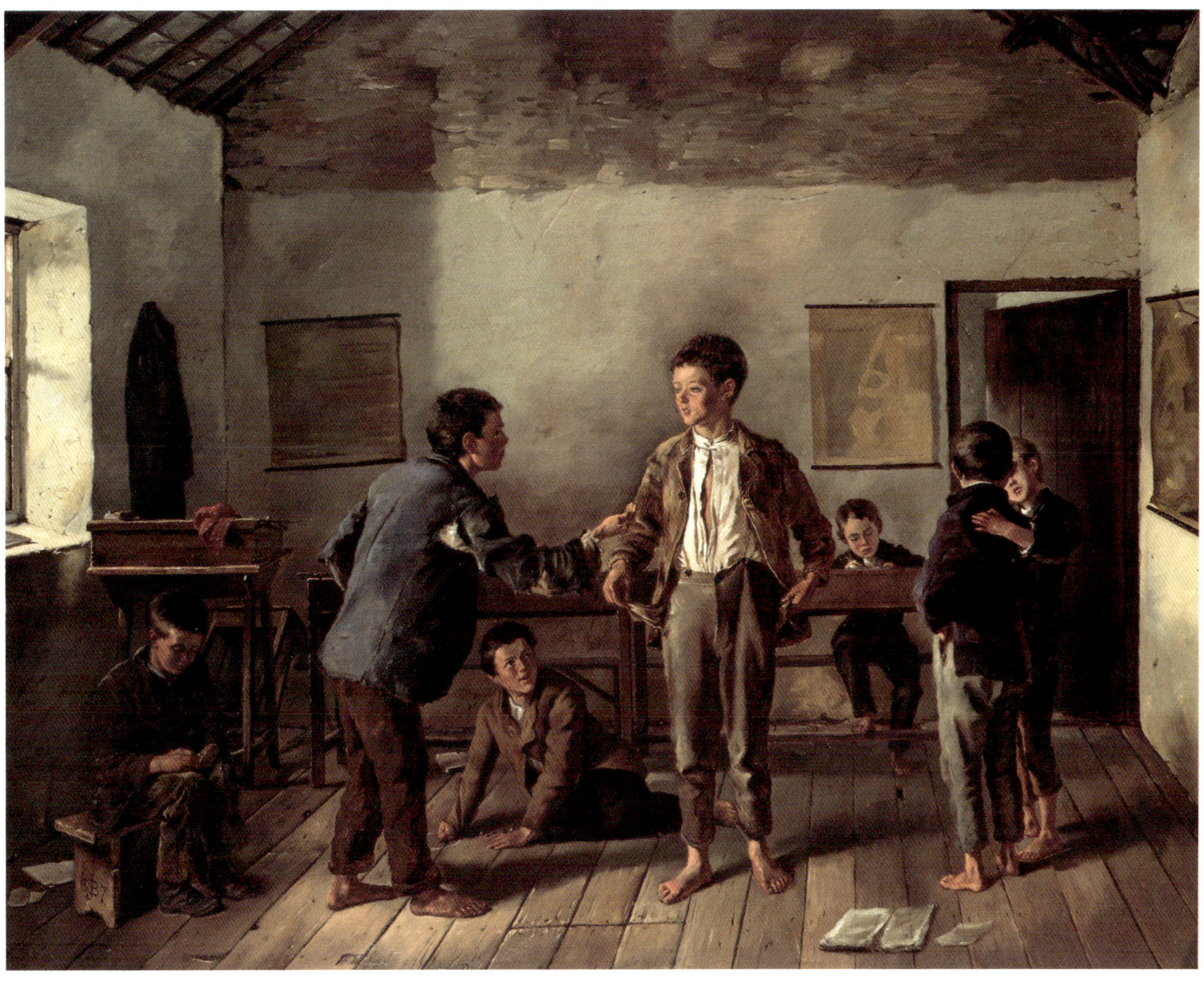

no. 14

The Schoolroom
(or Empty Pockets)
James Brenan, R.H.A.
(1837-1907)
1887
oil on canvas
27 1/2 in. x 35 in.

Signed and
dated
in monogram:
JB 87

Depicting a scene from daily life, this painting continues a genre initiated in Holland in the seventeenth century, and revived in Victorian Britain, most notably by the Irish artist William Mulready and the writer Charles Dickens. In this painting, Brenan portrays a school, not so much as a place for acquiring academic knowledge, but rather as a microcosm of the greater world beyond. In what may be a typical recess period, two main figures confront each other, probably over a supply of marbles. A third boy, sitting on the floor, pauses in his game of "jacks" to witness the event; another jealously guards his marble collection. Two younger boys on the right remain aloof, while a solitary small figure is absorbed in his lessons. Brenan records the event in a truthful manner, avoiding the Victorian tendency to sentiment-alize childhood.

State education was a hotly debated issue in Ireland throughout the nineteenth century. Catholic families avoided state-aided primary schools (established early in the century) for fear of proselytism by Protestant groups. Instead, "hedge schools," or schools in the open air, taught by itinerant schoolmasters, continued into the last quarter of the century. Children endured hardships to attend hedge schools, but the education they received was highly regarded, often encompassing classes in Latin, Greek, history and mathematics as well as literacy skills. By the 1860s, however, free primary schools, administered by several religious denominations, were established. The ragged, barefoot children shown here, whose broken and torn books are thrown to the floor, display none of the regard for learning which sustained the hedge schools.

CM

Maurice MacGonigal, P.R.H.A.
(1900-1979)

Maurice MacGonigal, one of the best-known academic Irish artists of this century, received his earliest art training in the stained glass studios of his uncle Joshua Clarke, whose son Harry would soon become a graphic and stained-glass artist. From an early age, MacGonigal was committed to painting rather than stained glass. The 1916 Easter Uprising in Dublin, and MacGonigal's activities with the Irish Republican Army that led to his internment at Ballykinlar, prevented his pursuit of an artistic career until his release in 1922.

MacGonigal attended the Dublin Metropolitan School, headed by academic painters Seán Keating (nos. 17-19) and Patrick Tuohy. Keating and Tuohy shared MacGonigal's nationalism, and also encouraged his insistence on high standards of craftsmanship. On a brief visit to Holland in 1927, he discovered Van Gogh's brushwork and exuberant color. He also found a way to unite his love of landscape with his need to forge a distinctively Irish identity. Just as the Dutch landscape school celebrated Holland's hard-won territory, MacGonigal traveled to the West of Ireland in search of a cultural identity. During the 1930s MacGonigal visted the West of Ireland. In Carraroe, MacGonigal found a living

Irish culture in which traditions continued unchanged for centuries, and where the Irish language was widely spoken. The costumes and buildings of his Connemara landscapes are more archaeologically correct than the expressionist interpretations of Jack Yeats, and more figurative and more realistic than the romantic images of Paul Henry.

MacGonigal won a silver medal for landscape from the Royal Hibernian Academy in 1928, the year of his first solo exhibition. Showing regularly at the academy beginning in 1924, he became an associate in 1931 and full member in 1933. Over the next decades MacGonigal would became a figurehead in Irish art, combining both professorship and later presidency of the academy with the more challenging roles of Professor of Painting and Deputy Director of the National College of Art. Despite the strongly academic tradition he inherited, MacGonigal took a surprisingly liberal approach to teaching: "Every kind of art expression should be encouraged in Ireland. There is little enough of it," he told The Sunday Independent in 1967. Nevertheless, MacGonigal felt obliged to resign after anti-academic student protests at the National College of Art in 1969.

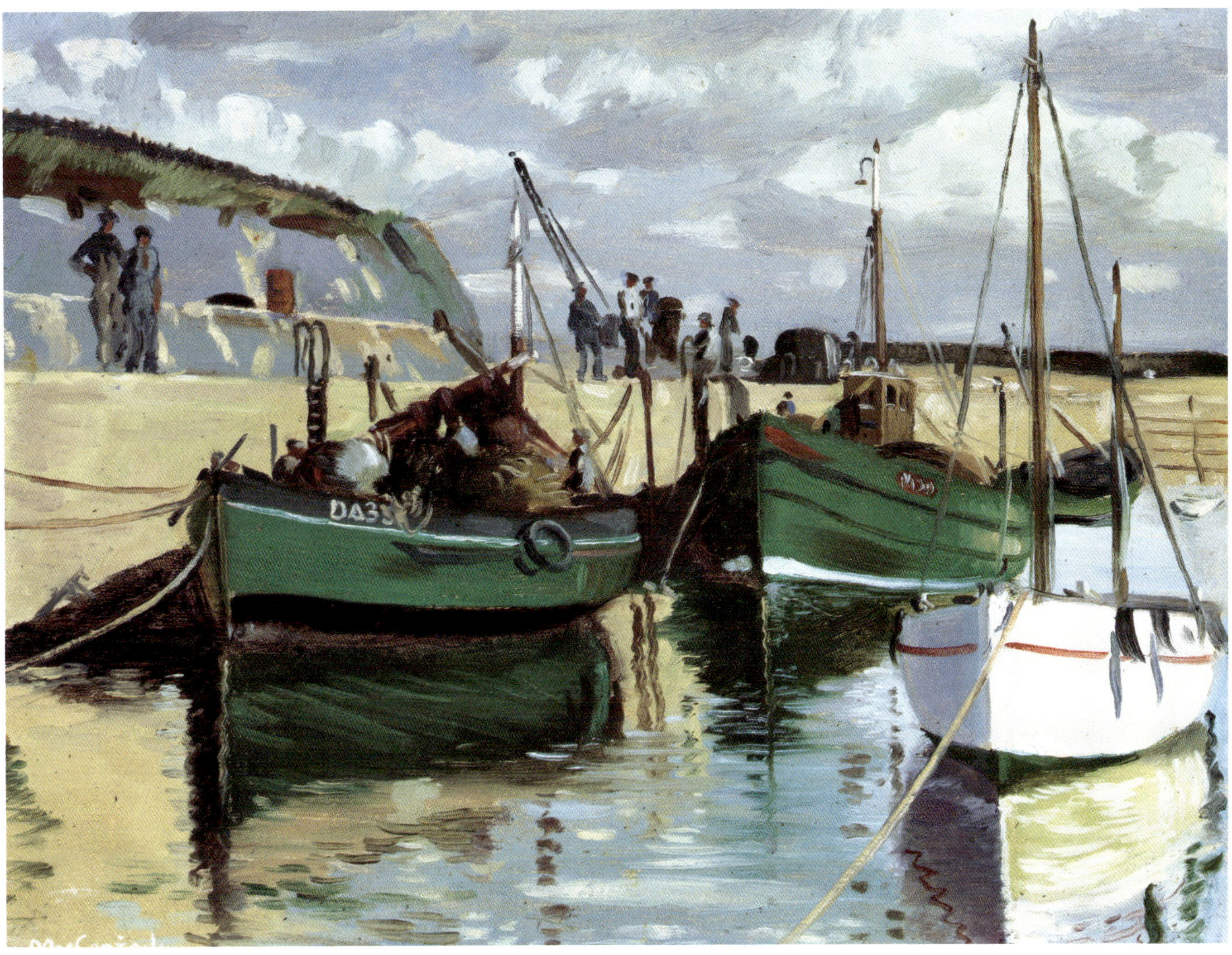

no. 15

Fishing Boats at Clogherhead
Maurice MacGonigal,
P.R.H.A.
(1900-1979)
c. 1943
oil on panel
12 in. x 16 in.

Signed, lower
left (in Irish):
Mac Congal

Provenance:
Dillon Antiques,
Dublin.

Exhibited:
Royal Hibernian
Academy, 1943.

The freedom of handling and looseness of brushwork at the expense of precise draftsmanship show the extent to which MacGonigal broke from the confining Academic tradition of his teachers. Working in his most intuitive manner, MacGonigal responds swiftly to the changing effects of light and color on the water in the foreground, but is apparently unconcerned that the tiny figure of the fisherman in the boat on the left is disproportionately small when compared to the more distant figures seen above the wall. The sparkling freshness of the pigments in this picture indicates MacGonigal's high standards of craftsmanship.

MacGonigal visited the little fishing port and resort of Clogherhead in County Louth regularly in the late thirties and early forties. The village is closely associated with Oliver Plunkett, who was beheaded for continuing to practice as a Catholic priest during the Penal Days.

CM

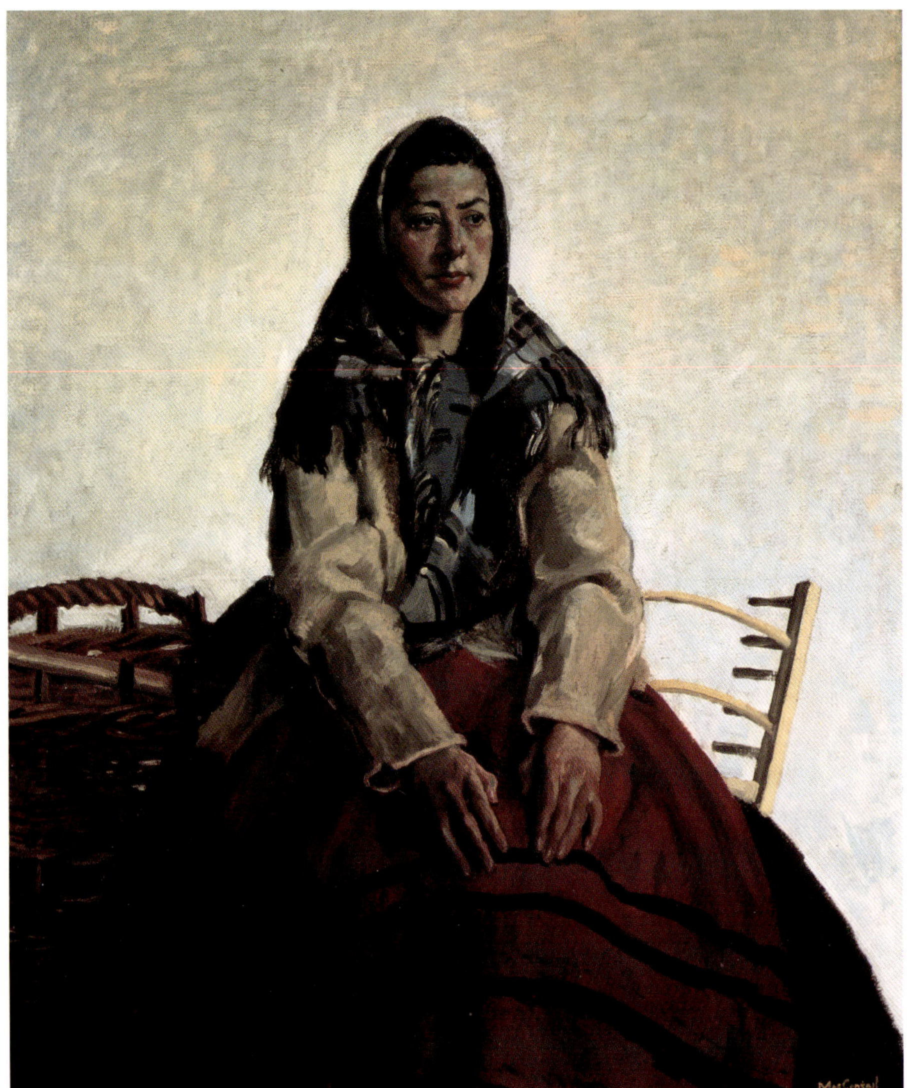

Wearing a blue check shawl over a Bainín jacket, a young woman, her hands stretched before her on her lap, rests between a willow hay rake and turf basket. A dark outer shawl has fallen away from her shoulders, framing a red flannel skirt; its three dark stripes indicate that she is married. Common dress for women of western Ireland in the early-twentieth century, the red outer skirt would be drawn up on either side to reveal a working petticoat underneath.

The model for this painting was MacGonigal's wife, painter Aida Kelly. The costume she wears, recently given to the National Museum of Ireland by her son, Ciarán MacGonigal, appears in a number of paintings, including *Cois na Farraige*, which was exhibited with *Cailín Og Iarthar* in 1938 at the Royal Hibernian Academy. Before her marriage, Aida Kelly campaigned for social activist Emma Goldman, and on behalf of the Republicans in the Spanish Civil War. She also designed a banner for the Socialist Workers' Party. Kelly retained a clearly distinct identity after her marriage, maintaining strong socialist and anti-clerical beliefs, even in the face of her husband's Catholicism and nationalism. She gave up her own aspirations as a painter to support his, devoting her energies instead to art criticism and family responsibilities.

CM

John (Seán) Keating, P.R.H.A.
(1889-1977)

John (Seán) Keating is best known as the artist who gave visual expression to the quest for national identity, initiated by literary revivalists Lady Gregory, J. M. Synge, W. B. Yeats, and George Russell. After early artistic training in Limerick, the city of his birth, he studied at the Metropolitan School of Art in Dublin, where he trained in the academic tradition under Sir William Orpen (no. 26). A promising pupil, the young Keating worked as model and assistant in his teacher's London studio in 1915.

After visiting the Aran Islands in 1914, Keating called for a national school of painting, which would draw upon traditional Irish life in the west. In a series of memorable works, Keating portrayed an idealized and heroic people. Through paintings such as *Men of the West* (Hugh Lane Municipal Gallery of Modern Art, Dublin) and *Men of the South* (Crawford Municipal Gallery, Cork) — the latter worked from actual portraits of those who participated in the ambushes of the War of Independence — Keating celebrated nationalist themes. After the War of Independence, Keating's paintings became the primary visual icons for the developing Irish Free State. His allegorical paintings, which treat both modern technology and traditional nationalist themes, illustrate the achievements of the new State as well as the economic hardship and emigration that survived Irish independence. Keating gained recognition painting heroic allegorical murals, such as those for the New York World's Fair in 1938.

Keating became professor at the National College of Art and Design in 1934. Between 1948 and 1962, as president of the Royal Hibernian Academy, he guided hundreds of young students in the standards of traditional figurative art, despite the increasing influence of modernist abstraction.

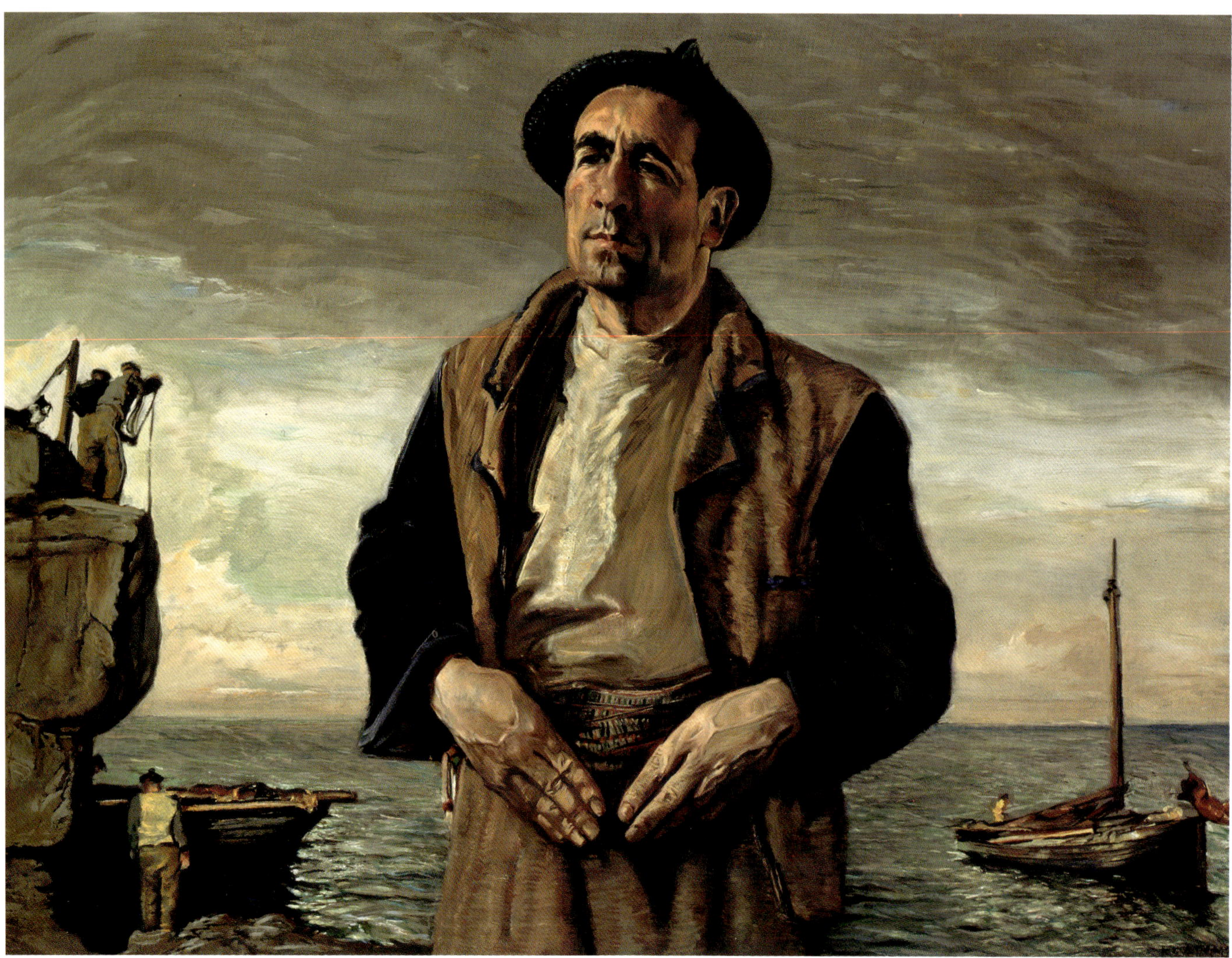

no. 17

An Aran Fisherman
John (Seán) Keating,
P.R.H.A.
(1889-1977)
oil on canvas
33 1/2 in. x 44 3/4 in.

Signed, lower right:
Keating

Provenance:
Dillon Antiques,
Dublin.

An Aran Fisherman depicts the heroic island-man – whom John Millington Synge, especially, among the literary revivalists – saw as the enduring exponent of traditional Gaelic values. Keating emphasizes the separateness of Aran culture from that of the mainland; in this painting, he portrays a heroic man, molded by hardship, who stands with pride and dignity. In his journal *The Aran Islands,* Synge reports that the Aranmen wear three colors: natural wool, indigo and grey flannel, as well as the woolen beret and colorful "crios" belt that we see in this painting. Keating's works painted on Aran reflect the luminous colors typical of that rocky limestone landscape. The graphic quality of this painting endows it with a sharp realism and heightens the intensity of feeling. The rugged man of Aran who eked a living out of stone and sea becomes for Keating a symbol of the nation's strength and resilience.

CK

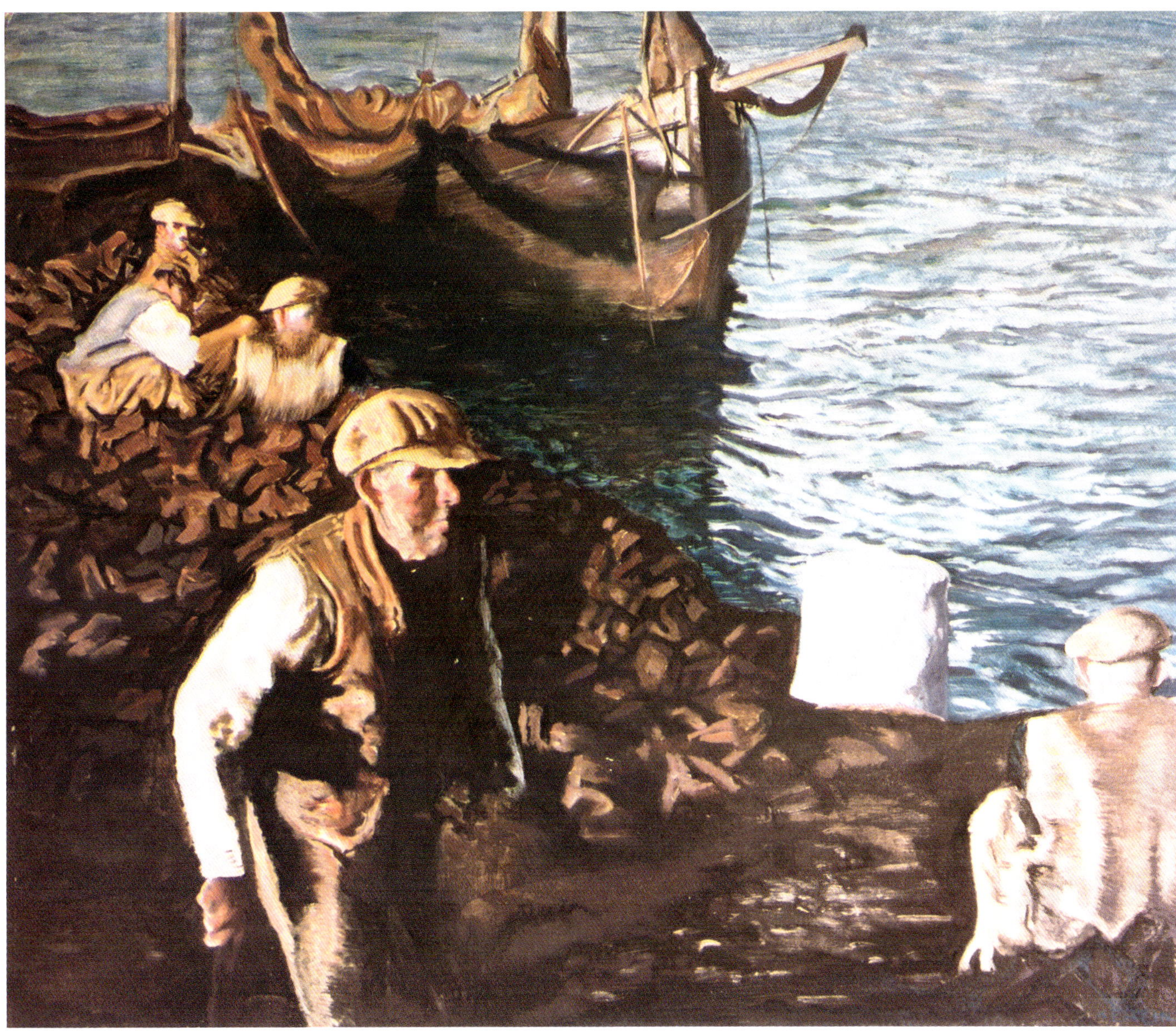

no. 18

The Port Authority
(or Connemara
Fisherman)
John (Seán) Keating,
P.R.H.A. (1889-1977)
c. 1940
oil on canvas
30 1/2 in. x 36 1/2 in.

Signed, lower right:
Keating

Provenance:
Dillon Antiques,
Dublin.

The Port Authority, probably painted during the 1940s, is typical of the quay-side views on the Aran Islands that Keating painted throughout his career. In these works, Keating depicts fishermen mending their currachs and nets under a pier wall, or loading red cattle onto hookers bound for Galway. Here, we see a crowded pier piled with turf, a scarce commodity on the rockbound islands, that was brought by the boat load from the Connemara mainland. The turf was unloaded and left heaped on the sandhills, later to be carried up to the cottages in panniers slung on donkeys or horses. The figure in the foreground, strong and determined, yet aged and bent by his labors, epitomizes Keating's acknowledgment of both the dignity and hardship of the traditional western islands.

The boat by the quay is a traditionally constructed hooker, made using wooden pegs to hold the timbers together. Such boats provided sole transport between the islands and the mainland until twice-a-week steamer service arrived in the early 1900s. Even then, hookers continued to ferry cattle and pigs to the Galway fair and horses to the mainland during the dry summer months when there was little grazing on the islands. They also carried large quantities of burnt kelp, valued for its high iodine content, to market in Galway.

CK

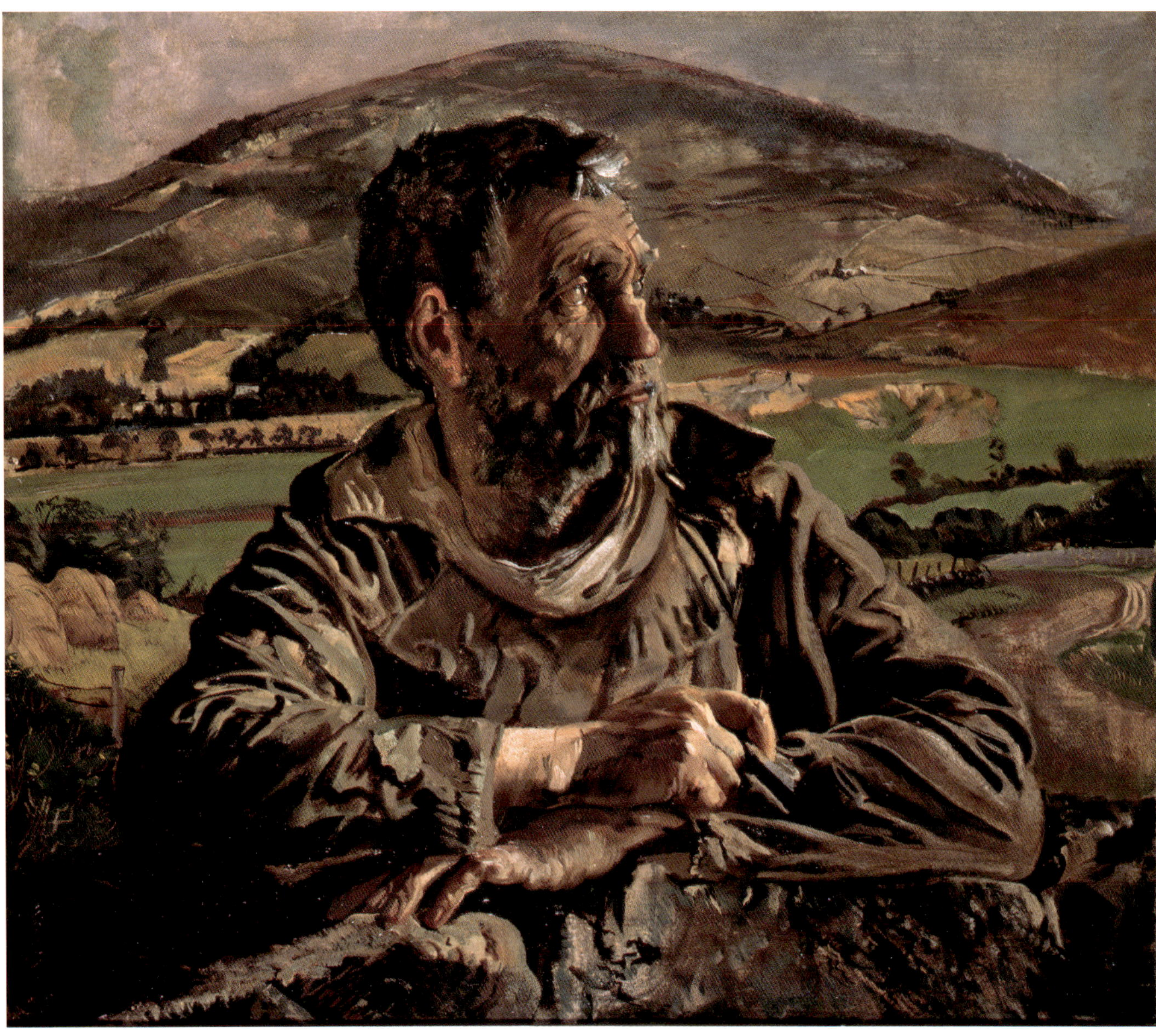

no. 19

King O'Toole
John (Seán) Keating,
P.R.H.A.
(1889-1977)
oil on board
26 in. x 30 in.

Signed, lower right:
Keating

Provenance:
Victor Waddington
Gallery, Dublin;
James Adam and
Sons, Dublin, 1991.

Exhibited:
Royal Hibernian
Academy,
1933, no. 10.

King O'Toole is another of Keating's heroic
figures, whose countenance conveys noble
suffering and perseverance. In its general
theme and style, the painting is related to *Holy
Joe on the Mountains,* completed in 1931
(Glasgow Municipal Gallery). A descendant of
a powerful ancient chieftain from County
Wicklow, Keating's O'Toole lives a life of poverty
and virtue, the qualities extolled by Eamon De
Valera's Ireland of the 1930s. Given the shabby
clothes and worn expression of this gray-
bearded figure, the title of the painting initially
seems ironic: that O'Toole is king of all he
surveys is improbable. His moral authority over
the Wicklow glen, however, emerges in the
way the figure echoes the mountain behind him
in size and shape. This monumentality, as well

as his sad but dignified repose, embody a
natural nobility. King O'Toole rests upon a stone
wall, and holds an empty pipe. In his isolation
and poverty, O'Toole epitomizes the reality
of life for those left abandoned in rural Ireland
by the emigrating young.

King O'Toole is one of Keating's great figure
paintings where setting is a backdrop for
a heroic narrative theme. The artist's respect for
masters of the past, such as Velasquez and
especially Hals (to whom he acknowledges his
debt in *Hommage to Franz Hals*) is evident in
his choice to render his subject's face in a
moment of expressive gesture.

CK

Henry Alken, Jr.
(1810-1894)

Samuel Henry Gordon Alken (known as Henry Alken Jr.), his brother Sefferien, father, three uncles, grandfather, and great-grandfather comprised a family prominent in the history of sporting art. Although the Alken family originally came from Denmark, Henry Alken, Jr. was born in Ipswich and later lived in London. Because Alken family members frequently imitated each other's style, their work can be difficult to identify. Henry Alken, Jr., however, is best distinguished by his careful rendering of detail.

The tradition of sporting art came to England in the late-seventeenth century with the arrival of Flemish artists who had a long tradition of painting hunting scenes. Prior to the arrival of the Flemish artists, animals may have been included in portraits, but were not painted for their own sake. With the increasing popularity of racing in the eighteenth and nineteenth centuries, a market for animal portraiture developed, and many artists specialised in this area.

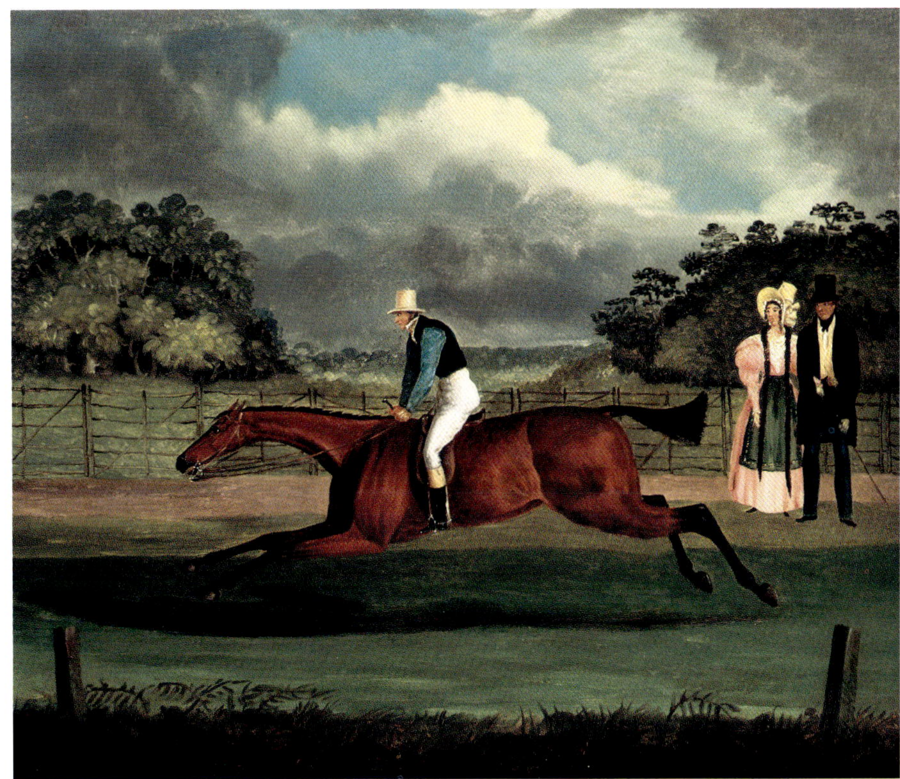

no. 20

S. Spode Training
Eastern Bere
Henry Alken, Jr.
(1810-1894)
1856
oil on board
11 3/4 in. x 13 1/2 in.

This painting shows trainer and equestrian artist Samuel Spode galloping Eastern Bere under the watchful eye of the owner and his wife. Spode wears the the blue sleeves and black body of the owner's silks. Instead of a jockey's cap, he wears a cream-color top hat. The trainer stands forward in the stirrups, allowing the horse to reach his peak speed. Eastern Bere moves at full gallop, his head strained forward, the rich chestnut color of the horse contrasting with the greens of the landscape. The artist carefully portrays the underlying musculature of the animal, particularly apparent in the front of its body. Alken's interest in physical structure suggests his familiarity with George Stubbs' studies of equine anatomy, first published in 1766.

Henry Alken, Jr. renders the owner and his wife's clothing in great detail. She wears a pink dress with leg-o-mutton sleeves; Alken captures the detailed pattern on her decorative apron, and the bow on her straw "poke bonnet." Although the crinoline, or hooped petticoat, was the height of fashion when this work was painted in 1856, the woman portrayed here wears a skirt of more practical dimensions, better suited to walking across fields. Alken treats the man's costume, especially the knot of his cravat, and his fringed scarf, with equal detail. The rather charming, cartoon-like faces, underline Alken's technical naïvity, as does the awkward treatment of the shadow under the horse, which is absent beneath the owner and his wife, who stand close by.

Little is known of Spode, who painted in both England and Ireland. His country of origin is disputed, but the suggestion that he was a trainer on the Curragh, in County Kildare, is borne out by this painting. Racehorse trainers emerged as a professional group in Ireland between 1800 and 1840. They needed a variety of accomplishments in addition to the ability to spot talent and develop it; they also needed veterinary and business skills. Despite these requirements, trainers were not necessarily wealthy, and they often needed to supplement their income with an additional job, often sheep farming, or, perhaps more unusually, as in the case of trainer and equestrian artist Samuel Spode (c. 1811-1858), by painting equestrian portraits.

DO

George Nairn, A.R.H.A.
(1799-1850)

Although George Nairn painted portraits
and landscapes, he is best remembered for
his portraits of horses and dogs. Nairn
entered the Dublin Society School in 1813
where he received his formal art training.
Thirteen years later, he exhibited at the
inaugural exhibition of the Royal Hibernian
Academy, becoming an associate member
in 1828. Although never elected to full
membership, he continued to show his work
at the annual academy exhibitions until
1849.

The genre of English sporting pictures,
especially involving horses, emerged from
the Newmarket races in the middle of
the eighteenth century. It was said that these
English patrons ranked portraits of their
horses second only to those of their families.
Their Irish counterparts were little different.
Hunting and horse-racing were, perhaps,
even more popular in Ireland. Nairn worked
largely on private commissions, commemo-
rating famous animals for their proud
country-house owners.

Nairn married well-known landscape artist,
Cecilia Margaret Nairn, daughter of the
artist John Henry Campbell. Their son, John
Campbell Nairn, also became a painter.

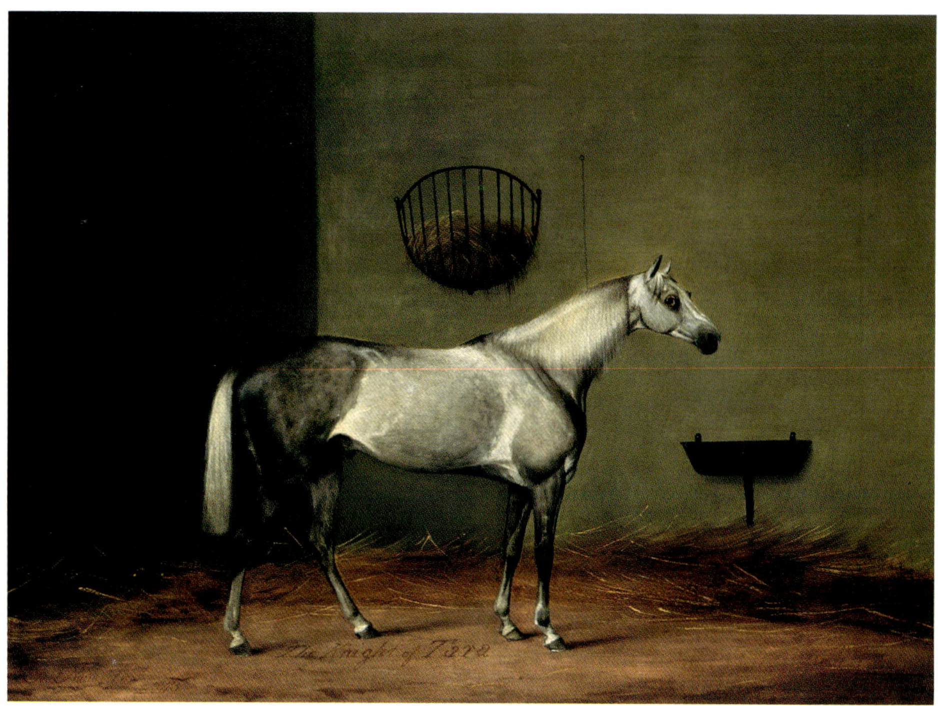

no. 21

Knight of Tara
George Nairn,
A.R.H.A. (1799-1850)
1843
oil on canvas
25 1/2 in. x 35 in.

Signed and dated,
lower left:
Geo. Nairn 1843

Exhibited:
Royal Hibernian
Academy 1843,
no. 133

Exhibited at the Royal Hibernian Academy
exhibition of 1843, *Knight of Tara* was
accompanied by the following information:

> The Knight of Tara, a grey horse, bred by
> Arthur Goslin Esq., got by 'Manfred' out of
> 'Anglesea' by 'Sir Harry Dimsdale,' the
> property of John Joseph Preston Esq., of
> Bellinter, Co. Meath.

Bellinter is situated near Tara, site of the
courts of the legendary high kings of Ireland.
It was here that St. Patrick first lit the pascal
fire to herald the conversion of the Irish
to Christianity in the fifth century. The Preston
family acquired nobility in 1800, when
John Preston was made Lord Tara in return for
his support for the Act of Union, which
removed the Irish legislature to Westminister.
The horse's name, then, carries personal and
historic associations for the owner.

Clearly influenced by English sporting artist
George Stubbs, Nairn blends observation with
convention. The dappled grey of the horse's
haunches and the tonal gradations along the
belly and head have been carefully studied.
Proportions, such as the title inscribed on the
stable floor, are part of the fashionable language
of early-nineteenth century horse portraits.
Horses of such obvious breeding would be kept
in impeccably clean and spacious stables,
accommodations far superior to those afforded
farm laborers and tenants at the time. John
Joseph Preston, proud of his fine stables,
commissioned George Nairn to depict them in
a painting the previous year.

CM

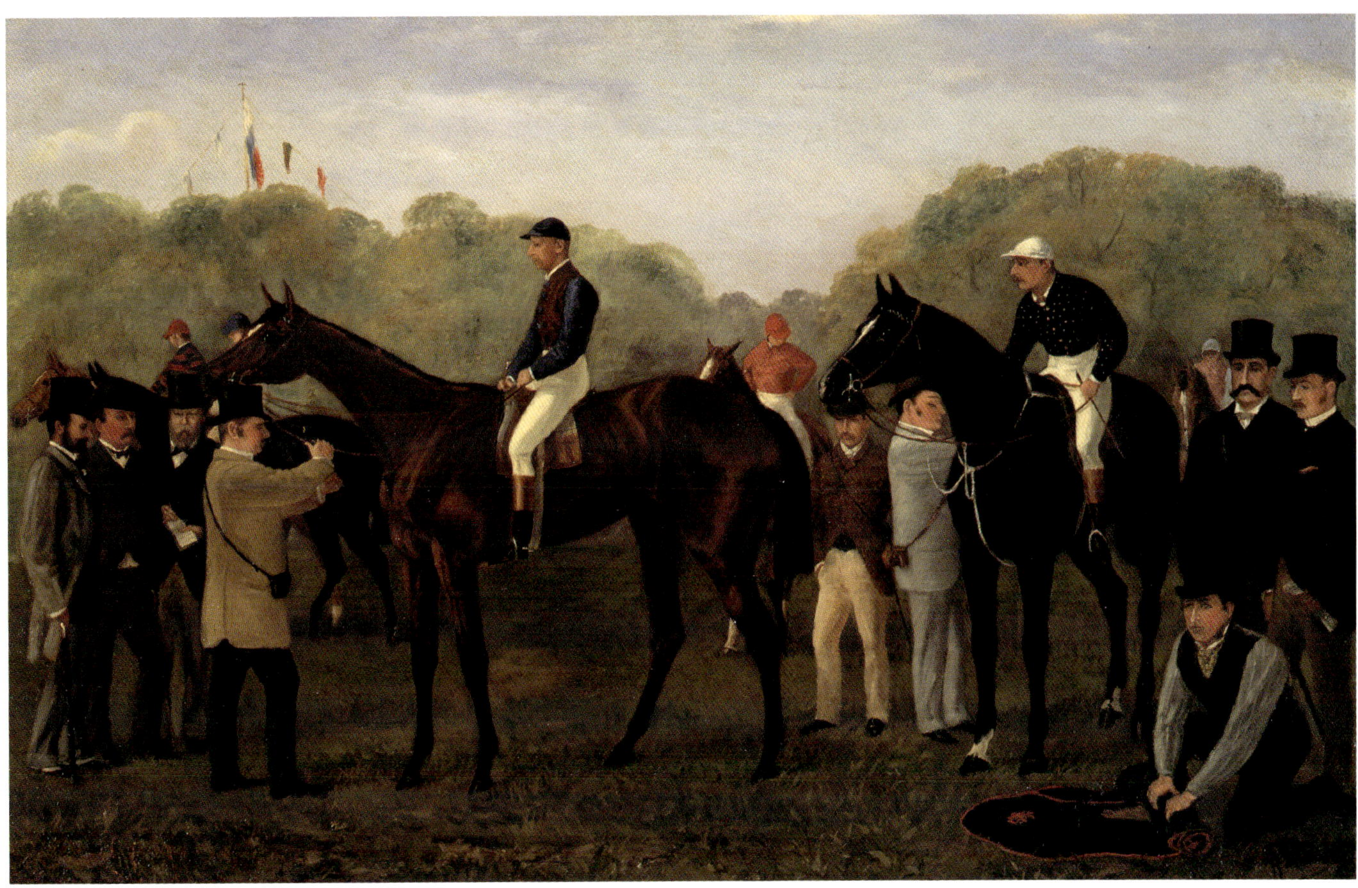

R. A. Miley
(active 1881-1888)

R. A. Miley exhibited briefly at the Royal
Hibernian Academy between 1881-1888,
which suggests that he was an amateur,
rather than a professional, artist. He lived
in Kingstown, now Dun Laoghaire, in
south County Dublin. The titles of some of
his exhibited works, for example, *A Cooling
Draft*, and *Across*, indicate that he favored
genre scenes, popular in the Victorian era.
Other exhibited works — *Ambush, Wounded
and Fugitives* — suggest that he spent time
in the army, furthering the supposition
that he was a part-time painter. *In the Quarry
near St Cloud* (1884) implies that Miley, like
so many of his Irish contemporaries, spent
time in France. He painted a number of
equestrian scenes in addition to *Down at the
Start*, including *The Tail of the Pack* (a
hunting scene) and *Watering Horses in the
Seine* (1886).

Horse racing was popular among all classes
throughout Ireland. From the early-
eighteenth century, many towns held racing
events that included entertainment for
ordinary people, as well as balls for the
gentry. The government disapproved of these
race meetings, however, believing they
encouraged drunkenness and idleness, and
might provide a focus for a riot during times
of political unrest.

no. 22

Down at the Start
R. A. Miley
(active 1881-1888)
c. 1880
oil on canvas
17 1/2 in. x 27 1/2 in.

Signed, lower right:
R. Miley 183

Miley depicts the last-minute preparations before a race; wearing the colors of their
horses' owners, mounted jockeys are ready to
enter the starting gate. The practice of
registering owners' colors first began at the Turf
Club in 1790. Wearing the registered colors
was compulsory, and penalties were imposed
if a jockey raced in the incorrect attire.

We can identify the owners, trainers, and
grooms by their distinct styles of clothing. In
the foreground, the groom, rolling a
rug, has removed his jacket, but his waistcoat,
cravat and bowler hat retain his air of formality.
The trainers, distinguished by binocular cases
and short, light-colored, practical jackets,
stand close to the jockeys and make last minute
adjustments to the tack. The trainer on the

right wears a light grey lounge suit, a style
only just coming into fashion when this
painting was finished. The more formally
attired owners stand apart, wearing traditional
dark frock coats and bow ties, rather than
cravats. As Miley shows us, moustaches and
beards were particularly fashionable among
men of all classes in the 1880s.

Miley carefully studies the horses; he effectively
depicts the glossy shine of their coats. The
animated expressions of the horses, eager to
begin the race, contrast with the wooden
appearance of the people, perhaps revealing
the artist's affinity for animals.

DO

Maria Spilsbury Taylor, R.A.
(1777- c. 1823)

Maria Spilsbury Taylor became a successful artist in an era when formal training in art schools was unavailable to women. Many eighteenth-and early nineteenth-century women learned painting as a polite pastime, but usually only those who came from artistic families, like Spilsbury Taylor, managed to become professional artists, exhibiting in established venues. London-born Spilsbury Taylor was the daughter of English engraver Jonathan Spilsbury and a niece of John Inigo Spilsbury, art master at Harrow. Before marrying and settling in Ireland in 1813, she made a reputation for herself as a genre and portrait painter in London, where she exhibited at the Royal Academy and at the British Institution. In Ireland, painting small portrait groups and single figures, she exhibited first at the Hibernian Society and afterwards with the Dublin Society.

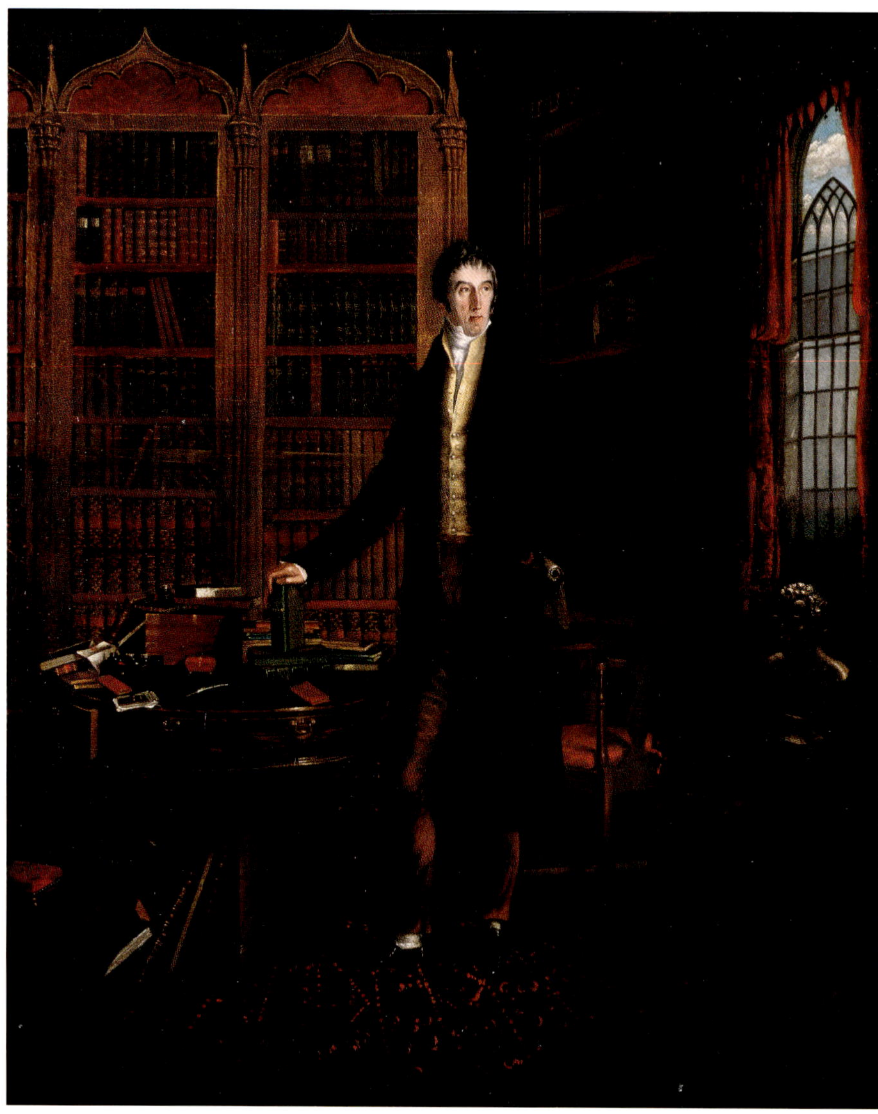

no. 23

Henry Grattan,
M.P., in a Library
Maria Spilsbury Taylor, R.A.
(1777- c. 1823)
c. 1815-1820
oil on canvas
37 in. x 30 in.

Spilsbury Taylor painted this portrait of Irish patriot and orator Henry Grattan (1746-1820) sometime between 1815 and 1820. Grattan is portrayed in the library of his home at Tinnehinch, Co. Wicklow, or that of his estate at Moyanna near Stradbally, Co. Offaly. Grattan was a leading member of the gentry-initiated "Irish Volunteer" movement which soon became militant in its demands for parliamentary reform of oppressive political and commercial restrictions in the late eighteenth-century age of revolution. Best remembered for his active membership in Ireland's parliament from 1782 to the Act of Union in 1801 — a period designated as "Grattan's Parliament" — this Protestant gentry leader unsuccessfully devoted his later years to the cause of Catholic emancipation.

Spilsbury Taylor's strangely attenuated, elegant, and somewhat frail portrayal of the aging leader typifies her delicate, highly detailed approach to fashionable costume and interiors, and her lack of concern with character description. The elongated figure of Grattan, surrounded by similarly elongated architectural features, is portrayed in his library, standing by a drum table that holds books, a brass bound wooden box, inkwells, a quill and blotter. His right hand rests upon a leather bound volume; in his left, he holds, perhaps, the text of one of his parliamentary speeches. His attire suggests that the portrait was painted between 1816 and 1820, when fashionable men began wearing tight, drab colored trousers instead of knee breeches. Grattan's surround-ings show the distinct influence of the "Gothicized" style of English architect Horace Walpole's famous house, Strawberry Hill. The open window suggests the importance of fresh air for one's health, an innovative notion at the time. Spilsbury Taylor also painted a small, full-length portrait of Mrs. Henrietta Grattan in mourning (fig. 2), which hangs in the National Gallery of Ireland.

CK

F. J. Davis

(active c. 1845)

We know so little about the artist F. J.
Davis, who is identified only by initials, that
we are unsure even of gender. Davis' mid-
nineteenth century painting portrays the
State Ballroom, renovated in the eighteenth-
century reconstruction of a medieval Dublin
Castle, and renamed St. Patrick's Hall in
1783. As the seat of imperial rule by the lord
lieutenant, the English monarch's representative in Ireland, nineteenth-century Dublin
Castle was, depending on one's perspective,
the respected center of social and government
life or a symbol of domination. The lord
lieutenant and his retinue spent winters in the
State Apartments of the castle, staging
lavish social events. When Davis recorded
this scene, the presiding lord lieutenant, the
Earl of Clarendon, held weekly "drawing-
rooms" — evening balls to present young
ladies to society.

Such extravagant social occasions continued
uninterrupted throughout the years of
the Great Famine (1845-1850), when over
one and a half million Irish died of starvation
or disease. The painting visually expresses
the prevalent attitude among castle visitors
when the Famine raged most cruelly; it
demonstrates that the national trauma had
little effect on the social life of the elite. In
1849, at the height of the crisis, Queen
Victoria and Prince Albert made an historic
visit to Dublin, encouraged by Lord
Clarendon's belief that their presence would
encourage trade and raise the spirits of the
people. Confirmation of the royal visit
prompted a flurry of activity, including the
substantial redecoration of the castle at
considerable expense.

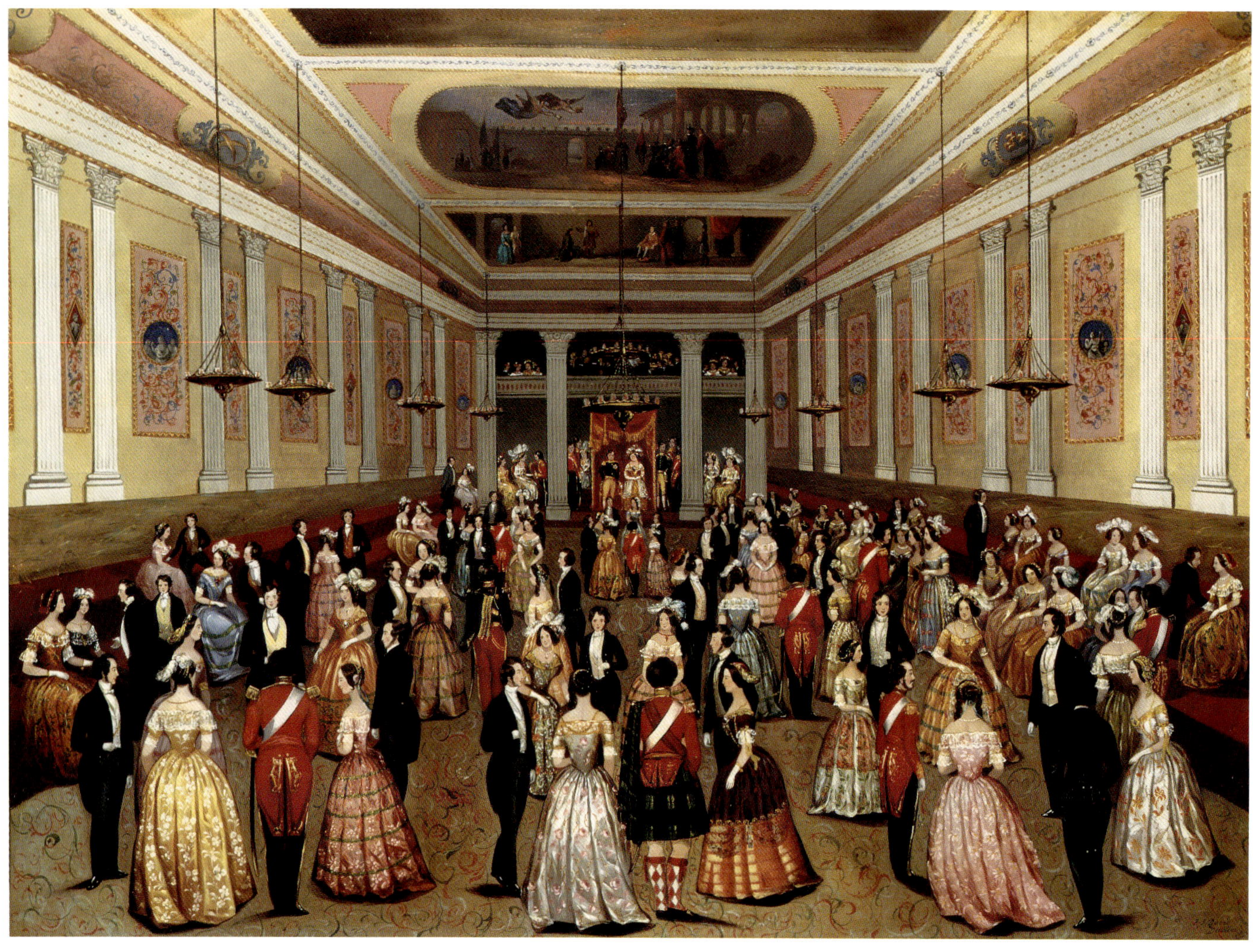

*The State Ballroom,
St. Patrick's Hall,
Dublin Castle*
F. J. Davis
(active c. 1845)
c. 1845
oil on wood
37 1/2 in. x 51 1/2 in.

Signed, lower right:
Dublin

Provenance:
Gorry Gallery, Dublin.

Painted in the mid-nineteenth century, this work records a "drawing-room," one of the major, formal social occasions of the Dublin Castle calendar. Couples, grouped together, prepare to dance, while Lord Lieutenant and Lady Clarendon are seated on chairs of state at the end of the hall. Behind them, and on the balcony above, are the peers, privy councellors, lord justices and some of the officers and ladies of the castle. Charming and naïve in quality, the painting reveals the artist's great care and attention to the details of a indulgent and luxurious dress etiquette. The ladies dress — particularly the white plume hair ornaments, jewelry, and ribbons of lace worn on the head— date the work to the mid 1840s. The male officers of arms and other office holders wear brilliantly colored court uniforms that indicate their position or rank.

A comparison of F. J. Davis's oil painting with an engraving of Queen Victoria's lavish

Drawing-room at the Castle, published in *The Illustrated London News* (August 11, 1849), indicates that the painting preceded both this visit and the rushed redecoration project. The engraving shows a carpet of Classical Revivalist style, while the Davis painting follows a Rococo style. The engraving indicates that, by the time of the royal visit, gas lighting had been installed; in Davis' painting argand oil-lamp chandeliers appear to hang from the ceiling. The cartouches, framed by pilasters on either side of the room, also appear to have been restyled. The chief Georgian architectural features of St. Patrick's Hall, such as the rows of corinthian pilasters which line the walls, the ornate classical cornices, and the screened ante-room with viewers balcony, however, appear to have survived the renovations unaltered.

CK

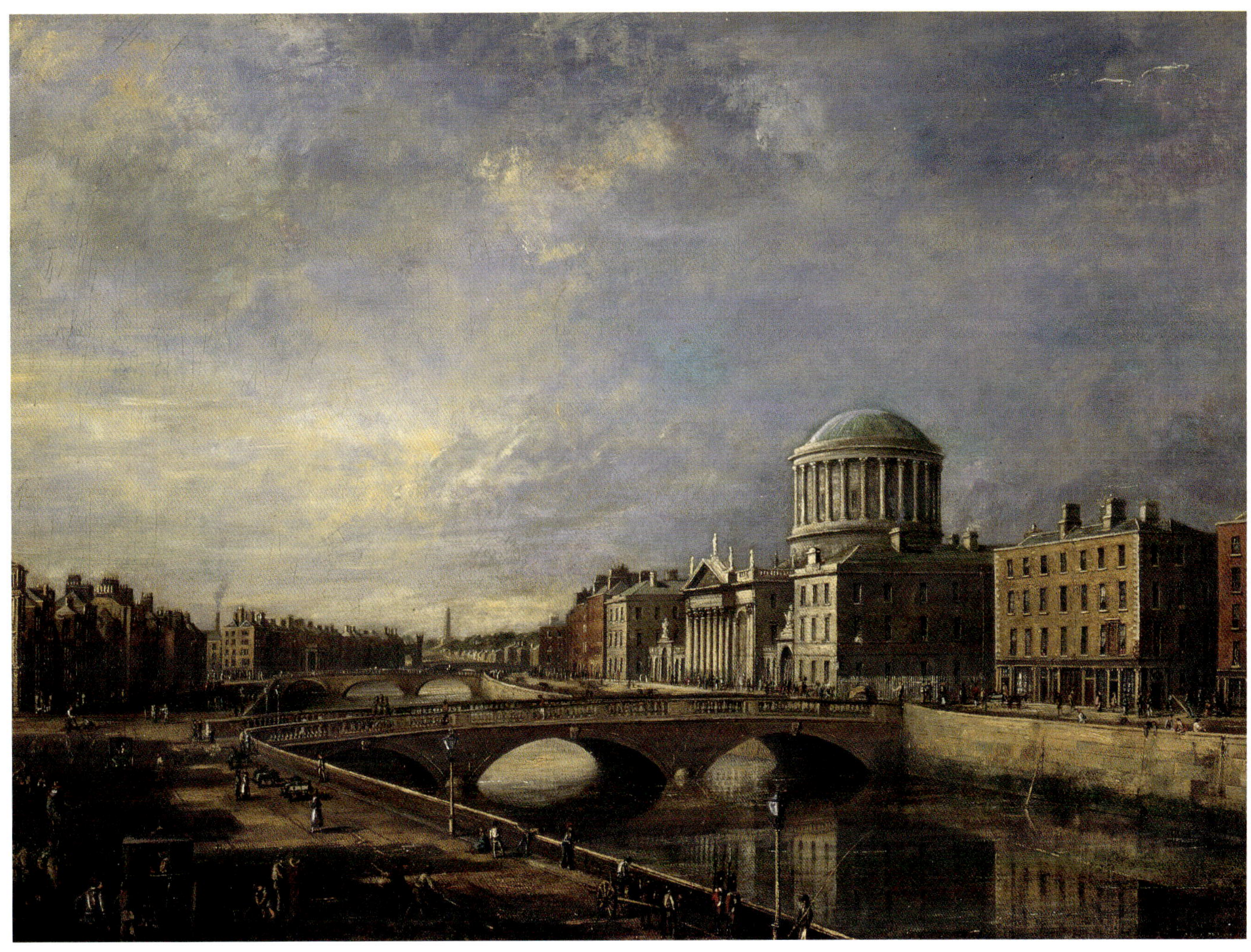

James Hore
(active 1829-1837)

James Hore is one of the better
topographical painters in the tradition
established by James Malton at the end
of the eighteenth century. Hore may
have belonged to a County Wexford
family of that name; however, precise
biographical information has proved
elusive. Documentary sources and
surviving watercolors attest that he was
in Rome in 1829. In 1837, at the Royal
Academy in London, Hore displayed
views of three prominent Dublin
buildings, *Trinity College with the Bank,
A View of the Custom House*, and,
discussed here, *The Four Courts*. In all
three paintings exhibited by Hore in
1837, the buildings are accurately
drawn, although architectural draftsmanship is subordinated to the more
painterly values of color and light.

no. 25

*The Four Courts,
Dublin, from
the Quay*
James Hore
(active 1829-1837)
oil on canvas
16 in. x 22 in.

Provenance:
Cynthia O'Connor
and Co., Dublin;
James Adam,
Dublin, 1992.

Exhibited:
Royal Academy
Exhibitors, London,
1837, no. 482

Literature:
Dr. Michael Wynne,
James Hore,
Gentleman View
Painter, Irish Arts
Review, vol. 2, no. 1,
Spring 1985;
Algernon Graves,
*Royal Academy
Exhibitors, 1769-1904.*

The Four Courts, one of the great Dublin
landmarks, was designed by James Gandon, an
English architect, who is responsible for some
of the finest classical buildings throughout
Ireland. Built in the late-eighteenth century, the
Four Courts was a bold expression of colonial
authority. The uncompromising juxtaposition
of the square central block and the huge circular
dome provides a metaphor for the unyielding
legal actions within. In Hore's painting, however,
the vast building is shown in a mellow early
evening light that casts long shadows on the
quay in the left foreground. The low horizon line
offers a panoramic skyscape, and the distant

vantage point from Wood Quay, on the opposite
bank of the River Liffey, reduces its dominance.
Reflections in the water and in the vertical lines of
the architecture provide geometric balance for
the strong diagonals of the river walls, which lead
the eye to the obelisk in Phoenix Park in the far
distance. A tall, smoking chimney on the left forms
part of the Guinness' Brewery, which, in 1837,
was already thriving. Artillery fire during the Civil
War in Ireland in 1922 seriously damaged the Four
Courts buildings. They were subsequently rebuilt
by the Irish Free State.

CM

Sir William Orpen, R.A., R.H.A.

(1878-1931)

Born in Stillorgan, Co. Dublin in 1878, William Newenham Montague Orpen entered the Dublin Metropolitan School of Art at the age of thirteen, and seven years later, he moved to London to attend the Slade School of Art. From his Slade days, Orpen evolved a rich eclectic style which synthesized many influences. An heir to nineteenth-century realist traditions, his style combined a reverence for the Old Masters, particularly of the Dutch and Spanish Schools, with an appreciation of the paintings of James McNeill Whistler, informed by an awareness of Modernism. In 1902, he established a teaching atelier with Augustus John in Chelsea, and from then until 1914 he taught part-time at the Dublin Metropolitan School of Art. His emphasis on the importance of draughtmanship fathered an academic tradition in Irish art, promulgated principally through his pupil Seán Keating (nos. 17-19) who, as Professor of the National College of Art and President of the Royal Hibernian Academy for almost thirty years, remained vehemently opposed to modernism.

From 1908, Orpen began to exhibit with the Royal Academy, which launched his career as a fashionable society portraitist and integrated him socially with the Edwardian elite. Although it is principally as a society portraitist that Orpen is most often remembered, his subject-matter was extremely varied; he painted group portraits, conversation pieces, allegories, narratives, devotional subjects, interiors and still-lifes. As Official War Artist he produced haunting, intensely poignant images of the plight of soldiers at the Front. He also focused on working class characters, such as his model in *Lottie from Paradise Walk*, who sat for him on numerous occasions. He painted a number of symbolic portraits, such as *Young Ireland*, a portrait of Grace Gifford whose striking features Orpen rendered as emblematic of courage and idealism and, ultimately, an idealized Ireland. Encouraged by his friendship with Hugh Lane and George Moore (and through them by his introduction to the Irish literary movement) the artist's exploration of his Irishness is further evidenced in paintings such as *The Holy Well*, and by his archetypal Irish gypsies and Arran Islanders who embody freedom of spirit.

After World War I, Orpen was knighted for his services as Official War Artist. In 1921 he was elected President of The International Society of Sculptors, Painters and Gravers. His publications included his War memoirs, *An Onlooker in France*, and also *Stories of Old Ireland and Myself*.

no. 26

*Portrait of
Miss Harmsworth
in a Landscape*
Sir William Orpen,
R.A., R.H.A.
(1878-1931)
c. 1908
oil on canvas
36 in. x 28 in.

Provenance:
Christie's, *Fine Irish
Paintings and Drawings*,
Dublin, June 28,
1995, lot 140.

Exhibited:
Royal Academy,
London,
Winter Exhibition,
1933.

Literature:
P. G. Konody and
S. Dark, *Sir William
Orpen, Artist and Man*,
London, 1932, p. 200,
268; B. Arnold,
*Orpen, Mirror to an
Age*, London, 1981,
p. 254.

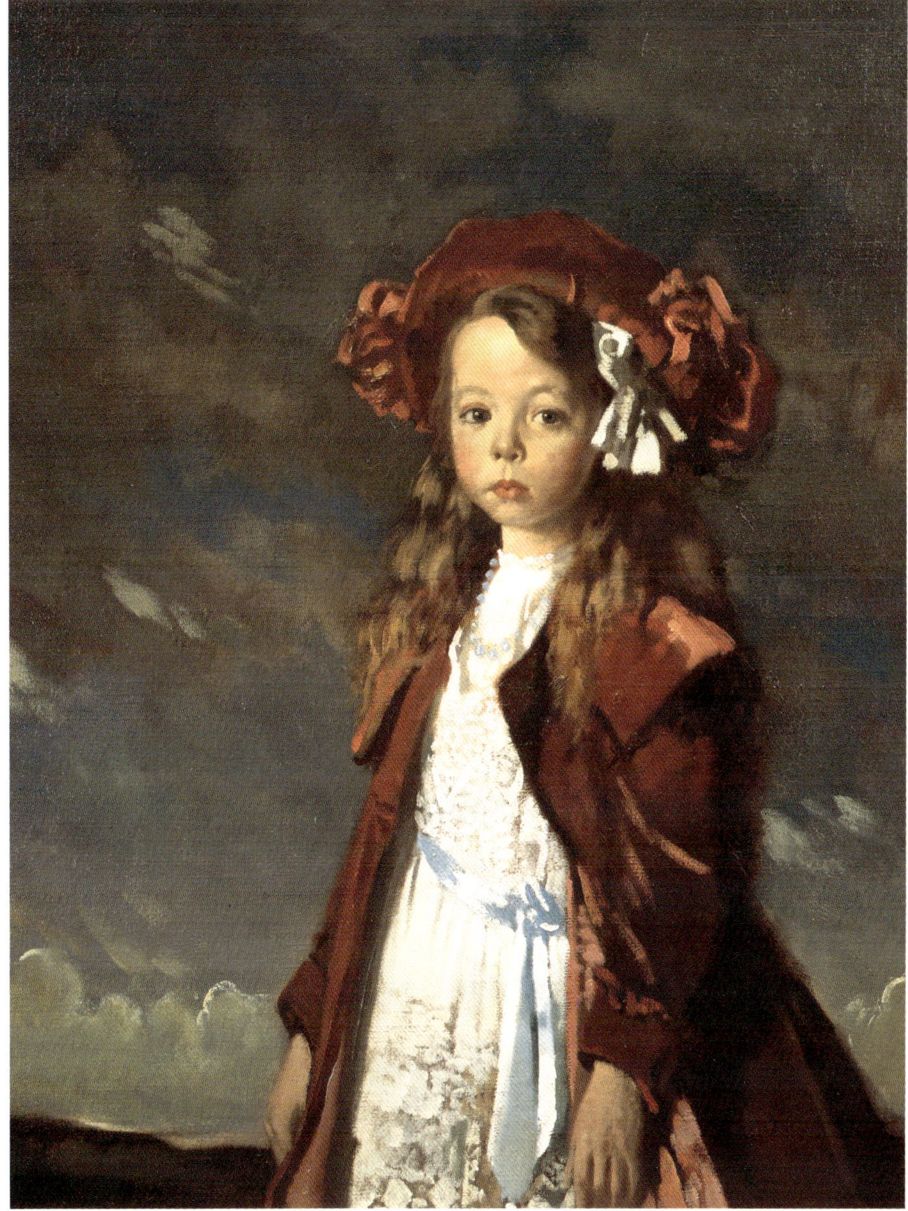

This is one of several child portraits painted by the artist during the early years of the century. Born in 1902, the sitter, Violette Lilian Rosemary Harmsworth, cannot have been more than five or six years old at the time, suggesting 1908 as a date for the portrait. Probably painted at Moray Lodge, Kensington, the family's London home, this portrait was one of a number of family portraits commissioned from the artist by Sir Robert Leicester Harmsworth.

Orpen was a rising star of society portraiture during the Edwardian era when this painting was completed, and rival of the lionised American-born portraitist John Singer Sargent.

He sensitively portrays the child's earnest expression and personality beyond sentimental prettiness. The artist was highly perceptive of young temperaments, having portrayed his own three children on various occasions. Orpen's broad virtuoso rendering of the child's red velvet coat and hat and treatment of her shimmering white satin and lace dress are reminiscent of the technique of seventeenth century Spanish painter Velasquez, whom the artist greatly admired, as is her location against a dark billowing cloudscape which affords her image remarkable presence.

CK

Richard Thomas Moynan, R.H.A.

(1856-1906)

Richard Thomas Moynan's work falls within the tradition of Victorian genre painting. He often depicts comfort-able, middle-class Dublin interiors, and poignant images of poverty-stricken, barefooted children at play, as in *Military Manoeuvres* and *Only a Waif! Cold and Wearied!* (National Gallery of Ireland). Born in Dublin, Moynan studied at the Royal College of Surgeons before deciding to become a painter. He enrolled in both the Royal Dublin Society's School of Art and the Royal Hibernian Academy's School. In 1888, with fellow student Roderic O'Conor (no. 38), he entered the Academie des Beaux Arts in Antwerp. There, with other Irish painters, such as Walter Osborne (nos. 34-35), he studied with realist painter Charles Verlat, winning first prize in the annual "Concours" com-petition. After working in Paris, he returned to Dublin in 1886 and established a successful portrait practice. For several years, Moynan was a leading and popular exhibitor at the Royal Hibernian Academy.

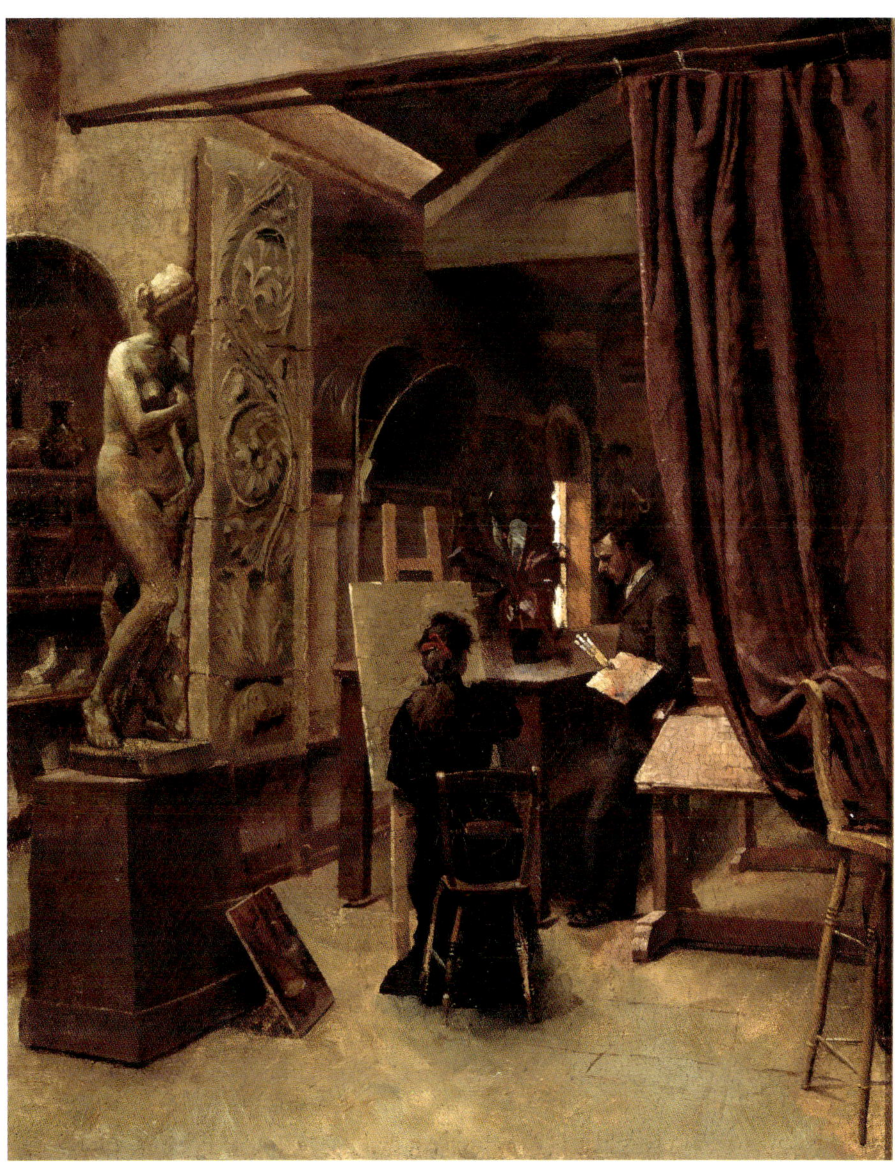

*Metropolitan
School of Art, Dublin*
Richard Thomas
Moynan, R.H.A.
(1856-1906)
oil on canvas
29 in. x 23 in.

Provenance:
Collection
of Knight of Glin.

A female student sits at her easel as a young man casually observes her work. The Royal Dublin Society School of Art (later the Dublin Metropolitan School of Art), the most likely setting for this painting, required rigorous formal training; students rendered studies from casts of classical statuary for a full year before admission to the life-drawing class and finally to painting — a routine sharply criticized by the poet W. B. Yeats and the painter William Orpen (no. 26), who studied there. From the plaster cast of the Medici Venus to casts of feet, hands, and other still-life props on the shelves, Moynan's work abounds in allusions to the Royal Dublin Society School of Art's classical curriculum.

The Dublin Metropolitan School (of which artist and educator James Brenan [nos. 13-14] was headmaster) lost many of its female students in 1893, the year the Royal Hibernian Academy first admitted women and offered a more flexible curriculum. The *Metropolitan School of Art, Dublin* may have been exhibited at the Royal Hibernian Academy, under the title *What Does it Want?* That may be the question which the young female student asks of her male colleague who, palette in hand, assesses her work. Moynan may be affirming the capacity of a young woman artist to do serious work at his own alma mater.

Moynan's textures, solid tonal realism, and attention to detail remind us of his Antwerp training, as does his portrayal of an even, honey-colored, form-bathing light. The vivid red bow in the young woman's hair, and the bright green foliage of the plant, enliven the otherwise mainly umber-based palette. The painting's spatial arrangement, lighting and classical elements recall Moynan's canvas entitled *Taking Measurements* (National Gallery of Ireland), which is set in the National Gallery of Dublin and portrays the artist in the sculpture hall, drawing from classical statuary.

CK

Theodor D. MacEgan
or *The MacEgan*
(1856-1939)

Theodor MacEgan was a descendent
of one of Ireland's ancient Brehon families,
the MacEgans of Bally-Mac-Egan. In
Gaelic Ireland, such families held heredi-
tary professions. The MacEgans were
a legal family and arbitrators of the ancient
Irish Brehon system of law from the
thirteenth century onwards. This learned
family also included a number of medieval
scholars who produced such works as
*The Annals of the Kingdom of Ireland
(The Four Masters)*, *The Leabhar Breac or
Speckled Book of the MacEgans*, and the
Book of Ballymote, Theodor MacEgan came
to his interest in historical subjects
naturally. In addition to his treatment of
historical themes, and renderings of scenes
of Dublin and its surrounding areas,
MacEgan was well known as a portraitist.
Exhibiting regularly at the Royal Hibernian
Academy, he produced striking images of
major figures of the day, including
Cardinal Rinnuccini, Archbishop Walsh,
Tim Healy, and Michael Collins. Early
in the twentieth century, the artist adopted
the title of "The MacEgan" as chief representative of the family who, in the early
eighteenth century, was one of the few
Catholic families whose original Coat of
Arms was confirmed by the Heralds
Office, Dublin Castle.

no. 28

*Interior National
Gallery, Dublin*
Theodor D. MacEgan
or *The MacEgan*
(1856-1939)
1932
oil on canvas
13 3/4 in. x 16 1/2 in.

Signed and
dated,
lower left:
MacEgan, 1932

Provenance:
Dillon Antiques,
Dublin.

Exhibited:
Royal Hibernian
Academy, 1933
no. 114; Gorry
Galleries,
*Souvenir Exhibition
of Drawings
and Paintings by
The MacEgan*,
1940, no. 12.

Literature:
Gorry Galleries,
*Souvenir Exhibition
of Drawings
and Paintings
by The MacEgan*,
1940, no. 12,
illustrated.

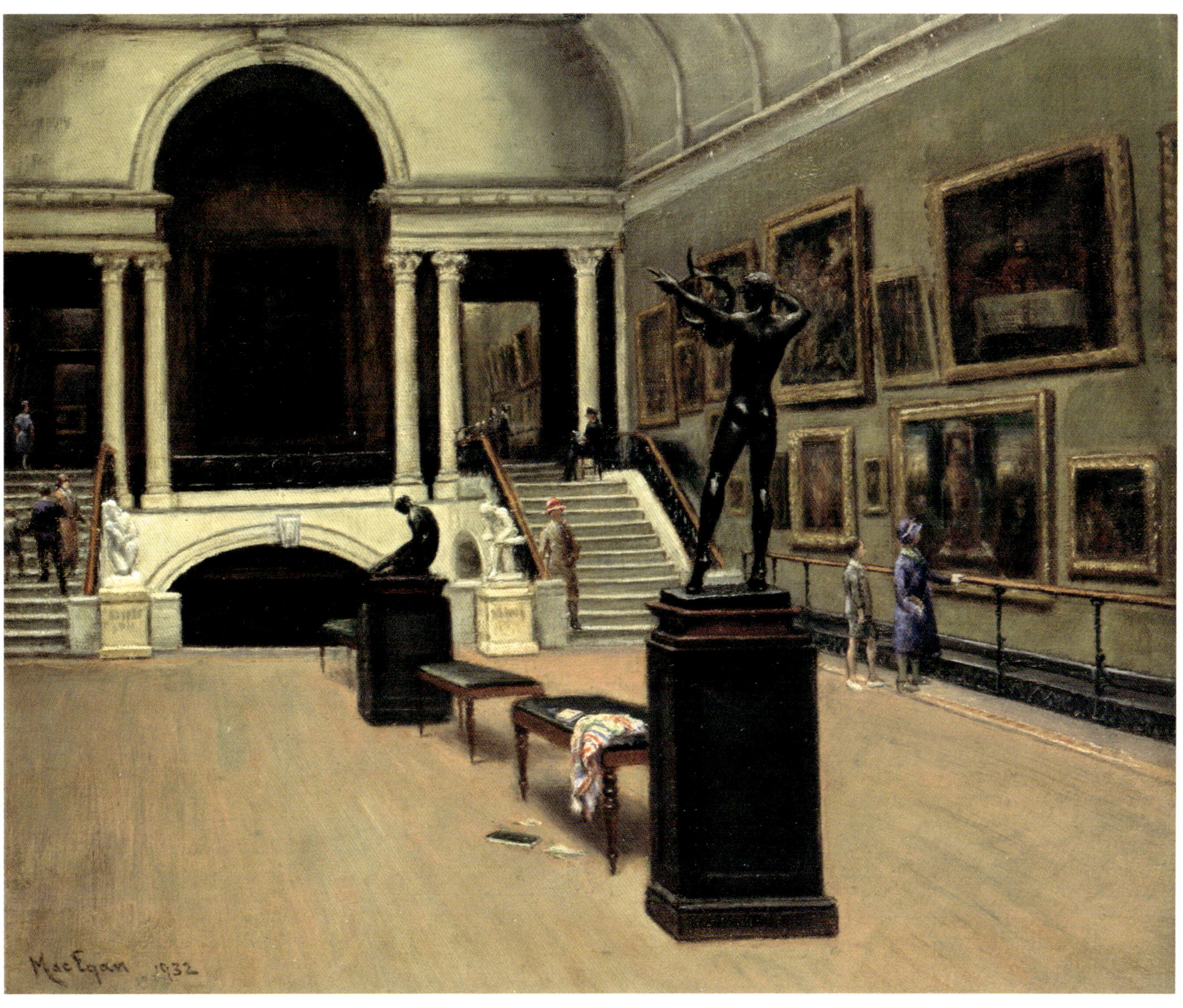

MacEgan's canvas depicts the main exhibition hall of Ireland's National Gallery, located in Merrion Square, Dublin. MacEgan painted two such interiors, exhibiting them in the Royal Hibernian Academy. In the foreground is the American John Donoghue's (1853-1903) bronze sculpture, *The Young Sophocles Leading the Chorus of Victory after the Battle of Salamis*. The two classical style marble works in the background are by the nineteenth-century Italian sculptor Giacomo Vanelli. On the right is *Spinario or Boy Extracting a Thorn* (copy of a Roman bronze, Capitoline Museums, Rome), and, on the left, *Crouching Venus* (copy of a Hellenistic marble, Uffizi Museum, Florence). On the walls, MacEgan has reproduced Titian's *Supper at Emmaus*, and Antonio Panico's *Christ on the Cross, with SS. Francis and Anthony of Padua*. Today, this room, although retaining the architectural elements of MacEgan's canvas, houses a selection of sixteenth-and seventeenth-century Italian paintings.

CK

Kathleen Fox

(1880-1963)

As the daughter of Captain Henry Fox of the King's Dragoon Guards, Kathleen Fox was part of an Irish Catholic upper-middle class family with a British Army tradition, a so-called Castle Catholic family. She entered the Dublin Metropolitan School of Art in 1903, a decision which, given her background, her family probably opposed. Her independence became particularly pronounced when she aligned herself with those involved in the 1916 Easter Uprising; Fox was the only artist known to have sketched actual scenes from that historic week. One of Fox's best known works is *The Arrest* (Sligo Museum), a large canvas that depicts the arrest of Michael Mallen and Countess Markievicz, leaders of the Irish Citizens Army, after their surrender to British forces.

Fox's interest in painting began when she worked with the London-based, Slade-trained, Irish painter Sir William Orpen (no. 26), who came to the Dublin Metropolitan School several times as visiting Fine Arts teacher, and who revolutionized the school with a rigorous system of drawing instruction. Kathleen Fox worked as his assistant in 1910, the year she was admitted to the Royal Hibernian Academy Life School. In 1911 she exhibited there for the first time with *Science and Power* (Hugh Lane Municipal Gallery), which shows sculptor Albert Power (no. 48), at work on the stone figure

Science, which would shortly adorn the new College of Science on Merrion Street. Between 1913 and 1915, Fox studied first in Paris, and later in Bruges. Five years later she traveled to London to paint her well-known portrait of *Cardinal Mannix* (Hugh Lane Municipal Gallery), the Australian churchman who supported Irish independence. The artist also depicted the incident commonly held to mark the beginning of the Irish Civil War, *The Ruin of the Four Courts*, which recalls the shelling in 1922, by the Pro-Treaty followers of Michael Collins, of the historic buildings occupied by Rory O'Connor and the anti-treaty forces.

During the First World War, Fox kept a studio in London where she met her husband, who was killed in action before their daughter, Therese, was born in 1918. The absence of submissions to the R.H.A. by Kathleen Fox from 1924 to 1944 seem to confirm Orpen's suspicion, expressed in *Stories of Old Ireland and Myself (1924)*, that she had given up painting during the late 1920s. When Fox took up her brush again later in the 1940s, her canvases manifested a remarkable change in subject matter. Assaulted by personal loss and the disasters of war, she had replaced the spirited, politically inspired canvases of the earlier years with the highly competent flower studies for which she is best known today.

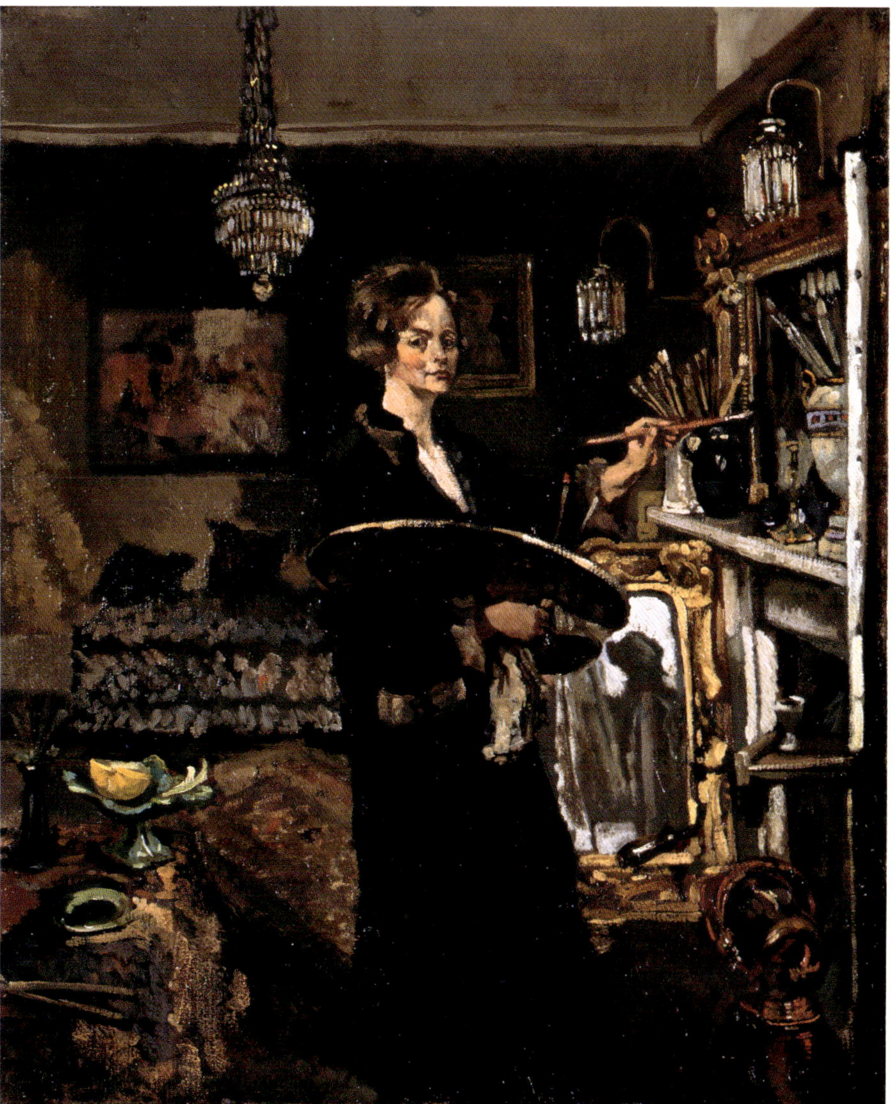

Self Portrait with Palette, painted before
1926, portrays the artist in her studio. Upon
her mother's death she inherited Brookfield, the
family home in Milltown, Dublin and painted
many of its interior views, of which this painting
may be one. The tonal realism of Fox's style
is close to that of William Orpen who, only two
years her senior, was her teacher at the Metropolitan School. Around 1910, Orpen painted
a number of interior views in which light,
falling through large windows, creates a lattice-
work pattern over the surfaces of fabrics and
furniture. This self-portrait demonstrates
the influence of those paintings. The viewer
occupies the position of the mirror, where the
artist studies her reflected image. On the
extreme right, the edge of a canvas on which
Fox is working is visible. A gilt mirror, propped
on the floor in the background, adds light
to the room and possibly displays a reflection of
the artist at her easel. Above left, crystal wall
sconces recall another leitmotif of Orpen's
interiors.

CK

Henry Robertson Craig,
R.H.A., R.U.A.
(1916-1984)

Henry Robertson Craig was born in Dumfries, Scotland of Scottish-Irish parentage, grew up in Perth and was educated at Perth Academy, and Dundee College of Art where he studied with James McIntosh Patrick. Conscription into the army in 1939 forced him to forego an award for further studies abroad. He spent the war years working on maps and camouflage, and performing other tasks for the underground forces of occupied Europe. In 1947 he took up residence in Dublin where he was elected to the Royal Hibernian Academy and quickly became part of the Irish art scene, and where he was elected to the Royal Hibernian Academy.

A highly accomplished portrait painter, Craig developed an impressionistic naturalism and cool elegance that appealed greatly to his society sitters, among them Lord Powerscourt, the Earl of Wicklow, Lord and Lady Glenavy and Lennox Robinson the playwright. He painted many canvases, both portraits and landscapes, on the estate of the Earl of Powerscourt and on the Kinsale estate of his patrons and long-standing friends Major Stephen Vernon and Lady Ursula Vernon.

Despite many portrait commissions, the artist struggled to make a living during the economic recession in Ireland in the 1950s. As a diversion during those days, Craig painted The *Regatta*, an outstanding portrait group depicting a number of his friends, including fellow Scotsman and artist Patrick Hennessy (his life-long partner), art dealer David Hendriks and his sister Yvette, businessman and patron of the arts, Gordon Lambert and former curator of the Dublin Municipal Gallery, Patrick O'Connor.

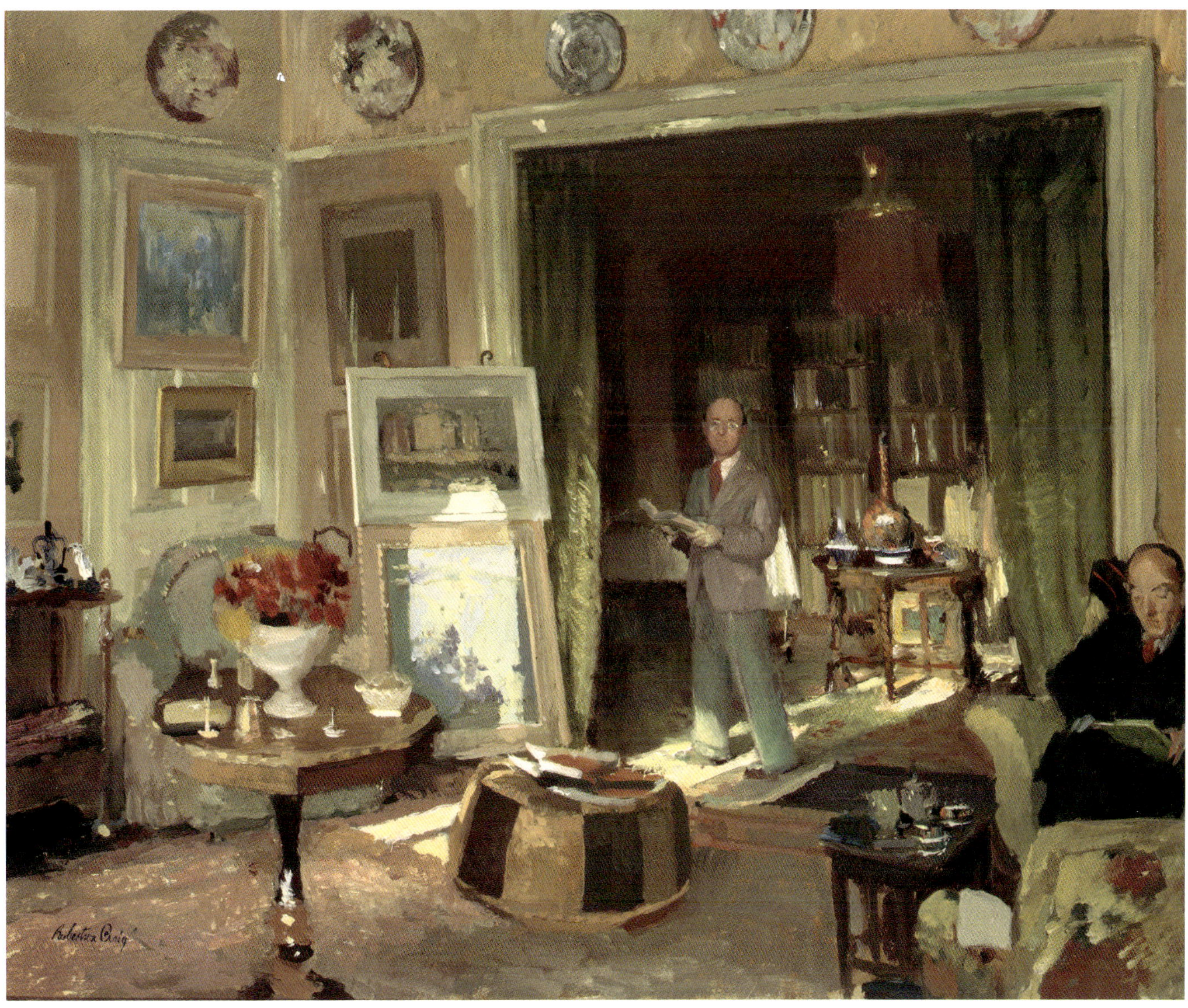

no. 30

*A Dublin Drawing
Room*
Henry Robertson Craig,
R.H.A., R.U.A.
(1916-1984)
c. 1958
oil on canvas
20 3/4 in. x 25 1/4 in.

Signed, lower left:
Robertson Craig

Provenance:
James Adam
Salesrooms, Dublin.

In a Dublin Drawing Room is a fine example
of the artist's interior group portraits, or
"conversation pieces." The standing figure
in this painting may be Sir Andrew Clutter-
buck, the British Ambassador to Ireland
from 1955 - 1959; the seated figure may be
the former's driver or body-guard. Craig's

other conversation pieces include those
of Dr. and Mrs. Lennox Robinson, and Major
Guillamore O'Grady and David Craig, each
set in a drawing room.

CK

William John Leech, R.H.A.
(1881-1968)

William John Leech was born into a comfortable middle-class family in Dublin, where
his father was Regius Professor of Law at Trinity
College. Like his teacher at the Royal Hibernian
Academy, Walter Osborne (nos. 34-35), Leech
studied in France first at the Academie Julian
in Paris, and then in Brittany. In 1914, he won a
bronze medal at the annual salon exhibition.
The outbreak of WWI forced Leech to move to
England where he settled in Guilford in Surrey
and remained for the rest of his life. He
continued to paint in France and to exhibit in
Ireland regularly. Leech avoided political
commentary during the war years, and rejected
the search for a national visual identity that
preoccupied so many of his Irish contemporaries. Instead, his paintings reflect the 'art for
art's sake' philosophy of James McNeil Whistler,
whose influence is particularly noticeable in
Leech's early work. Color and dramatic composition took precedence over subject matter
throughout the artist's career; yet, like his
mentor Whistler, Leech remained a representa-
tional painter. His artistic interests are best
exemplified in his aloe plant series, executed in
the 1920s at Les Martiques in France.

no. 31

*Morning Coffee
and Biscuits*
William John Leech,
R.H.A.
(1881-1968)
oil on canvas
30 in. x 25 in.

Signed, lower left:
Leech

Provenance:
John Duggan,
London, 1995.

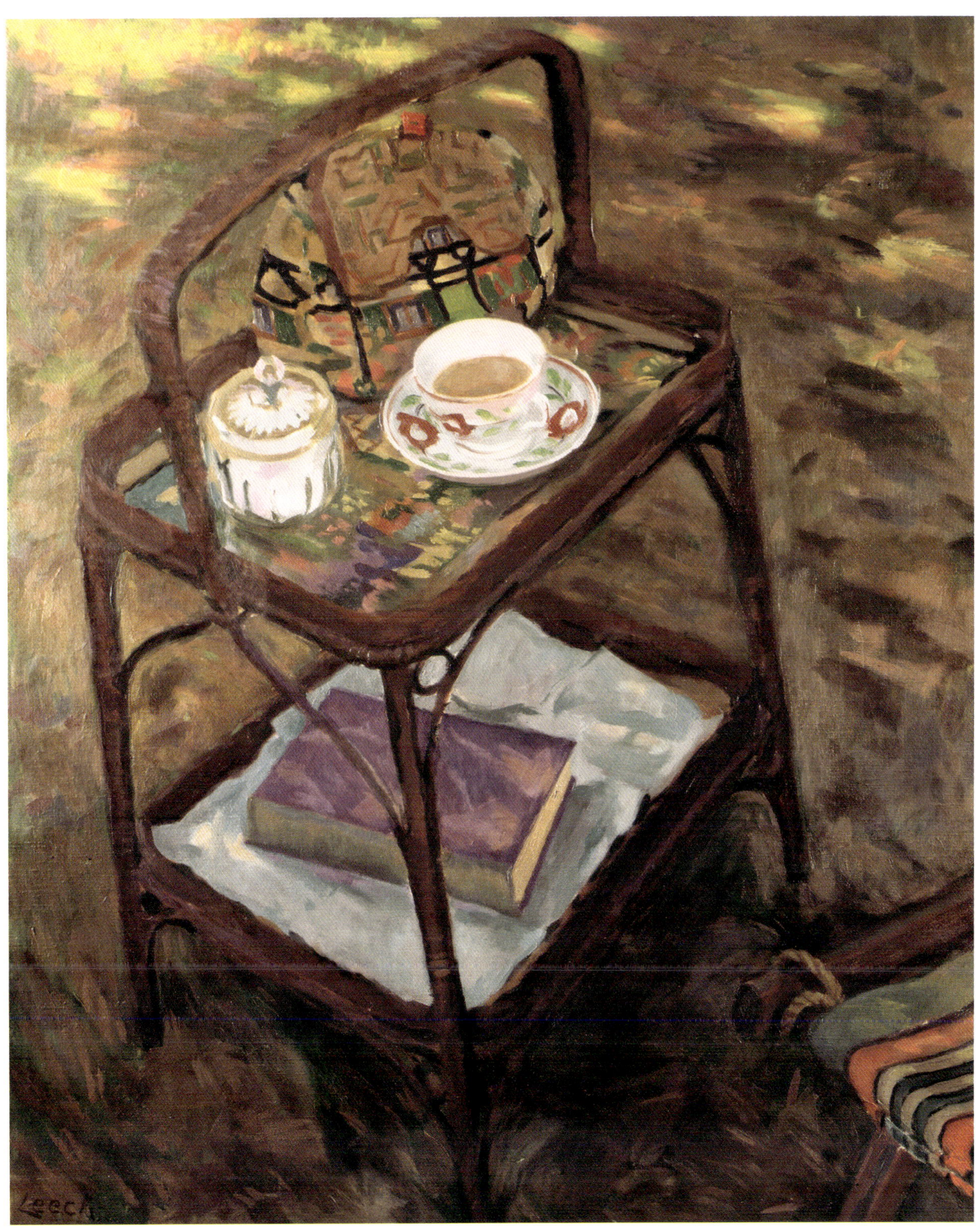

This painting is characteristic of Leech's later work. Seen from above — in the abrupt, angular perspective that Leech frequently employed — the tea trolley carries a single setting and English arts and crafts style teacozy. The loose, impressionistic treatment of the sunlit ground reveals his early training with Walter Osborne and offers a striking contrast to the more precise observation of the deck chair seen in the lower right of the painting.

CM

Frank McKelvey, R.H.A., R.U.A.
(1895-1974)

Born in Belfast in 1895, Frank McKelvey
was the son of a painter and decorator.
While attending evening classes at Belfast Art
College, McKelvey became an apprentice
lithographer and poster designer with the firm
David Allen and Sons. In 1917, he began
to exhibit at the Belfast Art Society; perhaps
his success in college competitions compelled
him to concentrate on painting rather than
design. The following year he made his debut
at the Royal Hibernian Academy, where he
showed work each year until 1973. In 1919,
McKelvey set up his own studio. By the mid
1920s, he was well established as an artist, and
his work made its way into public collections.

With his wife, Elizabeth Caldwell Murphy,
whom he married in February 1924, McKelvey
settled at the Maze, a rural area near Hills-
bourough Co. Down. At their home they kept
hens of various breeds and McKelvey made

time "to study poultry in all effects of sunlight,
a subject in which I have always been deeply
interested." His paintings reveal impressionist
influence in their effects of light and shade.
McKelvey mostly worked from a second-hand
knowledge of French art, for his first visit to
France came late in his career. Alfred Baker, his
teacher at Belfast Art College, worked in a
loosely impressionist style, and passed on to his
pupil his emphasis on working from nature.

Over the years he remained true to his
academic training, little distracted by the artistic
developments of the twentieth century. He
combined regular portrait commissions
with landscape painting, favoring the rugged
scenery of Counties Donegal and Mayo.

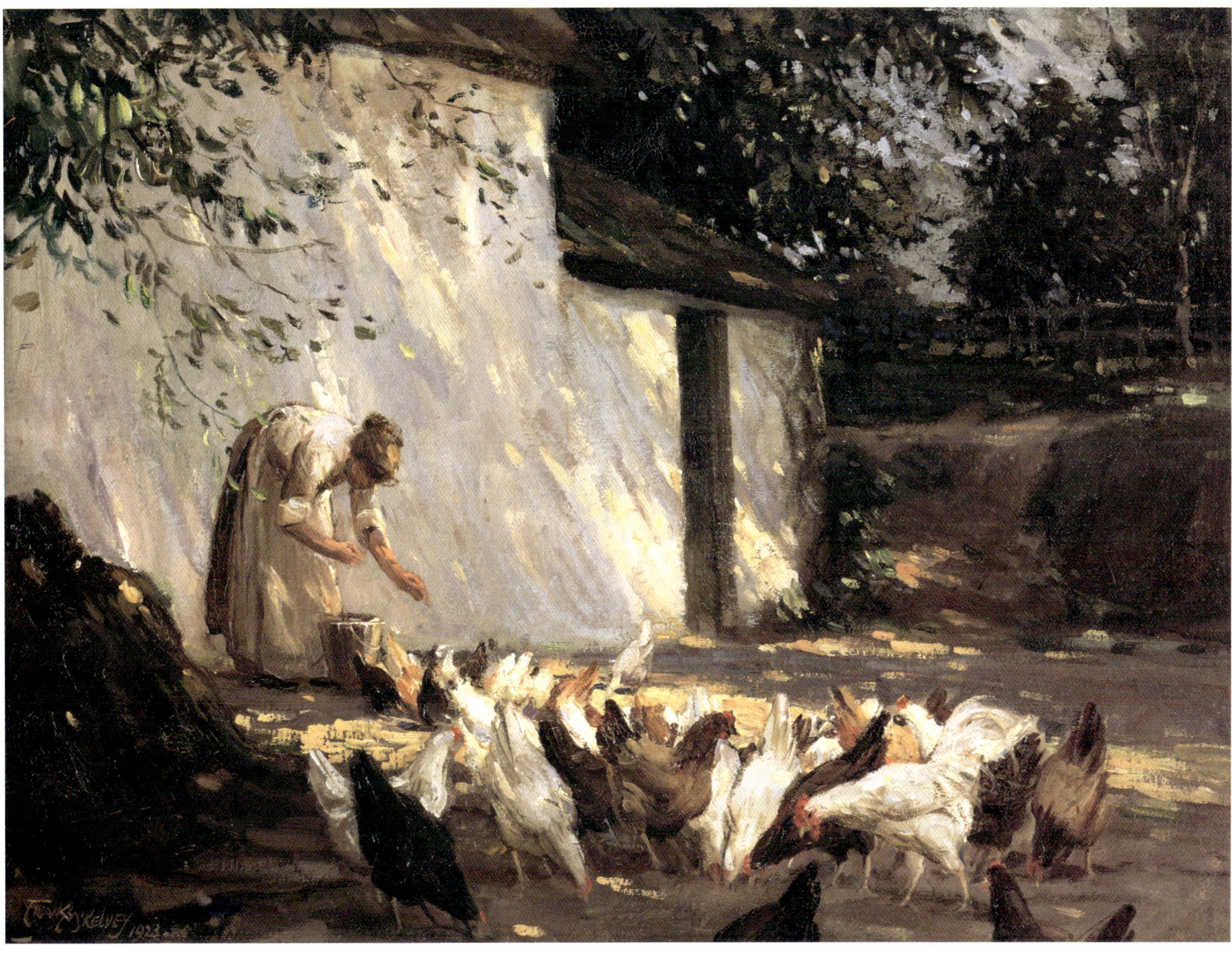

no. 32

The Poultry Yard
Frank McKelvey,
R.H.A., R.U.A.
(1895-1974)
1923
oil on panel
17 in. x 22 3/4 in.

Signed and
dated:
*Frank McKelvey
1923*

Exhibited:
Royal Hibernian
Academy 1923,
no. 211.

In *The Poultry Yard,* a woman reaches into a bucket of grain to feed an animated cluster of chickens, greedily pecking their food. This painting dates from 1923, the year before McKelvey's marriage, and most likely depicts his future wife at the family farm in Bessbrook, County Armagh. She is simply dressed; an apron protects her skirt, which is surprisingly long considering the date of the work.

From the left, light shines through the trees, creating a dappled effect across the whitewashed wall of the outhouses and the ground in front. Barely touching the trees in the background, the light draws our attention to the woman and the hens. Using the same broad painting style throughout the canvas, McKelvey makes no attempt to define the woman's features in any detail, allowing the light alone to focus on particular elements. However, he takes pains to depict accurately the different varities of poultry. McKelvey paints predominantly from a palette of earth tones with accented white and green; even the woman's white-and-fawn colored clothing blends in with the background. The splashes of red on the heads of the hens provide the only bright color.

DO

Walter Frederick Osborne, R.H.A.
(1859-1903)

Painting in Ireland, England, and the Continent, Walter Osborne became one of the nation's most highly regarded artists, in spite of his early death at the age of 43. Born in Rathmines, son of the painter William Osborne, he attended the Royal Hibernian Academy Schools in Dublin and the Academie Royale des Beaux Arts in Antwerp, where he studied under the influential French realist painter Charles Verlat. He moved to Normandy and then to Brittany, where he was drawn to the *plein-air* method of painting promulgated by Jules Bastien-Lepage. In France, Osborne painted scenes of provincial life in small, coastal towns, and moving from Brittany to England, he continued to produce rural landscape and genre paintings.

Osborne's portrait commissions, accepted initially to support his elderly parents and young niece, encouraged an enduring interest in the city's people and their activities. His works in the 1890s, combining portraiture and genre, portray ragged, barefoot city-children, charming garden scenes, and interiors with children. Osborne's later work shows impressionist influence; his palette is more adventurous, his brushwork more fluid, and his style more painterly.

While in Dublin, Osborne taught in the Academy Schools, where one of his most promising students was William J. Leech (no. 31).

no. 33

At the Breakfast Table
Walter Frederick
Osborne, R.H.A.
(1859-1903)
1894
oil on canvas
20 in. x 24 in.

Signed and dated:
Walter Osborne 94

Provenance:
Violet Stockley;
Sophia Mallin;
Gorry Gallery,
Dublin.

Exhibited:
Royal Academy,
1895, no. 631;
Dublin Arts Club,
1895, no. 112;
Royal Hibernian
Academy,
Memorial Exhibition,
1903-1904,

no. 143
(lent by Mrs.
Osborne); School
of Art, Cork, 1935,
no. 66; *Portraits*
exhibition,
National Gallery
of Ireland and Ulster
Museum, Belfast,
1983, no. 84.

Literature:
Academy Notes,
1895; Jeanne Sheehy,
Walter Osborne,
1974, no. 49; Sheehy,
Walter Osborne,
1883, no. 84, p. 146;
Sheehy, Gorry
Gallery exhibition,
October 1994,
no. 8, p. 7; Adrian
le Harivel and Michael
Wynne, *National
Gallery of Ireland
Acquisitions,
1984-85,* Dublin
1986, p. 57- 60.

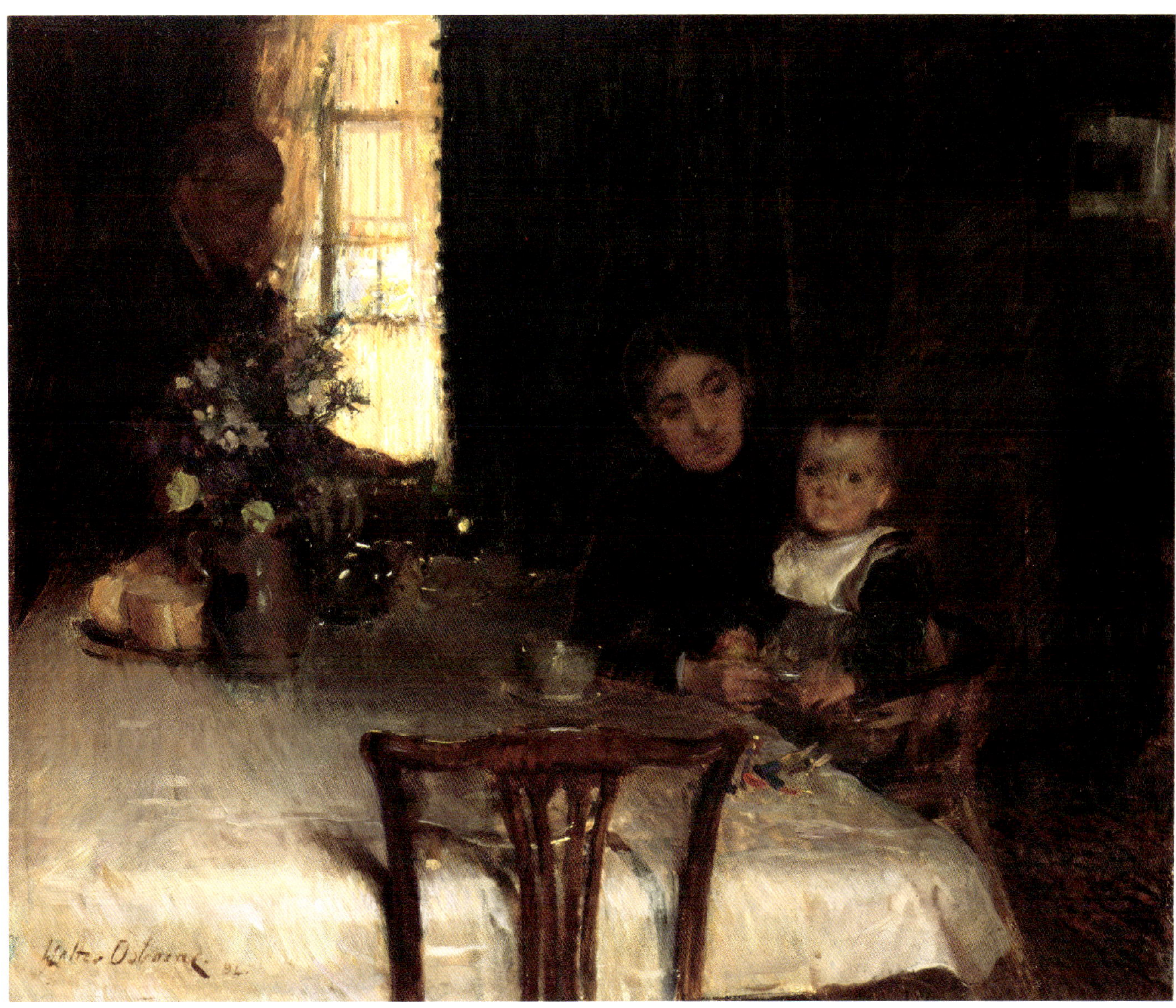

At the Breakfast Table is an informal depiction of Osborne's parents and his niece, Violet, whose mother died in childbirth. The death of Osborne's sister prompted him to return to Ireland permanently in 1892 to provide for his aging parents and the young child through his many lucrative portrait commissions. Painted at the family home in Rathmines, Dublin, *At the Breakfast Table* is a deeply personal work, combining Osborne's skill as a portraitist and genre artist. The child sits in her high chair; the artist's mother turns attentively toward her, and his father stands near the window. The empty place setting in the foreground, presumably the artist's, invites the viewer into the scene. As he did with many of his finished works, Osborne made a sketch from the painting which, in this instance, he forwarded to the child's father who remained in Canada.

The bachelor artist's new role as provider for a young child inspired him to create numerous sketches and paintings of his niece in his parents' house, in their garden, and at play with her friends. From then, until his death in 1903, he almost always included children on his canvases. In his indoor paintings of children, such as *The Goldfish Bowl,* 1900 (Crawford Gallery, Cork), *The Lustre Jug,* 1901 and *The House Builders,* 1902 (National Gallery of Ireland), the artist's lucidly painted subjects contrast with their glowing umber settings.

CK

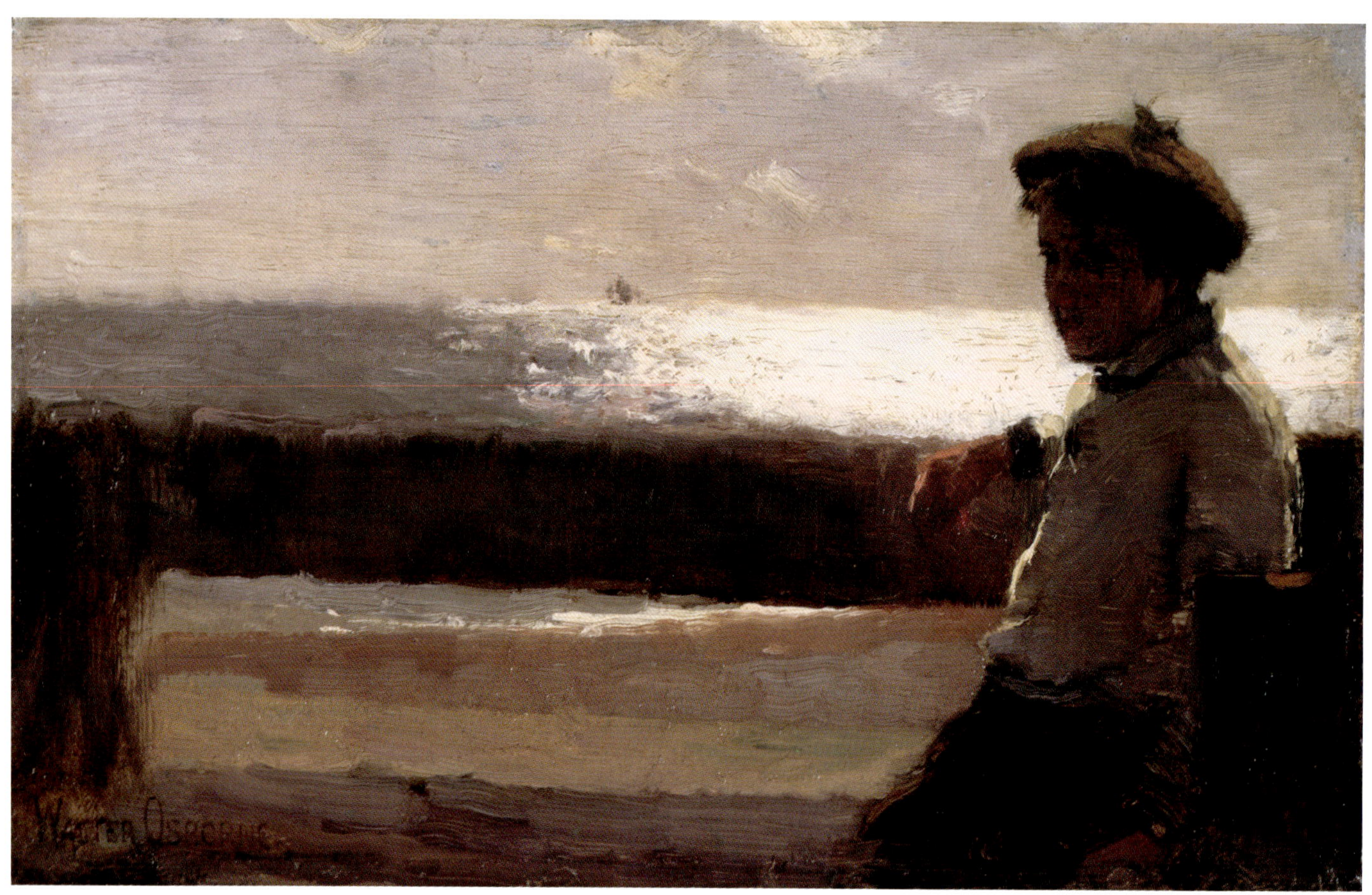

no. 34

Seated Boy and Sea
Walter Frederick
Osborne, R.H.A.
(1859-1903)
oil on board
5 1/2 in. x 8 3/4 in.

Signed,
bottom left:
Walter Osborne

Provenance:
a label on the
reverse suggests
that this picture
was in the
possession of Rev.
Charles Osborne,
the artist's brother,
who was Vicar
at Wallsend,
Newcastle-on-Tyne;
Mrs. Sophia
Mallin, stepsister
of Violet Stockley,
Gorry Gallery,
Dublin.

Literature:
Jeanne Sheehy,
*Gorry Gallery
Exhibition
Catalogue,* 1991,
no. 18, p. 7.

In 1884, Osborne moved to Walberswick, a coastal town in northeast England, where he painted genre scenes predominantly of children. *Seated Boy* is similar to *Boy on Shore,* 1886 (Hugh Lane Municipal Gallery of Modern Art, Dublin) which shows a boy wearing the same tam-o-shanter, white jersey and brown trousers shown here. Both paintings experiment with the effects of *contre jour* lighting, which renders the faces in deep shadow against strong sunlight. Osborne's brushwork is rapid, with traces of the "square brush" technique, especially in the treatment of the boy's left arm and the horizontal, timber railing on which he leans. Unlike *Boy on Shore*, this painting may be a study made for its own sake, rather than a preparatory sketch.

CK

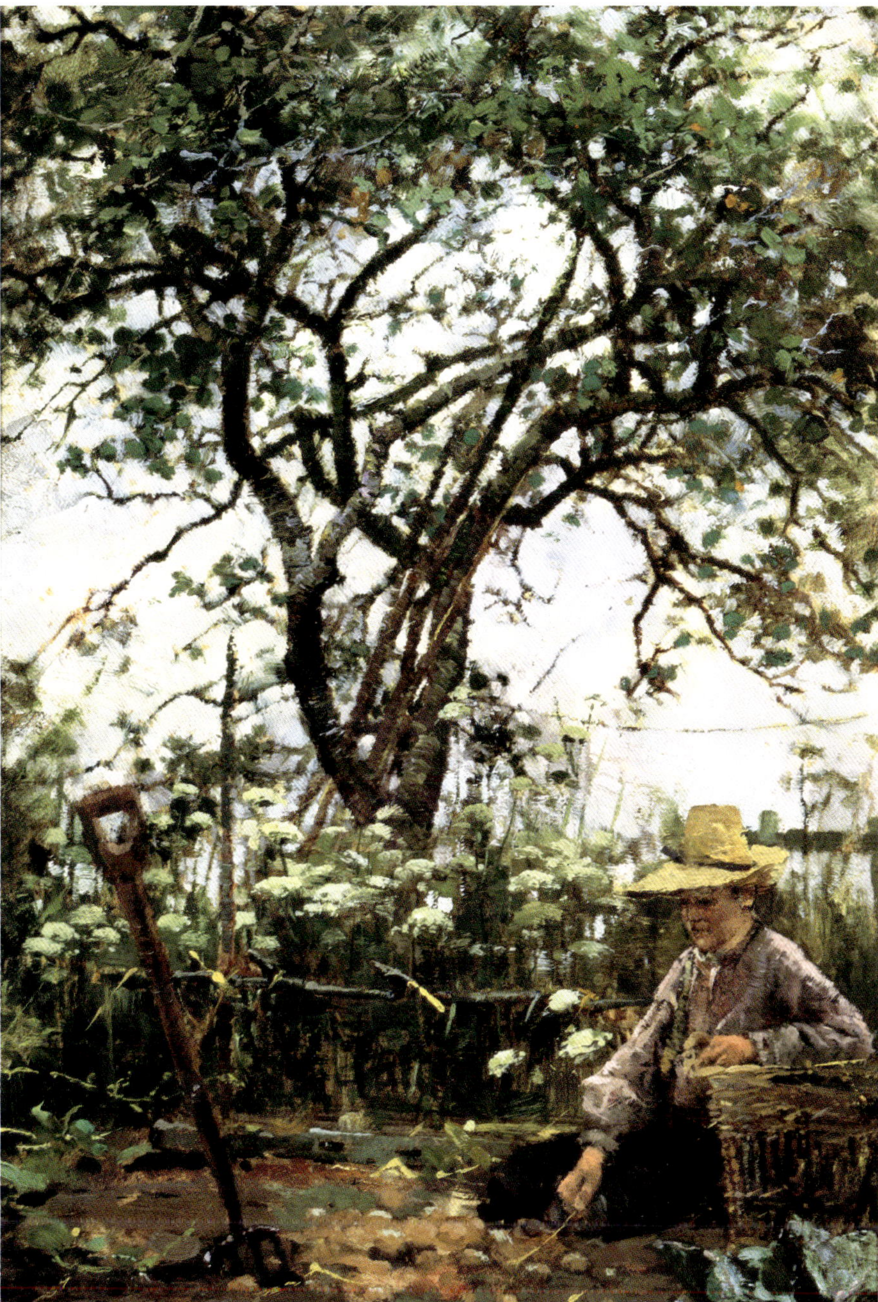

Like other Irish painters who worked in France in the late 1870s and early 1880s — such as John Lavery (nos. 4, 5), Frank O'Meara (no. 39), and Chetwood-Aiken (no. 36) — Walter Osborne was influenced by the naturalistic *plein-air* methods of Jules Bastien-Lepage. Osborne was drawn to Bastien-Lepage's simple compositional arrangements and highly detailed representations of nature executed out-of-doors. *Study of Nature,* painted either in Brittany or in one of the small, English villages where Osborne worked after 1884, depicts a woman working leisurely in her cottage garden; seated on the ground, she gathers freshly dug potatoes. The painting's limited range of subtle color, such as the distinctive blue-green color of the cabbages, and the pale light of the autumnal scene, typifies *plein-air* works. Bastien-Lepage's "square-brush" method, painted across forms to give them greater breadth, is evident in all elements of the composition, especially in the treatment of the figure's shirt, the branches of the apple tree and the garden-ing fork. Like other followers of Bastien-Lepage, Osborne often painted scenes of harvesting, turnip and fruit-picking, hoeing, and plowing.

CK

Walter Chetwood-Aiken
(1866-1899)

Walter Chetwood-Aiken died at the age of 33, before his work could be widely exhibited or, indeed, before he could produce a significant body of work. Works known to date by the artist, five large canvases and a number of chalk drawings, portray his interest in Brittany and the traditional dress of the white-bonneted Breton women. The majority of his paintings depict local religious ceremonies and rituals. Even his more secular subjects convey a calm spirituality and an almost visionary dreaminess.

Chetwood-Aiken was born of Anglo-Irish descent in Bristol in 1866. His father, a banker, inherited the family estate at Woodbrook, County Laois. Known to have painted at Burnham, Sussex, while in his early 20s, he probably studied in London before going to Paris around 1890. At the Academie Julian from 1890 to 1893, Chetwood-Aiken received conventional academic training with a heavy emphasis on life drawing in the atelier of William-Adolphe Bouguereau, where he worked alongside Henri Matisse. Like Matisse, Chetwood -Aiken was affected by the revolution in French art: the moody, naturalist style of Bastien-Lepage and, in particular, the works executed *en plein air* by the Impressionists.

Having completed his studies in Paris, Chetwood-Aiken joined the migration to Brittany where, since the early-nineteenth century, French and foreign artists were drawn to a remote countryside, dramatic coastline, and apparent cultural separateness from the rest of France. Brittany of the 1880s was viewed by city-dwellers as a remote, primitive, picturesque village, rich in local superstition and unusual religious customs.

One of the rare, large works by Chetwood-Aiken is *Le Pardon de Sainte Barbe au Faouet et la Fete du Saint Sacrament* (1897-1898), depicting the annual pilgrimage of peasants. Exhibited at the Salon of 1898, it received a *mention honourable* by art critic Antoin Proust. An earlier work, *Le Croix des Marins, Concarneau*, exhibited at the Salon of 1896, portrays five Breton girls and a young child on the quayside with a banner or cross in the background.

no. 36

A Song to Spring
Walter Chetwood-Aiken
(1866-1899)
1897
oil on canvas
27 1/2 in. x 66 in.

Signed,
lower left:
Walter Chetwood-Aiken 1897

Provenance:
Harold Chetwood-Aiken of Woodbrook, County Laois; Beatrice Chetwood-Aiken; Contents sale of Woodbrook, c. 1970; Christies, *Fine Irish paintings and drawings*, June 6, 1990.

Exhibited:
Royal Academy, London, 1897, no. 27.

Literature:
Dr. Julian Campbell, *Onlookers in France, Irish Realist and Impressionist Painters*, Crawford Municipal Art Gallery, Cork, 1993, p. 29; Dr. Julian Campbell, "A Forgotten Artist, Walter Chetwood-Aiken," *Irish Arts Review Yearbook*, 1994-1995, p. 165-67.

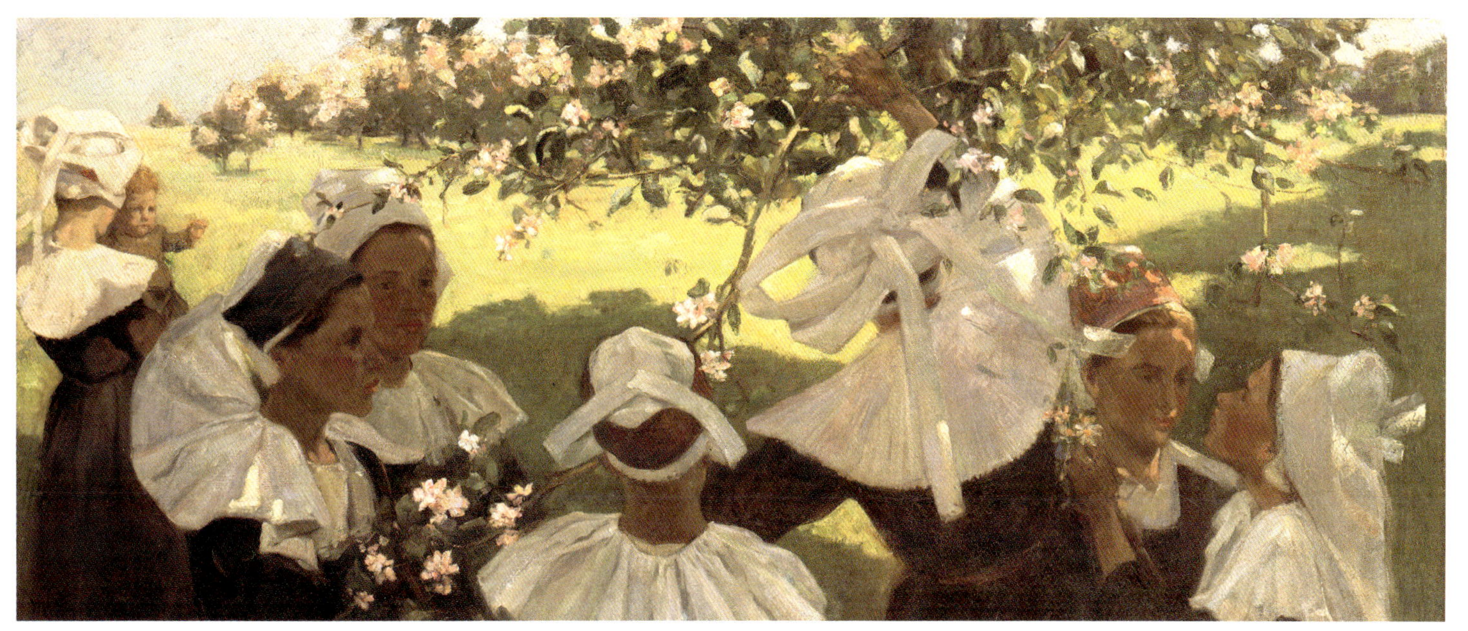

A Song to Spring portrays seven young women beneath a blossoming fruit tree. The profusion of blossoms, together with the rhythm of the bonnets, accentuates the alluring, almost hypnotic quality of this composition. Dressed in traditional Breton costume, the women are arranged across the canvas, as on a frieze; their distinctive white collars and headdresses create decorative arabesques, an exotic, symbolic effect that recalls Gauguin's *Breton Peasant Women* (1886) and *Vision after the Sermon* (1888). In each of the three paintings, the Breton women turn their backs to the viewer, suggesting a closed gathering, and creating subtle tension. The figures are dramatically cropped at shoulder or waist in Chetwood-Aiken's painting, as in Gauguin's *Vision after the Sermon*.

While *A Song to Spring* reveals Chetwood-Aiken's debt to impressionism, its emotional content distinguishes it from similar paintings by his Irish contemporaries who left Brittany around 1886, before the arrival of Gauguin. Here, Chetwood-Aiken reflects Gauguin's expression of ideas, mood and emotion in painting, but avoids his technique of using facets of brilliant color separated by black lines (cloisonnisme) and instead endorses naturalistic representation.

CK

Colin Middleton,
M.B.E., R.H.A., R.U.A.
(1910-1983)

Although Colin Middleton is a painter identified with the north of Ireland, he was also deeply responsive to a variety of European artistic movements. Born in Belfast, he worked for twenty years as a damask designer in his father's firm before devoting himself wholly to painting. Much praised for his technical virtuosity, Middleton was, above all, an eclectic artist, unique in the history of Irish painting for the sheer diversity of his style — as well as for his formal control, clarity of color and beauty of line.

His work displays the influence of many nineteenth and twentieth-century artists: from Monet, Cézanne, and Van Gogh to Miró, Picasso, and Salvador Dali. Middleton claimed that the complexity of his century demanded an openness to the experience provided by other painters. Early in his career, Middleton painted simply defined, sometimes surreal, street scenes. After the Blitz of Belfast in 1941, employing an impressionist technique, he painted views of Belfast streets with people at their daily endeavors, children at play, and aspects of the immediately surrounding countryside, but also intense expressionist renditions of landscape, musicians, and biblical scenes. Later in his life he experimented with severe geometric abstraction.

Cornfield was painted after Middleton left the damask business in 1947, and spent a year in East Anglia with his family — an experience that rekindled his love of nature. For the next seven years, Middleton lived in Ardglass, County Down, Northern Ireland, painting views in Counties Down, Antrim and Fermanagh, in a rich, neo-impressionistic style. The Ardglass period, as the artist himself described the years between 1948 and 1955, yielded several extraordinary narrative works, such as the bold, expressionistic *Jacob Wrestling with the Angel*, and *Isiah 54*. Inspired by Middleton's fascination with the bible and religion, these paintings symbolize his concern for the plight of refugees in Europe after World War II. This period also yielded several evocative landscapes in a style that echoes Jack B. Yeats's romantic expressionism.

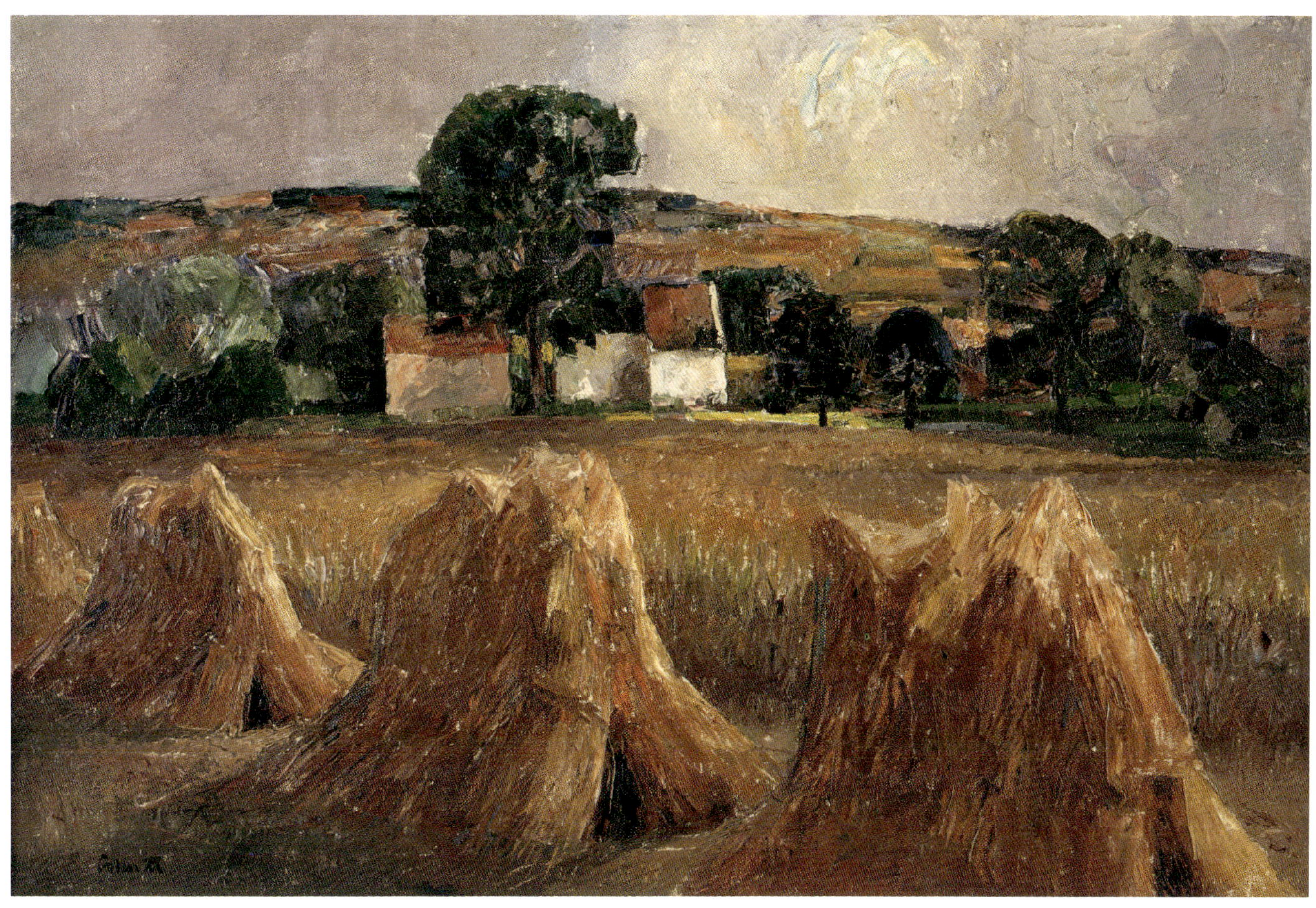

no. 37

Cornfield
Colin Middleton,
M.B.E., R.H.A.,
R.U.A. (1910-1983)
c. 1950
oil on canvas
20 in. x 30 in.

Signed,
lower right
with monogram:
Colin M

Provenance:
Dillon Antiques,
Dublin.

In this painting, strong directional brush strokes describe sheaves of corn which are gathered and tied tent-like, a subject and a treatment reminiscent of Van Gogh. Trees, some highly abstract, others more particularly rendered, frame the lower view of the composition. One large tree breaks over the horizon into the gray sky above, joining sky and landscape. The cubist rendition of the nearby houses, and the patchwork of fields on the distant hills, recall Cézanne. *Cornfield* has a strong sculptural quality, but Middleton's sensual use of paint and glowing color conveys an emotional quality inspired by Van Gogh's work.

CK

Roderic O'Conor
(1860-1940)

One of Ireland's leading painters, Roderic O'Conor was born in County Roscommon, the first son of a justice of the peace and high sheriff of the county, and a descendant of the ancient Irish family the O'Conor Don. He received a classical education at the Benedictine college at Ampleforth before studying at the Metropolitan School of Art in Dublin. Applying his early academic training, he copied the old masters in the National Gallery of Ireland and won several prizes for works drawn from both antique and live models. In 1883, he enrolled in the "Natuur" course taught by Charles Verlat at the Academie Royale des Beaux Arts in Antwerp. Verlat encouraged O'Conor to apply his paint vigorously and to experiment with bright pure color.

Moving to Paris, O'Conor probably arrived in time to see the last impressionist group exhibition in 1886, and certainly in time to see the work of various impressionists at the galleries of Durand-Ruel and George Petit. The impressionists' handling of light, color and atmosphere struck O'Conor forcibly; he began to paint in a bold 'impressionistic' manner soon after settling in Paris. He lived near the premises of art supplier and dealer Pere Tanguy, one of the few places to see the work of Cézanne and Pissarro, Gauguin and Van Gogh, Seurat and Signac — all that was avant-garde in painting.

From Paris, O'Conor moved to the artist colony at Grez-sur-Loing and from there to Brittany, where he came into contact with the Pont Aven School and befriended Gauguin. Although he undoubtedly admired Gauguin's palette and principles, O'Conor owed a greater stylistic debt to Van Gogh. When depicting the Bretons and landscape, O'Conor applied vibrant, contrasting color to the canvas in long, directional brush strokes to create a stripped effect that both describes and elongates the contours of his subject-matter.

After his father's death in 1893, O'Conor inherited the Roscommon estate, and from then enjoyed financial independence. He declined the invitation to accompany Gauguin on his venture to the South Seas, and went, instead, in 1895 to Rochefort-en-Terre, where he painted highly expressionistic canvases from his imagination and was inspired by the turbulent seas off the rugged coastline of Finistere. His work from this period anticipates the paintings of the Fauve and expressionist painters of ten years later.

O'Conor moved back to Paris in 1904 and, in 1908, was invited to serve on the selection jury for the Salon d'Automne. From this period he began to paint still-lifes, portraits, self-portraits, flower studies and nudes. Tones of red, pink, violet, and pale blue stain parts of the canvas, while other parts are left bare. In pose and mood, such paintings are reminiscent of the intimist works of Bonnard, whose influence is again perceptible in O'Conor's glowing canvases painted at Cassis on the French Riviera c. 1912 - 1914.

no. 38

Lovers in a Moonlit Garden ("Romeo and Juliet")
Roderic O'Conor
(1860-1940)
c. 1898-1900
oil on canvas
21 1/4 in. x 25 1/2 in.

Stamped, verso:
Atelier O'Conor

Exhibited:
Manchester and Leeds City Art Galleries,1962, no. 87; Bristol City Art Gallery,1969, no. 28; Turin, Museo Civico, 1969, (L); Cork, Crawford Municipal School of Art, 1971, no. 103; Guildford Festival, 1973, no. 24; Birmingham City Museum and Art Gallery, 1974, no. 31; Folkestone Arts Centre, 1975, no. 66; London, Camden Arts Centre, 1976, no. 98; Edinburgh, Scottish Arts Council Gallery, 1976, no. 21; Rochdale Art Gallery, July 1978, no. 42; Arts Council at the Courtauld Institute Galleries, London and U.K. tour, 1979, no. 34; Pont-Aven Musée, 1984, no. 34; Edinburgh, Scottish National Gallery of Modern Art, 1985, no. 75; London, Barbican Art Gallery, and tour to Belfast, Ulster Museum; Dublin, National Gallery of Ireland; Manchester, Whitworth Art Gallery,1985, no. 50.

Provenance:
Studio of the artist, sold Hotel Drouot, Paris, 7 February, 1956; Roland, Browse & Delbanco, London; Henry M. Roland Collection; Laurence Powell, Donegal, Ireland, 1995. Roland affectionately referred to this painting as his "Romeo and Juliet," hence the literary subtitle.

Literature:
Cyril Barett, "Irish Art in the 19th Century," *Conoisseur*, December 1971, p. 235; Anne Crookshank and the Knight of Glin, *The Painters of Ireland, 1660-1920*, London 1978, p. 262-63; Jonathan Benington, "From Realism to Expressionism: The Early Career of Roderic O'Conor, *Apollo*, April 1985, p. 257-58; Henry Roland, *Behind the Facade: Recollections of an Art Dealer, London 1991*, cover illustration; Jonathan Benington, *Roderic O'Conor: a Biography, with a Catalogue of His Work*, Dublin, 1992, p. 200-01, no. 90.

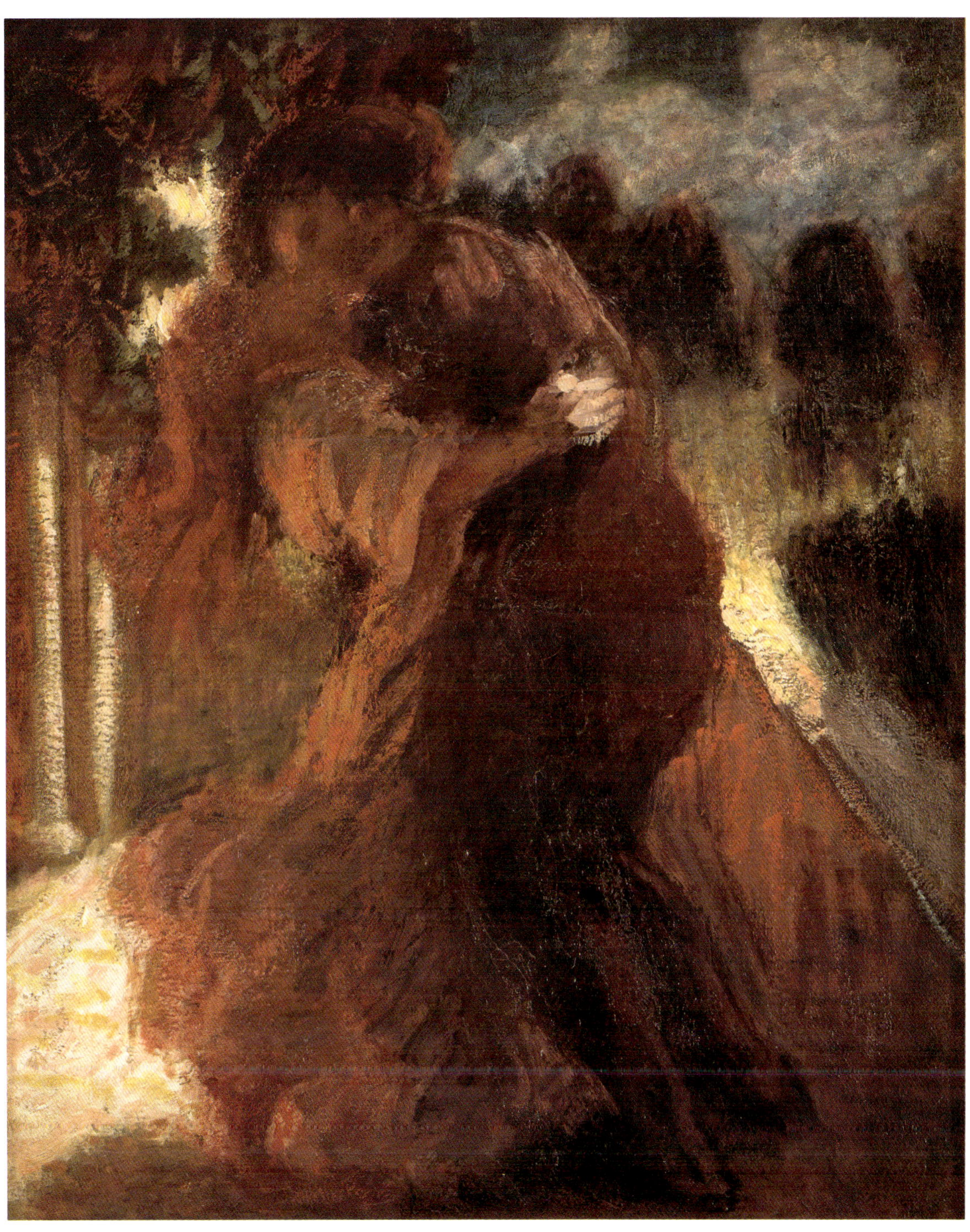

Lovers in a Moonlit Garden ("Romeo and Juliet") is one of a unique series in this artist's oeuvre, remarkably different in approach from all else he painted throughout his career. While O'Conor usually worked directly from the subject, this is one of the works which he painted from his imagination. In 1895, O'Conor moved to Rochefort-en-Terre, an inland village in Morbihan. Here he reflected on the direction of his work, relative to that of Gauguin and the Pont-Aven School. He seems to have also examined and assessed the painterly investigations of other contemporaries, such as Edvard Munch and James Ensor. Certainly *Lovers in a Moonlit Garden* strongly recalls Munch's *The Kiss,* a composition of a faceless, entwined couple that O'Conor may have seen at the Salon des Independants in 1897, and must surely have known from the widely published prints of the painting. *Lovers in a Moonlit Garden* is romantic, mysterious and dramatic. In a dimly lit landscape, two lovers rush into each others arms, their embracing figures melding into a hallucinatory image. The rich and sensual reds, pinks, oranges and yellows emphasize the couple's passion. That O'Conor never exhibited or sold this painting suggests its personal nature. Its erotic subject matter, reiterated in the intensity of its paint work, makes it unique among the body of O'Conor's work.

CK

Frank O'Meara

(1853-1888)

Frank O'Meara was born into a medical family in Carlow in 1853. The artist's grandfather, Dr. Barry Edward O'Meara, was Napoleon's doctor and confidante during the latter's imprisonment in St. Helena.

O'Meara developed an early interest in art, and in the early 1870s, went to Paris to study. In about 1874, he entered the atelier of Carolus-Duran and the following summer he visited the artists' colonies of Barbizon and Grez-sur-Loing, near the Forest of Fontainbleau.

While at Grez, O'Meara absorbed the lessons of French "plein-airists" and their concern for evocation of mood. He was also inspired by the flattened forms and symbolism of Puvis de Chavannes, in particular his still, religious figures in sparse landscapes and tilted perspectives. O'Meara's mature style, which coincided with an increased tendency towards solitariness, is characterised by a preference for isolated figures, usually young or elderly women, who move along the water's edge, shrouded in mist and dim gray light, alone with their thoughts. The artist's use of seeping, autumnal hues and quiet greens imbue his works with a sense of sadness. For eleven years, O'Meara made Grez the location of most of his mature work, becoming more and more solitary as his friends dispersed. After contracting malarial fever at Grez, O'Meara returned to Ireland in 1888 and died in Carlow on 15th October at the age of 35.

Although dying young, O'Meara was one of the most important Irish artists of the 1880s. He was an early exponent of "plein-airism," and developed from it a mysteriously romantic style. O'Meara influenced artists who visited Grez, including William Stott of Oldham, American painters Alexander and Lionel Birge Harrison, Scandinavian artists Larrson and Skredswig, as well as fellow Irish painter and friend John Lavery (nos. 4, 5), through whom he came to exhibit his Grez compositions in the Glasgow Institute of Art, and thus to inspire the development of the "Glasgow School" style.

A limited number of works by the artist have been traced, five of which are in the Hugh Lane Municipal Gallery of Modern Art, Dublin, and one in the Ulster Museum, Belfast. Other rare examples, like *Old Mill at Grez*, reside in private collections or remain untraced.

no. 39

Old Mill at Grez
Frank O'Meara
(1853-1888)
c. 1878
oil on canvas
18 in. x 22 in.

Inscribed on reverse of stretcher:
Frank O'Meara-Carlow-Ireland

Provenance:
David Smithers O'Meara, grandnephew of the artist; Milmo-Penny Fine Art Ltd., Dublin, 1990.

Exhibited:
Old Mill at Grez may be the picture entitled *Rest at Evening,* which Frank's eldest sister Sara loaned to the *Exhibition of Irish Art* at the Guildhall, London in 1904.

Literature:
J. Campbell *Frank O'Meara and His Contemporaries,* Hugh Lane Municipal Gallery of Modern Art, Dublin, 1989, Appendix 1, no. 5 (entitled *Landscape with Mill*).

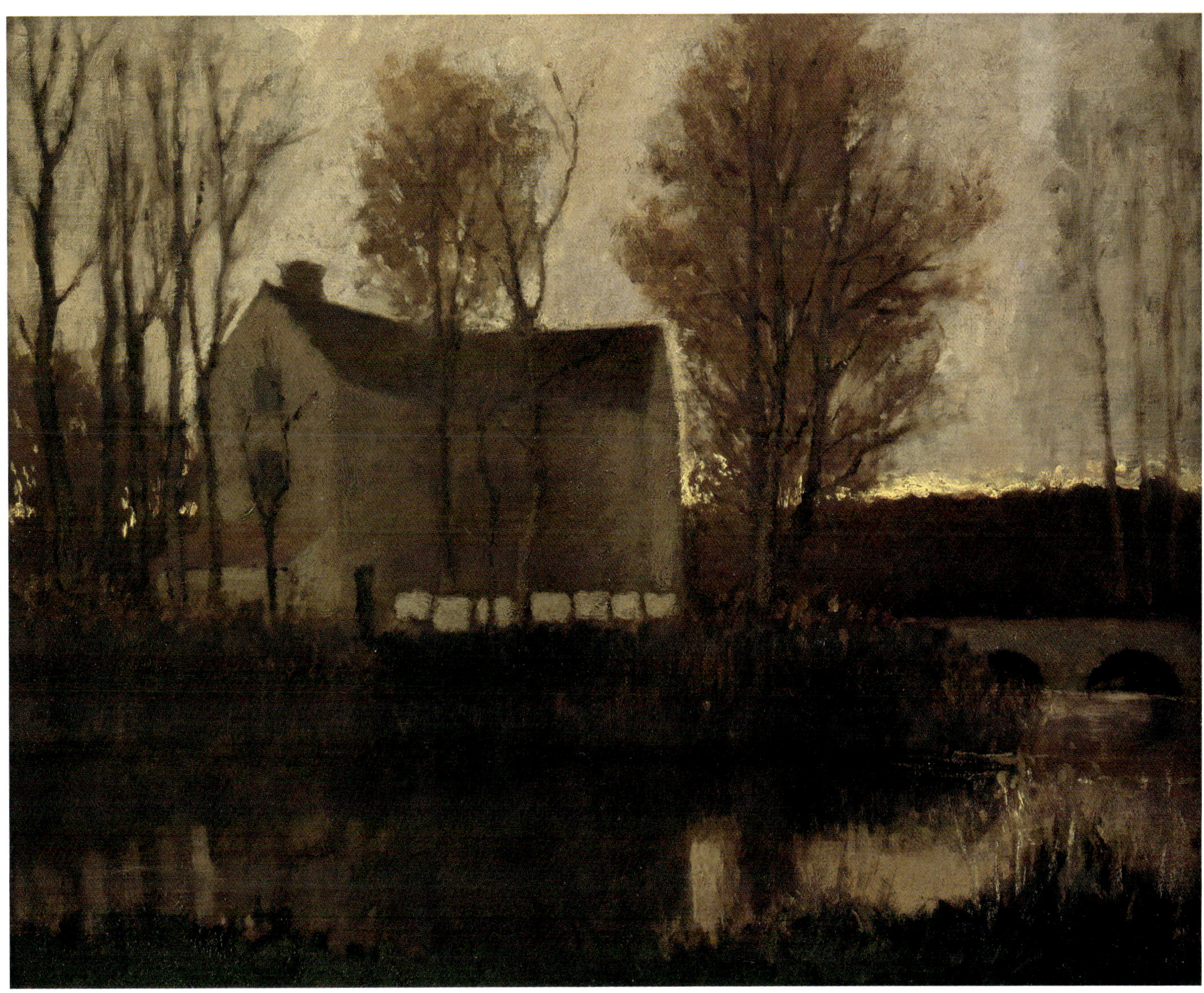

Old Mill at Grez is unusual among this artist's known oeuvre as it lacks the presence of a figure. This painting may be an early work, probably painted in the late 1870s, and contemporary with *Autumnal Sorrows*, 1878 (Ulster Museum, Belfast), a poetic composition with two figures.

Painting river scenes, O'Meara captures that time of day when light fades and color drains from the landscape. His use of silvery greens, grays, and browns to portray the trees, riverbank foliage, and their reflection in the still water, evokes a silence and melancholic mood typical of his paintings of Grez. The general "grayness" of Grez's streets and stone houses was observed by all who visited the village during this period. Its sleepy character, medieval church, ruined castle, slow flowing river and old stone bridge seem to have well suited O'Meara's temperament.

The yellow rim of light above the trees and the off-white blocks of paint at the base of the mill are characteristic of O'Meara's style. This painting could depict a mill scene on the river Barrow, near O'Meara's home town of Carlow, but, more likely, it is a French landscape of the mill and bridge at the village of Grez, where O'Meara painted the majority of his works. (The art dealers' stamp and luggage label, "Baggages Bourron" on the reverse of the painting, seem to confirm a French provenance, for Bourron was the local station for Grez-sur-Loing.)

The bridge at Grez was probably the most portrayed bridge in France in the late-nineteenth century. Robert Louis Stevenson remarked in his essay "Fontainbleau: Village Community of Painters," in *The Magazine of Art* (1884), that "the bridge is a piece of public property, anonymously famous; beaming … from the walls of a hundred exhibitions, I have seen it in the Salon; I have seen it in the Academy." Of his known works, O'Meara seems to have included the bridge in only two paintings, *Old Bridge at Grez* and *Autumnal Sorrows*. His fellow countryman John Lavery, on whose artistic development he exerted much influence, also portrayed the bridge on several occasions, and in one painting entitled *On the Bridge at Grez*, of 1884, the figure leaning against the parapet of the bridge in beret and knee-breeches is thought to be O'Meara.

CK

Jack Butler Yeats
(1871-1957)

Although Irish writers have achieved promi-
nence in modern times, visual artists often
receive less than their fair measure of attention.
Nowhere is this more obvious than in the
Yeats family. In one generation, John Butler
Yeats, himself a painter and a writer, and Susan
Pollexfen, produced not only Ireland's best
known poet, William Butler Yeats, but also the
most innovative and independent figure in
Irish art between 1850 and 1950, Jack Butler
Yeats. Their two sisters, Susan and Elizabeth,
moreover, were the founders and directors
of the Cuala Press.

Jack B. Yeats received only a minimum of
formal training as a painter during his short
attendances at the South Kensington,
Chiswick and Westminster schools of art before
he worked as a graphic artist for a number
of London periodicals. His real academies,
however, were the town of Sligo, the home of
his Pollexfen grandparents (with whom he
spent most of his boyhood) and his immediate
family.

Yeats lived in Surrey, England, and, after his
marriage to Mary Cottenham White in 1894,
in Devon. But he kept in regular contact
with Ireland, touring the west with John
Millington Synge (author of *The Playboy of the
Western World*) in 1905. He moved back to
Ireland in 1910 where he remained for the rest
of his life.

Throughout his artistic career, Yeats worked
alone. Although sympathetic and supportive of
young artists he joined none of the avant-
garde art circles in Dublin. Seen as strongly
"modern" in his treatment of paint and in his
expressionism, he never-theless continued
to exhibit regularly at the conservative Royal
Hibernian Academy, and, like Picasso, he
never espoused abstraction.

His paintings have a strong narrative content,
inspired by his reading of popular stories,
of the sea, the American West, and closer to
home, by the mythical heroes of folk life
and ballads. His memories of Sligo, a small, old
town on the edge of the Atlantic populated
by seafaring adventurers and traveling showmen,
were an endless source of subject matter.
Yeats believed that all artists work from memory,
not necessarily their own memories, but those
that are deeply felt. His passion for Sligo is
intense and conspicuous. His equally intense
sympathy for, and identification with, the poorer
people of his homeland, manifested in his
commitment to the cause of Irish Independence
from Britain, led him to learn the Irish language
and to attend Sinn Fein meetings. In 1920,
he closed his Dublin exhibition as an expression
of sympathy for those seeking political status
for Irish Republican Army prisoners. He
received much recognition in the 1940s and
1950s from contemporary artists and critics,
such as Kokoshka and John Berger, while his
writing was greatly admired by Samuel
Beckett and Flann O' Brien.

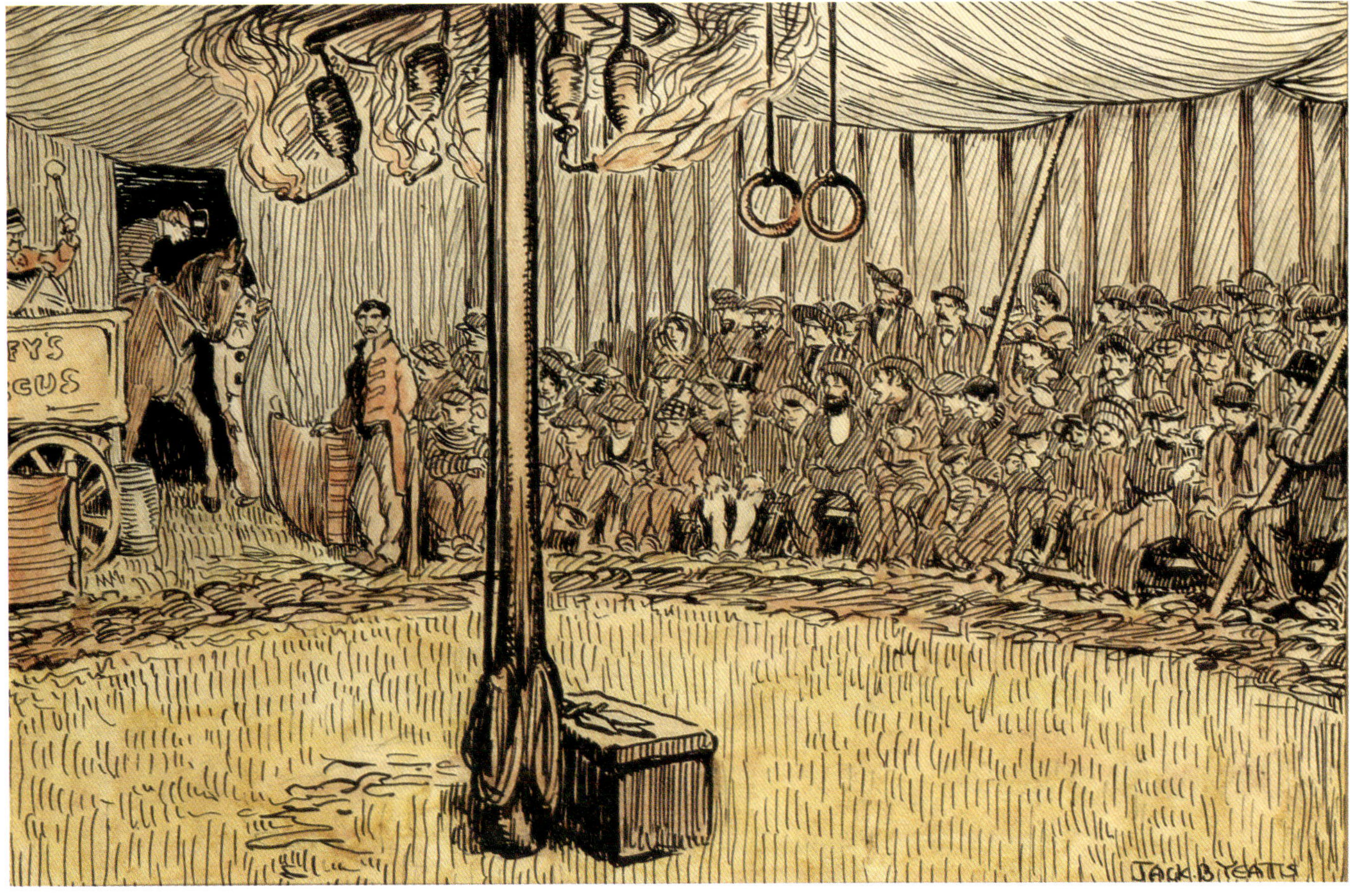

no. 40

Duffy's Circus
Jack Butler Yeats
(1871-1957)
c. late 1890s
watercolor,
pen and ink
5 1/2 in. x 8 1/4 in.

Signed,
lower right:
Jack B. Yeats

Provenance:
Mrs. Kitty O'Neill,
Dublin.

The Circus fascinated Jack B. Yeats, just as it clearly absorbs the audience, which jostles and strains to catch its first glimpse of the horse and rider entering the big top, on the left. Yeats was attracted to the circus, as he was to popular sporting entertainments, by the excitement they aroused in the local community. Here was the outsider who comes for the performance and is gone, who is daredevil and glamorous and yet one of the people.

This is Duffy's Circus, which toured the smaller towns and villages of Ireland until the 1960s. It was small, concentrating on equestrian acts and performing clowns and jugglers, subjects which recur at regular intervals in Yeats's work. Here, however, the concentration is on that moment of expectation in the crowd before the event begins, the last whispered exchange between the bowlered equestrienne and the baggy-trousered clown. Many of Yeats's familiar types can be seen in the audience: the grim pirate with his broad-brimmed hat, the excited youngster in front of him, and the well-dressed gentleman in the center front.

The picture may be dated to the late 1890s, when Yeats was still more committed to expressive line than color, but the composition — the swaying fabric of the tent, the pole just off center and the packed house — is one he used often in both oils and watercolors. Its closest parallel is the print that accompanied this poem in the *Broadside* of June 1908, published by the Cuala Press:

The Travelling Circus

Trumpets and fifes in the street, the circus is coming to town
There's a fine blue peacock's plume in the tall white hat of the clown
And the piebald horses' feet
Go sounding, sounding, sounding round and around the ring
And the lady leaps and hoops like a swift white bird on the wing
And bandsmens' drums are pounding.

CM

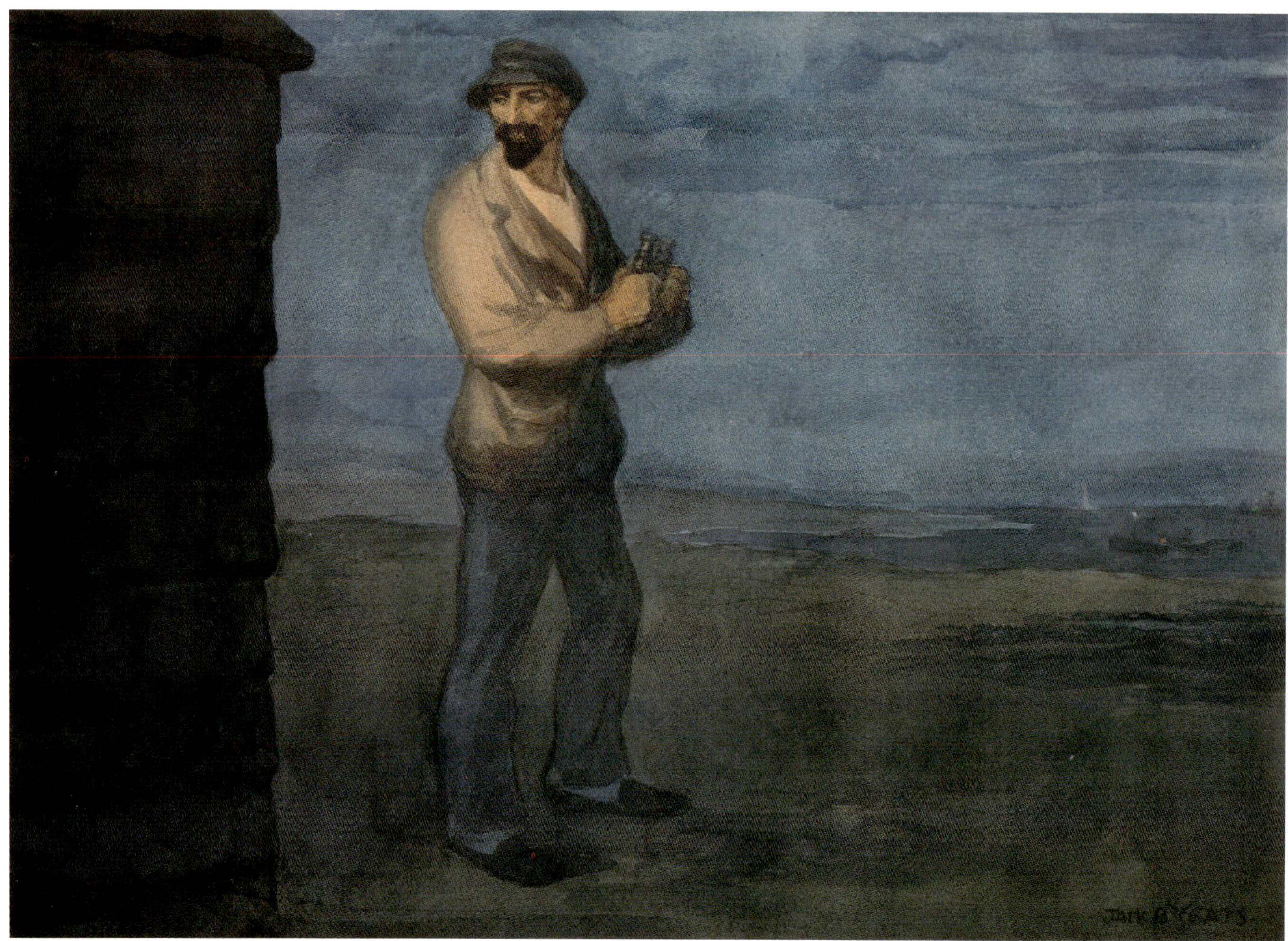

no. 41

*The Lookout
(or The Pilot House)*
Jack Butler Yeats
(1871-1957)
c. 1911
watercolor
13/4 in. x 13 1/2 in.

Signed,
lower right:
Jack B. Yeats

Exhibitions:
Dublin 1911,
London 1912,
Paris 1912.

Provenance:
W.T. Howe,
Cincinatti,
McInerney, Dublin;
Christie's Sale
at Carrickmines
House 1986,
Dillon Antiques,
Dublin.

Literature:
H. Pyle,
*Jack B. Yeats,
His Watercolors,
Drawings
and Pastels*,
Dublin
1993, no. 692.

This watercolor is rare, completed during Yeats's later period when he painted mostly in oils. The pilot stands in contraposto, binoculars in hand, enveloped by the soft blue light of evening. The glow from the station casts light on his jacket and face. In the distant harbor, boats pass along and below the horizon.

Jack B. Yeats walked with the rolling gait of a sailor and this trait, combined with his lifelong love of the ocean, led to the myth that he had spent years at sea as a boy. Yeats painted and wrote about the sea and those whose lives were connected with it. For him it represented freedom and adventure, but also challenge. The pilot, who confronts the sea to safeguard sailors and their cargoes, is one of Yeats's heroes. This watercolor is Yeats's best representation of the pilot and his lookout station at Rosses Point, in County Sligo, a subject that he painted several times.

CM

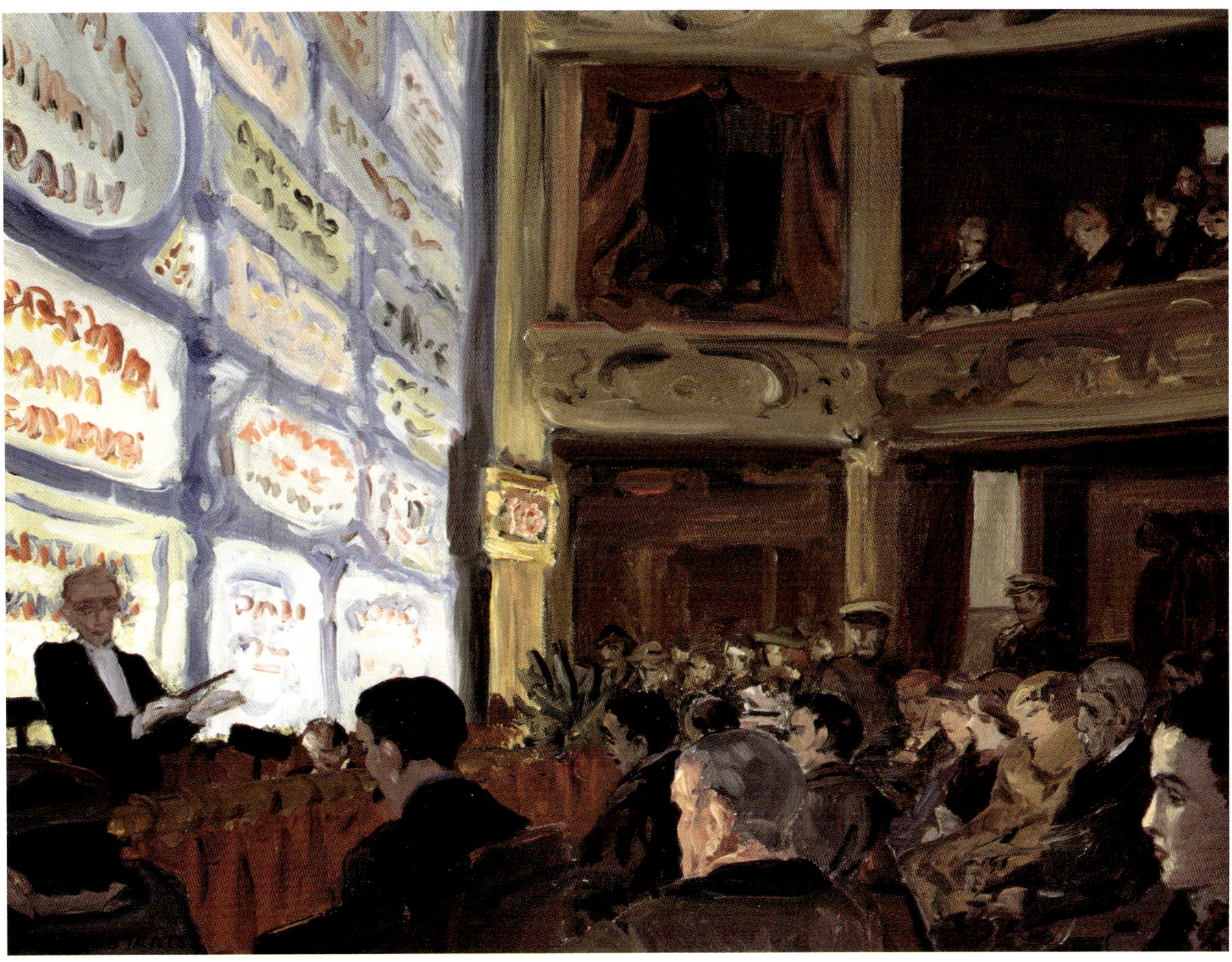

The painting shows early twentieth-century Dublin's Gaiety Theatre during an interval in the performance. The conductor, as was customary, leads the orchestra in a medley of national tunes. Behind him, the lowered safety curtain is covered with barely-legible advertisements. To the left of the screen, an empty box framed by curtains looks like a small stage, creating an atmosphere of expectancy.

Although Yeats painted this scene from memory, no detail is overlooked, and the mood is immediately convincing.

The graphic journalistic techniques of Yeats's early pen-and-ink work is evident in the faces of the theater-goers, which he brilliantly combines with the more expressive handling of oil paint in the screen and the red drapes. With his usual wit, Yeats mercilessly records the boredom and lassitude on some of the faces of the prosperous Dublin theater-goers, a sharp contrast to the palpable excitement of his humbler audiences at sporting events, country fairs and circuses.

CM

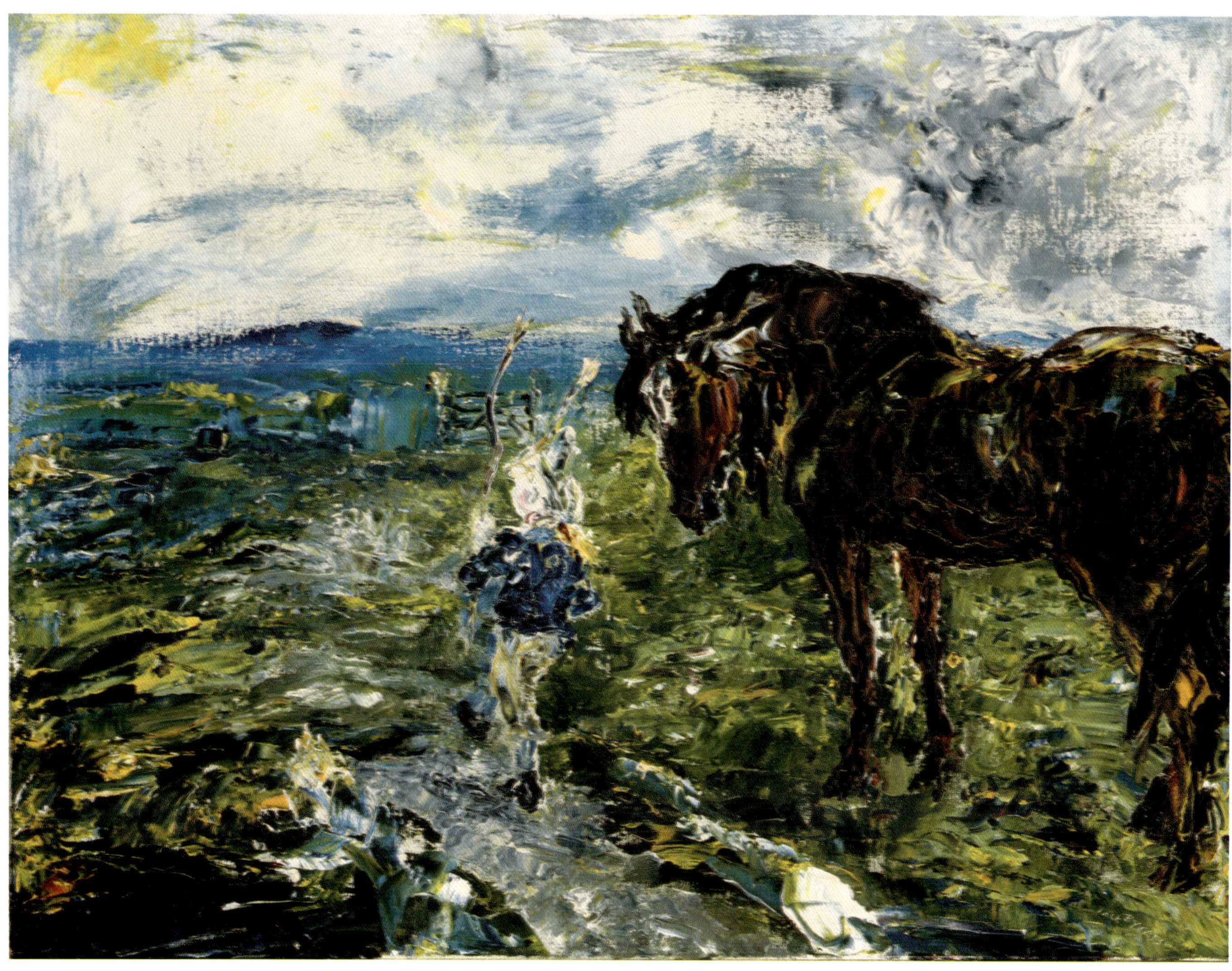

no. 43

On To Glory
Jack Butler Yeats
(1871- 1957)
oil on canvas
18 in. x 24 in.

Signed, lower right:
Jack B. Yeats

Provenance:
Sold by the artist
to Leo Smith,
Dublin, 1948;
M.J. Doran
(Davy Byrne's Pub)
Dublin, Dillon
Antiques,
Dublin 1986.

Literature:
H. Pyle, Jack B.
Yeats, *Catalogue
Raissonne of
the Oil Paintings*,
Dublin 1992,
no. 879, p. 795.

The mood of *On to Glory* is considerably lighter than that of *The Lonely Sea*. The golden-haired child — Yeats's ideal youth, has a companion now in the magnificent chestnut pony, which lowers its head submissively toward the bridle in the child's hand. The horse is another powerful and recurring motif in Yeats's work. It symbolizes freedom and adventure and, for the artist, carries associations with travel, the excitement of the race day and the pioneering dreams of the Wild West, which he so loved to read about. In *On to Glory,* the combination of roadway and open sea in the distance invites the child and his horse to venture into the unknown. Yeats remembers his youthful dreams of heroic figures who traveled the world beyond the confines of normal society, whether in a circus wagon or on board a pirate ship. The landscape is reminiscent of Sligo, the place of Yeats's golden childhood, where the perfect rapport between child and horse, which we see here, is possible.

CM

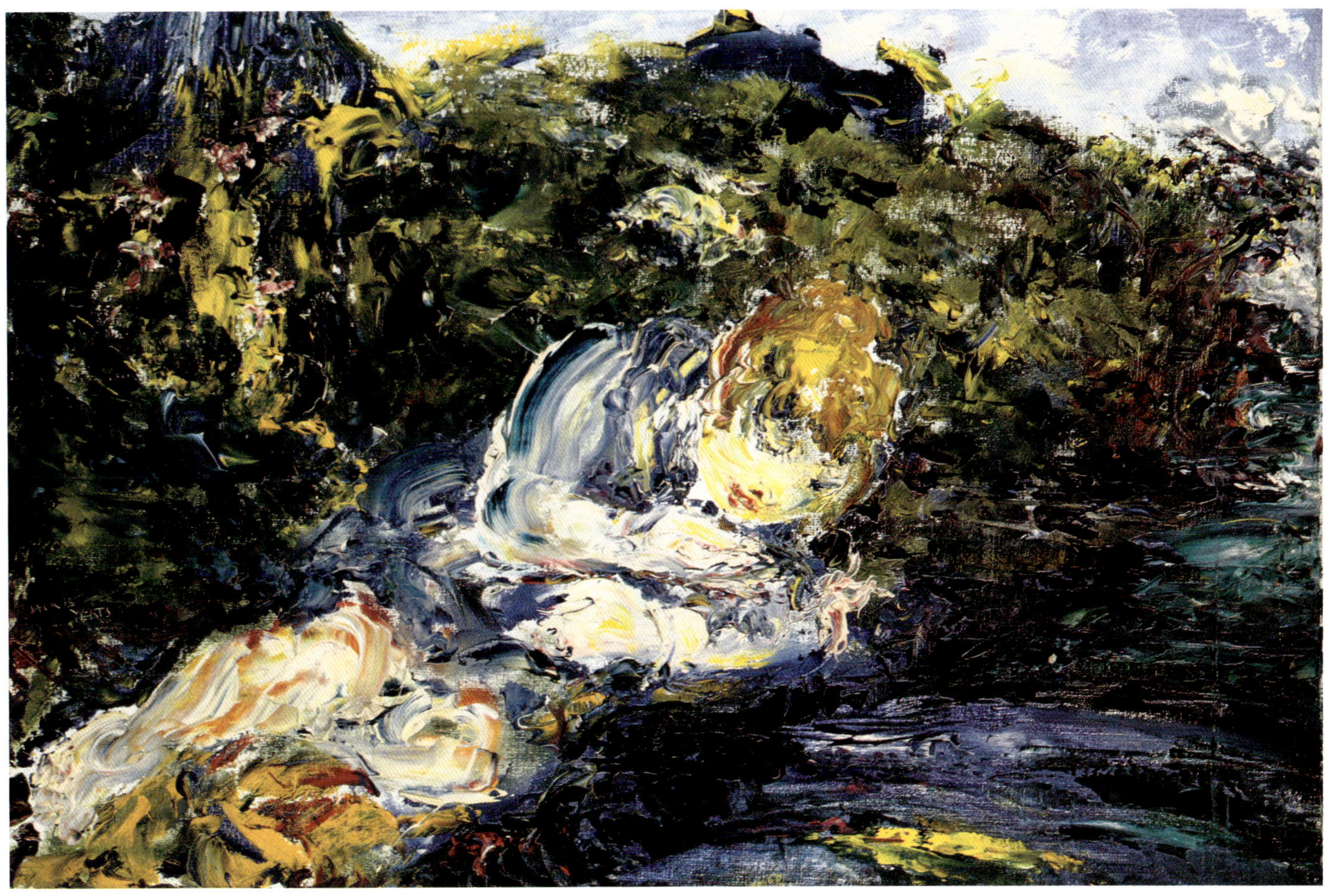

no. 44

The Lonely Sea
Jack Butler Yeats
(1871- 1957)
c. 1940
oil on canvas
14 in. x 21 in.

Signed, lower left:
Jack B. Yeats

Provenance:
Leo Smith,
Dublin 1948;
M. J. Doran
(Davy Byrne's Pub)
James Adam,
Dublin 1976;
Dillon Antiques,
Dublin.

Literature:
H. Pyle, Jack B.
Yeats, *Catalogue
Raissonne of
the Oil Paintings*,
Dublin 1992,
no. 854.

All of Yeats's main preoccupations through-out his life come together in *The Lonely Sea*. A golden-haired child, symbol of innocence and hope, crouches, gazing into the shadowy water at the seashore. The child holds the pink rose that Yeats used as a personal emblem in many paintings, beginning in 1915 with *Bachelor's Walk/In Memory*. In that picture a Dublin flower girl drops a rose on the site of a shooting incident in which the British army opened fire on the Volunteers, killing three people. In the same year Yeats and the Cuala Press published another *Broadside* containing a poem by G. N. Reddin, in which the rose is an analogue for Ireland as the extract clearly indicates:

> So weep no more but feed your
> heart with hope,
>
> More men shall rise who scorn the
> tyrant's rope,
>
> My little Rose.
> And they shall fight and win your
> freedom back

> And all you had, you'll have,
> and all you lack,
>
> My Little Rose.

In the 1930s and 40s the rose also came to be associated with the mysterious, unfathom-able nature of beauty in Yeats's work. In *The Lonely Sea*, now old and saddened by the recent death of his wife, Yeats looks back at the dreams of youth, his idealism, his aspirations for freedom and, inseparable from these, his dream of beauty.

The mood of the painting is sad, as was so much of Yeats's painting in the 1940s. In addition to his bereavement, Yeats was also depressed about war. The child in *The Lonely Sea* cradles the rose protectively in his arms as if to defend beauty and idealism from a threatening world.

CM

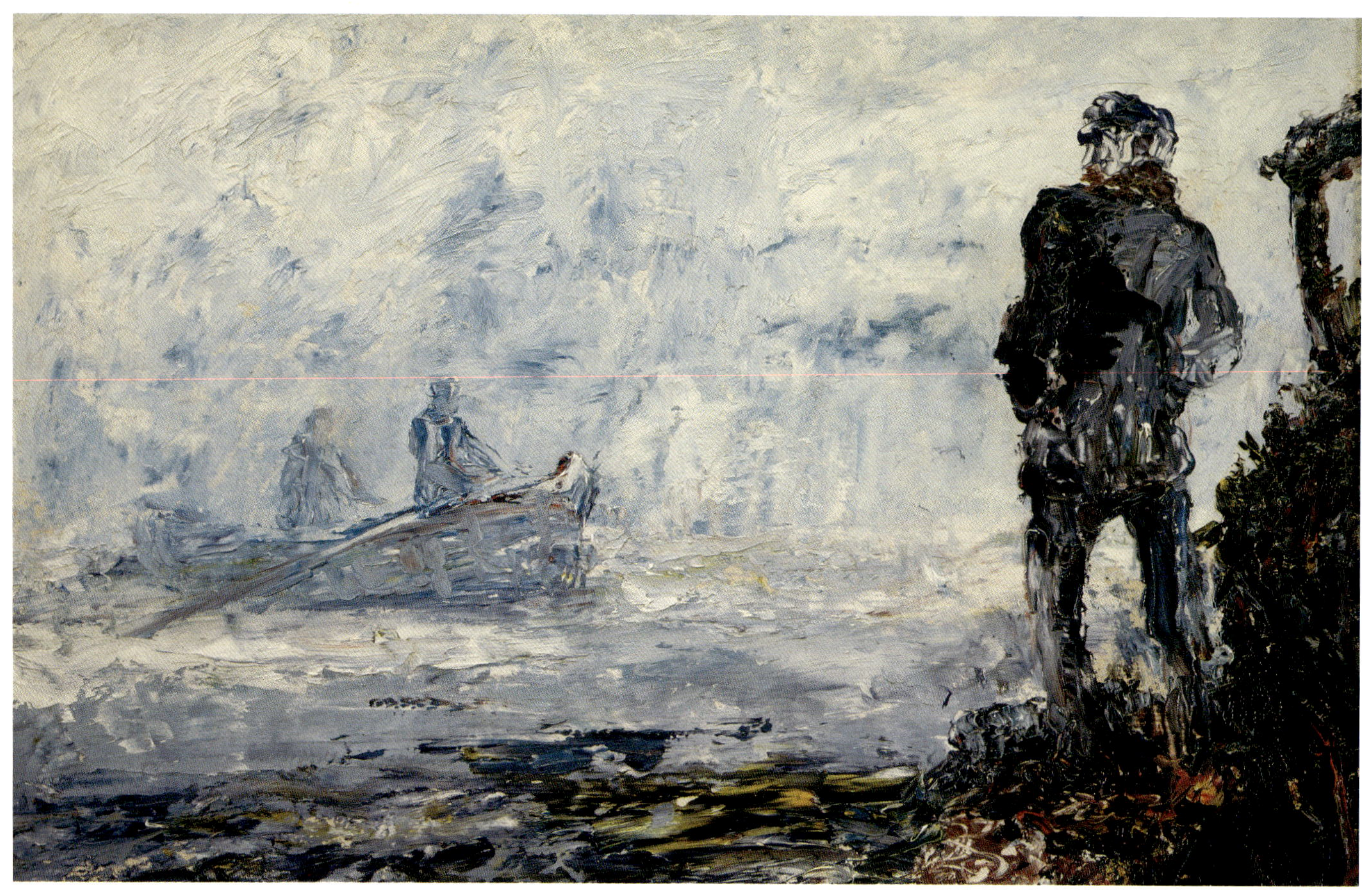

no. 45

Misty Morning
Jack Butler Yeats
(1871-1957)
oil on panel
9 in. x 14 in.

Signed:
Jack B. Yeats

Provenance:
Sold through
Victor Waddington
Galleries
in 1943 to Jack
Toohey, Dublin;
Private collection.

Literature:
Hilary Pyle,
*Catalogue
Raisonne of the
Oil Paintings*,
Dublin 1992,
no. 350, p. 486.

The small panel painting entitled *Misty Morning* brings together a number of familiar Yeatsian themes. A solitary figure on the shore, reminiscent of the figure in *The Pilot House*, gazes out through the early morning fog at an approaching rowboat. The watcher is clearly visible in the right foreground, in contrast to the two dimly silhouetted figures in the boat. The relative obscurity is a device prominent in Yeats's later work; it suggests distance in time as well as in space. The watching man can be read as a symbol of the artist, grown older now, and looking back into his storehouse of memories. *Many Ferries*, painted in 1948, refers to a similar moment from Yeats's earlier life, when he and the playwright John Millington Synge, traveling through Connemara together, encountered an old ferryman who told them of his life as an emigrant and of the hardships he endured on his return to Ireland.

The watcher is typically Yeatsian, lean, but strong and square-shouldered, and made monumental by virtue of the low horizon above which he stands. In the early works, such characters faced forward, at once confronting the viewers and introducing them to the narrative, like the linking figures in a Renaissance altarpiece. In the late works, their backs seem to lead us into the remembered past.

CM

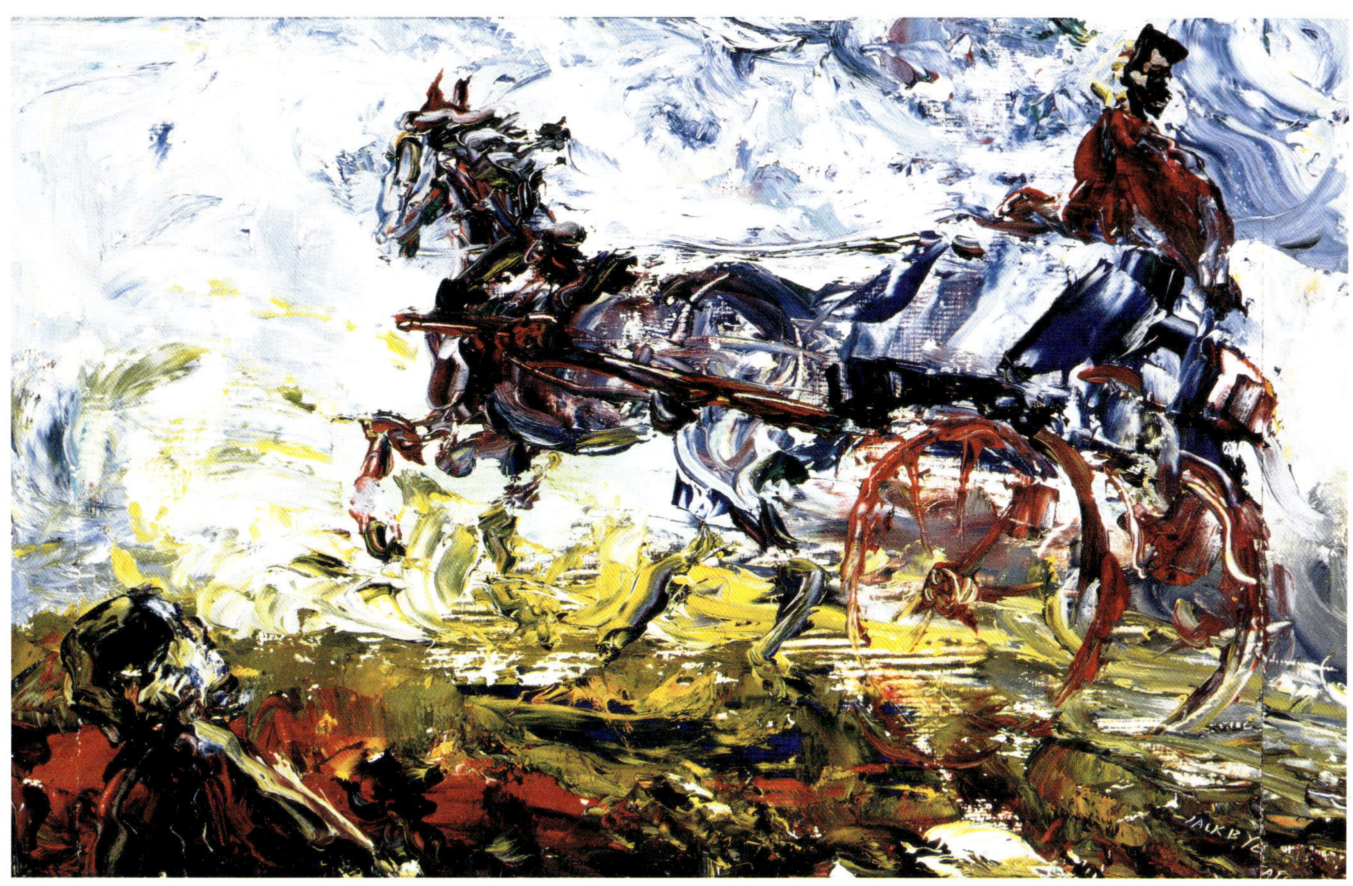

no. 46

The Embanked Road
Jack Butler Yeats
(1871-1957)
c. 1945/6
oil on panel
9 in. x 14 in.

Signed, lower right:
Jack B. Yeats

Provenance:
Mr. Leo Smith
Dublin, 1946;
Mrs. Tim O'Neill,
Dublin; Dillon
Antiques, Dublin.

Literature:
H. Pyle,
Jack B. Yeats,
*Catalogue Raisonne
of the Oil Paintings*,
Dublin 1992,
no. 788, p. 710.

Like the sea, roads are symbols of freedom for Jack Yeats. *The Embanked Road* is a small panel, but the dynamic movement represented renders its effect almost apocalyptic. A single horse and driver hurtle along an open road, their heads directed unwaveringly toward the unknown distance ahead. They seem to rush into another world, an impression Yeats has deliberately created with the low horizon and the hostile, even jealous, gaze of the watcher concealed in the bank on the left. Speed and urgency are suggested in the swirling brushstrokes and by the lack of definition at the points where the horse's hooves and the wheels of the carriage meet the road's surface. Yeats's use of color also evokes apocalypse. Turbulent streaks of blue in the sky around the driver's head and patches of unmixed primary color in the left foreground give way to opaque white light, beckoning the rushing pair.

The picture was probably painted in 1945-1946, when Jack B. Yeats's career was at its height. Only three years earlier he had a major exhibition in London, and been honored by the National College of Art National Loan exhibition of his work at home. In 1946 he was awarded an Honorary Doctorate of Letters by Trinity College Dublin.

CM

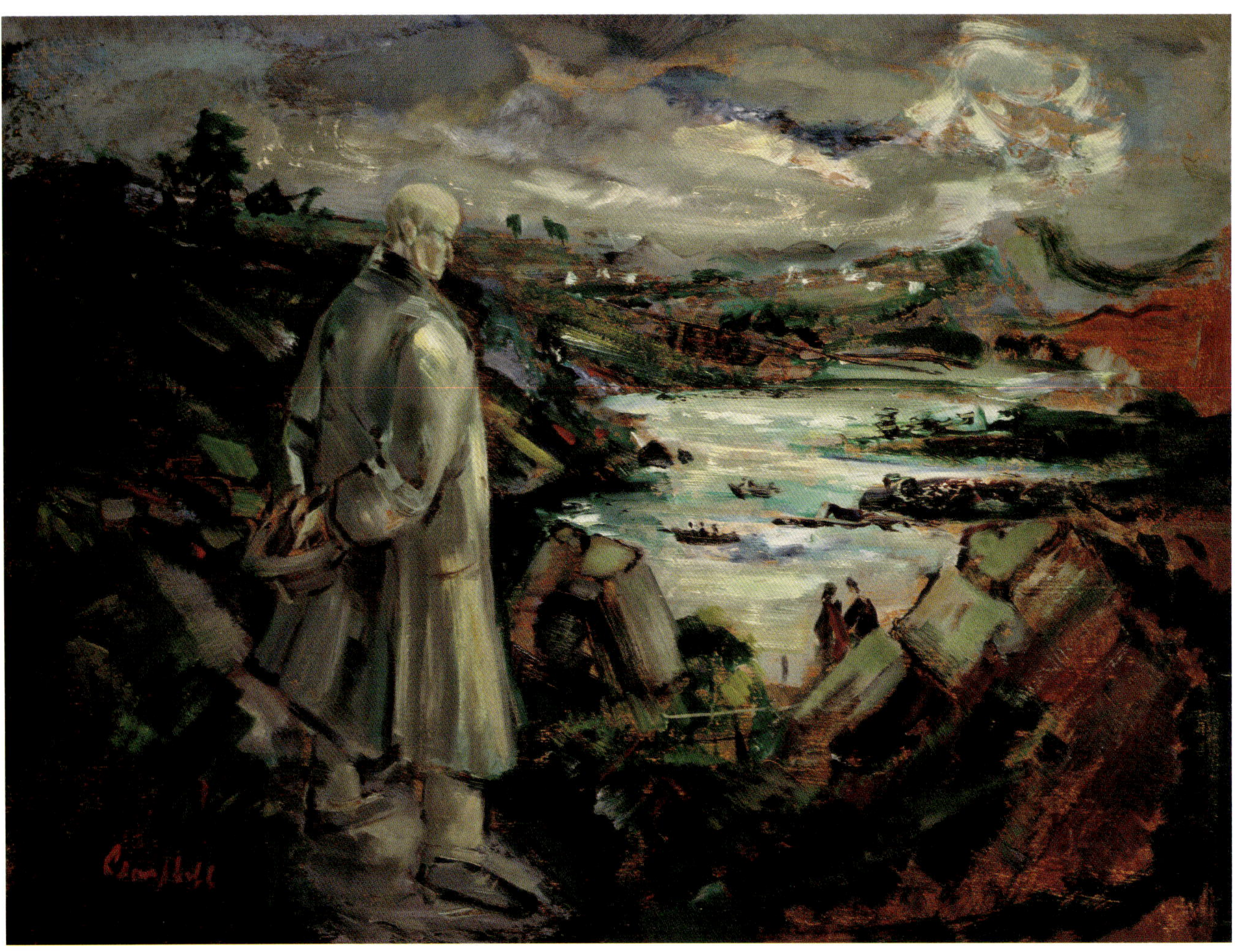

George Campbell, R.H.A.
(1917-1979)

George Campbell, born in County Wicklow and raised in Belfast, was a self-taught artist who began painting relatively late. The bombing of Belfast by the Luftwaffe in 1941 inspired his first pictures, although his deep interest in the culture and landscape of Spain inspired much of his later work. Attracting critical notice, Campbell's work was shown in 1944 at joint exhibitions in Belfast, with his brother Arthur, and in London, with Gerald Dillon. Campbell and his brother were important figures in the artistic life of Northern Ireland. Along with Dillon, the brothers were founding members of both the Progressive Painters Group and a branch of the Artist's International Association. Campbell, Dillon, and fellow artist Dan O'Neill, were to dominate Irish Art during the 1950s.

Campbell was a respected contributor to the Irish Exhibition of Living Art, a movement founded to provide a forum for avant garde art in opposition to a conservative art establishment. Although his work shows influences of cubism and continental expressionism, he rejected abstraction.

no. 47

Jack B. Yeats,
An Impression
George Campbell,
R.H.A.
(1917-1979)
oil on board
18 in. x 24 in.

Signed,
lower left:
Campbell

Provenance:
Gorry Gallery,
Dublin, 1995;
Victor Waddington
Galleries, Dublin.

Exhibited:
Royal Hibernian
Academy,
1951, no. 48.

Literature:
Gorry Gallery
sale catalogue,
May/June 1995,
no. 54, color
illus. p. 14.

Jack B. Yeats, an Impression was painted at the request of Victor Waddington. The art dealer who hosted George Campbell's first one-man exhibition in Dublin Waddington owned the gallery that presented Yeats's work as well. It was through him that the two men met.

Madge Campbell, the artist's wife, recalls when her husband sought permission to sketch Yeats. In his seventy-third year, Yeats shrank from publicity. He eventually agreed, however, and Waddington, learning of the sketches, suggested that Campbell add a Yeatsian Sligo landscape. This picture is the result. Although Campbell carefully reconstructs Yeats's west-of-Ireland landscape, the vibrant palette and cubist brushwork are unmistakably Campbell's, as is the separation of the figure from its natural surroundings.

CM

Albert Power
(1883-1945)

A student at the Dublin Metropolitan School, Albert Power inherited the academic sculptural tradition of his instructors John Hughes and Oliver Sheppard. Power occupied a conservative role in Irish sculpture, before modernism had become a vital force. His career flourished after 1911, when he was awarded the National Gold Medal for Sculpture at the Dublin Metropolitan School. From then, until his death in 1945, Power received some of the most important commissions by church and state in Ireland. More interested in national issues than in current debates about modernism, he refused to participate in the 1938 exhibition at the Royal Hibernian Academy, arguing that there was too little emphasis on Irish identity. He was a full member of the Academy of Christian Art, oddly named since it accepted only Roman Catholics. Despite Power's strongly nationalist and Catholic sympathies, his large political and religious works appear inert when compared to his delightfully spontaneous small pieces, such as the marble *Icarus*, 1940 (National Gallery of Ireland). He was equally proficient in marble and bronze, as his significant output of bronze portraits attest.

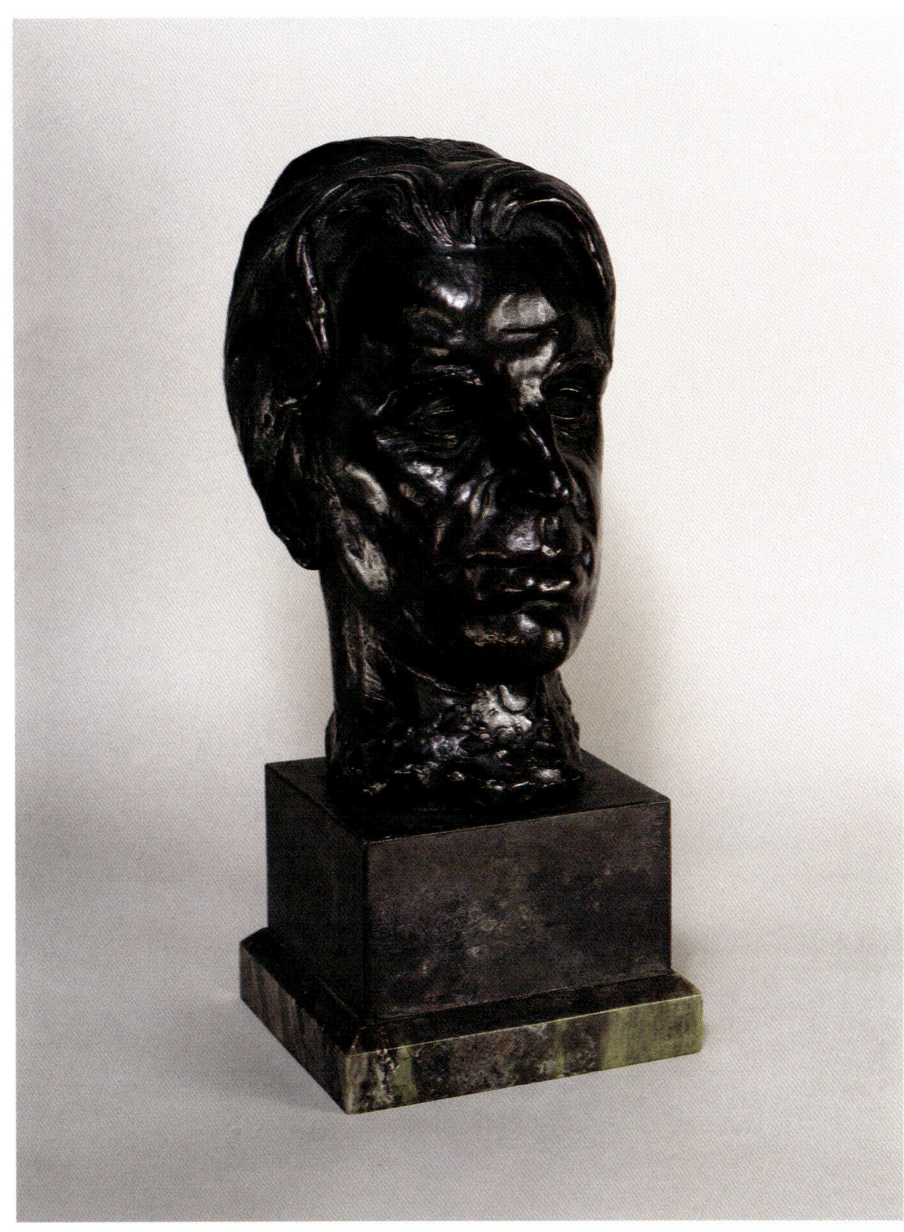

no. 48

Head of William Butler Yeats
Albert Power
(1883-1945)
1918
Bronze
17 1/2 in.

Signed and dated:
Albert Power 1918

Provenance:
Oliver St. John Gogarty, Renvyle; Carrick-mines House, Dublin.

Literature:
Ed. Daniel J. Murphy, *Lady Gregory's Journals*, New York: Oxford University Press, Gerrard's Cross, 1987, vol. 2, books 30-44, p. 388.

This bronze head of William Butler Yeats is the first of several representations that Albert Power executed of the great poet and playwright. In his fifty second year, just five years before he was awarded the Nobel Prize for Literature, Yeats was already well known for his part in the Irish literary renaissance, and the founding of the Abbey Theatre.

The economy of the simple rectangular plinth and green Connemara base focuses attention on the densely modeled head and acts as a foil for the sensuous treatment of the face. The variety of the surface modeling, which derives ultimately from Rodin, intensifies the poet's steadfast gaze.

CM

Laurence Campbell, R.H.A.
(1911-1968)

Born into an artistic Dublin family in 1911, Laurence Campbell began his career as an apprentice with a commercial stone cutting firm. He received more formal training at the Dublin Metropolitan School of Art from Oliver Sheppard creator of the 1798 memorial bronzes in Wexford and Enniscorthy, and the Chuculainn statue in Dublin's General Post Office. The Taylor Prize and the Henry Higgins Scholarship, which Campbell received in 1935 and 1936, respectively, enabled him to travel to Stockholm to study under Nils Sjorgen, and to Paris to study under Aristide Maillol. In the 1940s, he was named acting professor of sculpture at the National College of Art. Classical and academic by nature, he declined an invitation to join the Irish Exhibition of Living Art Group in 1943 — an organization established to promote modernism in Ireland. Although Campbell did participate in its first exhibition, he was more at home in the ambiance of the Royal Hibernian Academy, to which he was elected in 1940.

Campbell's travels in Europe did little to challenge his conservatism. His most avant-garde work is best exemplified by a stone mother-and-child group completed in 1933. His debt to the continent is more obvious in the simple, classical massing of his commemorative bust of the rebel Seán Huston, who was executed for his part in the 1916 Easter Uprising.

no. 49

*Bust of Jack B.
Yeats, #9*
Laurence Campbell
(1911-1968)
1944
bronze on
marble base
19 in.
(excluding base)

Signed:
*Laurence Campbell
R.H.A. 1944*

Foundry mark:
C '90 and numbered.
Limited edition
of nine, cast by
C.A.S.T. Ltd.
from the original
plaster.

Provenance:
Gorry Gallery,
Dublin.

Exhibited:
Royal Hibernian
Academy,
1945, no. 265
(plaster);
National Loan
Exhibition,
National College
of Art, 1945.

Literature:
*National Loan
Exhibition
Catalogue 1945*,
National College
of Art, Dublin,
1945; *Capuchin
Annual 1945-
1946*, illus. p. 166
and 122;
*Gorry's Sale
Catalogue*, Dublin,
Nov. - Dec. 1990,
p. 3 and 9,
color illus. p. 9.

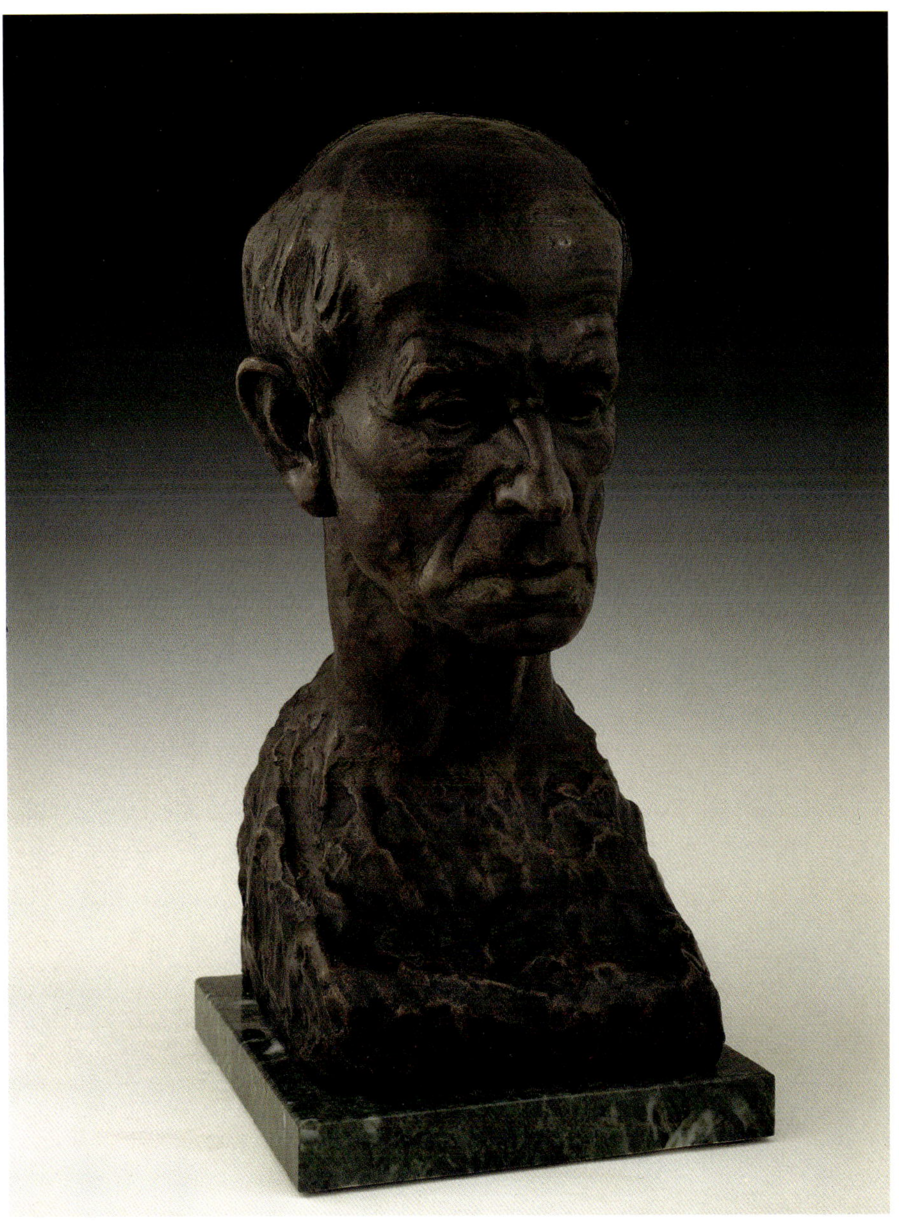

Campbell executed figurative works in wood, bronze, woodcuts and etchings. He is best remembered, however, for his smaller bronze portrait busts, of which this *Bust of Jack B. Yeats* is a fine example.

The original plaster bust from which this bronze was cast was exhibited in 1945 at both the Royal Hibernian Academy and the National Loan Exhibition, when Jack B. Yeats (nos. 40-46) was at the height of his fame. Sir Kenneth Clark, Director of the National Gallery in London, considered Yeats to be among the three most important "modern" artists in the British Isles, and exhibited his work in 1942. A solo exhibition at the Tate Gallery followed in 1948.

Campbell chooses to present Yeats's melancholic side, reflecting the preoccupation in his painting at that time. Throughout the mid-1940s, Yeats painted scenes of the past in which the dreams of childhood are tempered by adult experience and his personal sorrow over the outbreak of a Second World War. Reclusive and introspective himself, Campbell was highly sympathetic to Yeats's mood at the time. The massing of the bronze, sloping downward to the green marble base, combines with the somber tilt of the head to render this a highly expressive sculptural portrait.

CM

Additional Works

from the
Collection of Brian P. Burns

A Quick Shod
Anonymous, Irish
oil on canvas
13 in. x 18 1/2 in.
acc. no. 1011

A Training Tout
Anonymous, Irish
oil on canvas
13 in. x 18 1/2in.
acc. no. 1012

*Lady Conyngham's Royal
Pomeranian at Bifrons, Kent*
Anonymous, Irish
oil on canvas
19 1/2in. x 24in.
acc. no. 1090

Lest We Forget
Anonymous, Irish
oil on canvas
26 in. x 30 in.
acc. no. 1046

*Sprig of Shillelagh and
Shamrock So Green*
Anonymous, Irish
ink drawing with watercolor
11 in. x 9 in.
acc. no. 1046

Testimony (Witness)
Anonymous, Irish
ink silhoutte and drawing on paper
16 3/4 in. x 12 1/2 in.
acc. no. 1048

The Boot Boy
Mildred Anne Butler, R.W.S.
(1858-1941)
oil on canvas
12 in. x 9 in.
acc. no. 1052

Bust of Jack B. Yeats (#1)
Laurence Campbell, R.H.A. (1911-1968)
cast bronze
H: 19 in. (excluding base)
acc. no. 4019

Come On
M. Collyer
17 1/2in. x 24 in.
oil on canvas
acc. no. 1025

Fair Day in Connemara
Comyn
oil on canvas
17 1/2 in. x 29 in.
acc. no. 1026

Rory O'Moore
Charles H. Cook, R.H.A. (1830- 1906)
oil on canvas
11 1/2 in. x 9 1/2 in.
acc. no. 1053

Achill Sound, County Mayo
Michael J. De Burca, R.H.A.
oil on canvas
17 1/2 in. x 20 1/2 in.
acc. no. 1054

Edmund Burke
John Henry Foley, R.A., R.H.A.
(1818-1874)
cast bronze
H: 38 in.
acc. no. 4012

Oliver Goldsmith
John Henry Foley, R.A., R.H.A.
(1818-1874)
cast bronze
H: 38 in.
acc. no. 4013

A Moving Scene on the Road to Slane
W. Heath (1795-1840)
color engraving on paper
8 1/2 in. x 12 3/4 in.
acc. no. 3048

Mare and Foal
John Frederick Herring Jr. (1820-1907)
oil on canvas
20 in. x 24 in.
acc. no. 1097

*Horse Drawn Carriage and Four Figures
with Windsor Castle in the Background*
after John Frederick Herring Jr.
oil on canvas
23 in. x 35 in.
acc. no. 1030

*Cartoon for the Left Hand Stained Glass
Panel, Naithi's Baptistery, Dundrum,
County Dublin*
Evie Hone, (1894-1955)
gouache on paper
13 in. x 9 1/2 in.
acc. no. 1125

Sun and Shadow Donegal
William Jackson, R.H.A.
oil on canvas
20 in. x 24 in.
acc. no. 1057

*Morning Light, Cobh Harbour,
County Cork*
Paul Kelly
oil on canvas
40 in. x 30 in.
acc. no. 1134

Breton Woman Knitting
Charles Vincent Lamb, R.H.A. R.U.A.
(1893-1964)
oil on canvas
23 in. x 18 1/2 in.
acc. no. 1060

Flaherty's Pub
Charles Vincent Lamb, R.H.A. R.U.A.,
(1893-1964)
oil on canvas
20 1/4 in. x 24 1/4 in.
acc. no. 1061

Sunset the Caravan
Sir John Lavery, R.A., R.S.A., R.H.A.,
(1856-1941)
oil on canvas
30 in. x 25 in.
acc. no. 1126

Renaissance Man
Louis Le Brocquy, H.R.H.A, (b. 1916)
oil on canvas
36 in. x 24 in.acc. no. 1123

After the Storm, The End of a Coaster
Patrick Leonard, A.R.H.A (b. 1918).
oil on canvas
39 in. x 45 1/2 in.acc. no. 1031

Boats in Harbour
Maurice MacGonigal, P.R.H.A., (1900-
1979)
oil on canvas
15 in. x 22 in.
acc. no. 1099

Harbour View
Maurice MacGonigal, P.R.H.A., (1900-
1979)
oil on canvas
12 in. x 16 in.
acc. no. 1065

Great Courtyard, Dublin Castle
James Malton, (c. 1760-1803)
color engraving on paper
10 in. x 14 1/2 in.
acc. no. 3054

Leinster House, Dublin
James Malton (c. 1760-1803)
color engraving on paper
10 in. x 14 1/2 in.
acc. no. 3055

The Grandmother
Frank McKelvey, R.i¹.A., R.U.A., (1895-
1974)
watercolor on paper
24 1/4 in. x 18 1/4 in.
acc. no. 1101

Marble Hill Strand, County Donegal
Frank McKelvey, R.H.A., R.U.A., (1895-
1974)
oil on board
12 in. x 17 in.
acc. no. 1101

Mourne Mountains
Frank McKelvey, R.H.A., R.U.A., (1895-
1974)
oil on canvas
10 in. x 15 in.
acc. no. 1068

Map of Kerry
Richard Molloy
ink and watercolor on paper
9 in. x 8 1/2 in.
acc. no. 1071

Writer with Pipe
Erskine Nicol, A.R.A., R.S.A.,
(1825-1904)
oil on canvas
14 in. x 18 in.
acc. no. 1104

On the Racecourse
Walter Frederick Osborne, R.H.A.,
(1859-1903)
watercolor on paper
13 1/2 in. x 20 1/2 in.
acc. no. 1119

Looking Back
Daniel O'Neill, (1920-1974)
oil on canvas
18 in. x 23 in.
acc. no. 1115

Bust of Dean Jonathan Swift
Albert Power, R.H.A., (1883-1945)
marble
H: 24 in.
acc. no. 4015

Home from the War
E. de Saisset
oil on canvas
31 in. x 25 1/2 in.
acc. no. 1106

Pembroke a Thoroughbred Horse
Samuel Spode, (active 1850)
oil on canvas
19 in. x 23 1/2 in.
acc. no. 1076

Portrait of a Young Man on Horseback
Samuel Spode (active 1850)
oil on canvas
18 3/4 in. x 23 in.
acc. no. 1109

Cloon Lake, Glencar, County Kerry
Bartholomew Colles Watkins, R.H.A.
(1833-1891))
oil on canvas
13 1/2 x 20 in.
acc. no. 1077

Kylemore Lake, Connemara
Bartholomew Colles Watkins, R.H.A.,
(1833-1891)
oil on canvas
13 1/2 in. x 20 in.
acc. no. 1078

Bantry Bay
James Whaite, (active 1860-1890)
watercolor on canvas
23 in. x 37 in.
acc. no. 1079

Financial Argument
Sir David Wilkie, (1785-1841)
oil on canvas
27 1/2 in. x 35 3/4 in.
acc. no. 1110

Teeing off at Portmarnock
Alexander Williams, (1837-1930)
watercolor on paper
9 in. x 13 1/2 in.
acc. no. 1111

Draw on Him Now
Jack Butler Yeats, R.H.A., (1871-1957)
ink drawing with color on paper
11 1/2 in. x 8 1/2 in.
acc. no. 2000

Envelope illustrated with a Sailing Vessel
Jack Butler Yeats, R.H.A., (1871-1957)
ink on paper
5 in. x 8 1/2 in.
acc. no. 2001

Autographed Letter to John Mansfield
Jack Butler Yeats, R.H.A.,
(1871-1957)
ink on paper
letter: 9 3/4 in x 7 1/2 in.,
envelope: 4 in. x 4 1/2 in.
acc. no. 2002